CLASSICAL ISLAM

Classical Islam

A HISTORY 600–1258

by G. E. VON GRUNEBAUM

translated by KATHERINE WATSON

ALDINE PUBLISHING COMPANY, *Chicago*

First U.S. edition published 1970
by ALDINE PUBLISHING COMPANY
529 South Wabash Avenue, Chicago, Illinois 60605

George Allen and Unwin Ltd.

Library of Congress Catalog Card Number 78-75049
SBN 202-15016-X
Printed in the United States of America

PREFACE

THE title of this book implies a judgment. The classical represents a model. It is, in fact, a model whose reconstitution is by definition both an obligation and an impossibility.

To the Muslim, man has declined below the measure of the heroic ancestors; their greatness is as much an incentive as an embarrassment. And yet it is to their past that recourse must be had in contemporary predicament, their strength, their modes of action which must be reappropriated and relived.

The normative period does not, however, in common Muslim consciousness, extend all the way to the end of the ʻAbbāsid caliphate in Bagdad. What terminates in 1258 is the major chain of political legitimacy to which reality had failed to conform for rather more than four centuries when the extent of the Muslim empire had ceased to be coterminous with the rule of Islam and the unity of tradition had become no more than a postulate.

None the less, the fall of Baghdad did more than bring home the precariousness of all human structures, even those erected on the true faith and devised to safeguard it. It demonstrated that the 'Abode of Islam' had become saturated with Islam, that the community no longer required a caliphate to give it a political and religious centre of gravity, that the vitality of Islam as an interpretation of man and the world, a way of life, and a style of thinking and feeling was now independent of any institutional support. Such support would henceforth be welcome as comfort and excuse to relax but no more needed for spiritual self-assurance. In future, states might not see themselves as aides and instruments of the glory of Islam; but the community was to view them precisely as such and so to identify with them rather than merely to tolerate them as a trial or a convenience which, in fact, they mostly were.

Periodization will always be open to criticism. The change from power to civilization as the dominant aspect of the Islamic development did not, of course, occur suddenly when the heathen stormed the psychological centre of political Islam; but the very irreparability of the calamity made the faithful realize that the abiding of their world, its beliefs and manifestations, had outgrown any particular political form and had indeed become too wide to be contained in history. In this realization the epigones undoubtedly rejoined the innermost intent of ancestors and founder.

The essence of a society is in a sense identical with its history;

and yet its history may detract from that essence as is the case of Islam, despite its triumphs on the fields of battle and rulership. Nevertheless telling its history is the only way open to us to render that essence accessible, to circumambulate it and show it from all sides.

Some of the facts, observations, and ideas presented in this book may seem to the specialist to be in need of documentary corroboration. The author agrees but has decided for once to expose himself to scepticism in the interest of an unbroken narrative and to keep the evidence in his desk whence he shall be glad to spread it out if the critics become too restive. For the moment, however, he has adopted the immediate interests of a hypothetical readership, scholar and lay, and the student in between, which he feels is primarily in receiving order in chaos rather than laborious arguments for one particular order in preference to another. Secretly, he is wondering from what front he will be challenged and refuted.

By her translation Mrs Watson has somehow lightened the sternness of the original. What persuasiveness the present text possesses is to no slight extent owed to her. The reasonableness and the aesthetic ambition of the publishers are gratefully appreciated. So is the co-operation of the Propyläen Verlag in granting permission for an English edition.

I should not wish this book to go out without an expression of gratitude to Professor Stanford J. Shaw of the University of California, Los Angeles, to whom I am greatly indebted for his generous assistance on the Bibliography. In conclusion, I should perhaps state that the present book was prepared as part of the publication program of the Near Eastern Center, University of California, Los Angeles.

G. E. von Grunebaum

CONTENTS

ILLUSTRATIONS

MAPS

Pre-Islamic Arabia

'In studying the writings of the ancients we become their contemporaries; in reflecting and pondering on their circumstances it is as though we also witnessed them and experienced them. Thus study of this kind can take the place of a long life, supposing death should hastily snatch us away.'

ABŪ SHĀMA OF DAMASCUS, d. 1267

THE devout Muslim is inclined to see the appearance and rise of his religion in the light of a miracle; the overwhelming success of the Prophet's mission is for him the most compelling confirmation of its truth. Even the non-believer is prepared to see if not a miracle at least something miraculous in the fact that such a towering and finely developed structure should arise on a foundation as narrow from the point of view of population and civilization as pagan Central and North Arabia; a structure which derived its survival and its greatness from its ability to transform itself from a religious community possessed of a national political character into a commonwealth of culture which was both religious and supranational, while yet retaining its existence and validity as a state. The political history of Islam contains a paradox peculiar to this religion alone: it is the history of the transformation of an Arab sect into a community dominating an empire, and furthermore a universal religious community which was primarily non-political, yet was the determining factor in political events and imposed its own qualities on whole cultures. In other words it was not the physical domination but the cultural power of the new teaching, not its origin in a particular geographical and intellectual zone but its immanent universality, which proved the deciding factors in its development. In the same way the new experience of the divine which it brought with it proved more inflammatory than the sense of identification with the Arab nation which was disseminating it. Yet, a further paradox, the Arabs have until the present day always claimed and been conceded a kind of privileged position within the Islamic community.

Arab pride and at times the townsman's periodic access of romantic feeling for the desert have served to keep within bounds the tendency to despise pre-Islamic paganism and all its works which followed the conversion. Yet the animosity of the subject peoples, who could only vent it against the pre-Islamic Arabs, the Arab

Muslim's consciousness of progress, and the obvious difference of cultural level between the Syrian and Mesopotamian border lands and the peninsula have all fostered the attitude that the pagan period was one not far removed from general barbarism. This attitude is one shared by the Islamic community and by Western scholars. South Arabia, the *Arabia felix* of the ancients, with its city states and its nomads, kept in check by kings, often priest-kings, is of course excluded from this condemnation. The kingdoms of the Yemen had been involved in world politics for centuries. They were a natural focus for land traffic as well as for the ships plying between the Red Sea and the Indian Ocean, and they lay at the end of the caravan routes from Syria and Egypt. Their economy was fed by a carefully maintained irrigation system. Intellectually and politically, and to some extent linguistically, they were cut off from the rest of the peninsula, although South Arabian colonies appeared all along the caravan routes and history records more than one successful sally from the south into the centre. But it was not with the Yemen that pre-Islamic Arabdom felt at one. Notwithstanding certain parallels or influences from the south, Islam is the creation of Central and Western Arabia, just as its Prophet came into the world in the most important settlement of this area.

Power in the south was centred in the towns, whereas in the rest of the peninsula it lay with the nomads; in the south the dominant tendency was towards concentration into states whereas it was everywhere else towards dispersion into tribes and a few small urban units. Conditions of life in the bare steppe lands restrict to an average of six hundred the size of a viable permanent community of nomads who can camp together; the towns of course were larger and lived mainly by trade and the money spent by pilgrims, unless, like Ṭā'if in the south-west and Yathrib in the north-west, they were placed in an environment unusually favourable by Arab standards. The nomads seemed to be self-sufficient but were in fact dependent on the peasants and townsfolk they so much despised. These in their turn, suffering from the depredations of the nomads, returned their contempt, though in fact they shared their outlook and cherished the same prejudices, being most of them only separated from nomadism by a very few generations. Even tribal organization was preserved by the sedentary populations of the peninsula. Only among the peasantry or fully settled peoples of the borderlands was a person's descent described by where he lived rather than by his tribe.

Thus the individual, in the oases as much as in the steppe, felt himself first and foremost a member of his tribe. Only in and through the community of the tribe was his existence made possible and an indispensable minimum of personal security assured. It was not only the respect which he enjoyed outside which depended on the status of his tribe and within it, the standing of his sub-group; he was not as yet sufficiently recognized as an individual in isolation from his group for him not to be considered exchangeable with any other member of his tribe of the same standing by the law of the blood feud—the only brake on unbridled violence between the tribes. The tribe was certainly an effective unity, but it was not firmly bound together. Both splits and amalgamations of originally unrelated groups who camped together were frequent and subject to firm legal forms; sooner or later their occurrence is mirrored in the official genealogy; it reflects equally the earlier history of the tribe and its temporary political alliances. This loose form of organization was accompanied by a lack of authoritative leadership. The chief (*sajjid*, lit. 'speaker') exercised hospitality and took care of the tribe; he led the migrations whose broad regional and seasonal lines were laid down traditionally and he was often, but not necessarily, the leader in war. He exercised his leadership more by influence and standing than by power. There was no right of succession, but the *sajjid* frequently came from the same family. He represented the tribe in extra-tribal dealings but, except for a quarter part of any war loot no income was provided for him to meet his various obligations.

The tribes were autonomous, not to say sovereign, in their relations with each other; alliances were formed as easily as they were dissolved. The aristocracy of the 'great families' cut across these divisions; the north and central Arab world was in a certain sense, despite all its divisions and differences of custom, a unity whose members felt themselves bound together in a hierarchical order; they might even marry outside the tribal group, although the woman in these cases never joined her husband's kin entirely and the children might be exposed to the problems and dangers of divided loyalties. Forms of marriage vary, traces of matrilineal organization are not hard to recognize; but in the periods accessible to us patrilineal descent seems to have become increasingly dominant. Polygamy was as customary as easy separation, reports of polyandry belong in the realm of ethnological legend. Hard conditions led to hard customs, in disputes the arbiter (*ḥakam*) had no more to support him than his prestige and the pressure of opinion.

It is at the least extremely unlikely that the Arabs are autochthonous in the peninsula to which they have given their name. But they were installed there long before they appear in history, and sometimes because of internal pressures and sometimes lured by the political weakness of their neighbours they were continually spreading into the fertile borderlands of Syria and Mesopotamia in larger or smaller groups. Changes in the balance of power and the opportunities for cultivation, especially in South Arabia (where the question must remain open whether political or economic decline more effectively created them) led regularly to an increase in the internal migrations which were frequent at all times. These seemed on the whole to prefer the south-north axis to the west-east.

The Arabs, a name which can be approximately translated as passer-by or nomad, probably opened up the peninsula in the not too distant past. Since their tribes depended on small stock and (later?) asses their nomadism was confined to the borders of the steppes; the form of life of the camel-breeding Bedouin, to which ancient tradition ascribes an unfathomable antiquity, is in reality a relatively recent development and is only known with certainty from about the eleventh century BC. It was the camel which first made the deserts passable; it is able to carry 250 kilogrammes—and even, according to some authors, substantially more; above 600 kilogrammes. It can cover up to 160 kilometres in a day (the average day's journey of a loaded animal lies in the region of 40 kilometres) and keep this up in a maximal temperature of 57 degrees centigrade for as long as eight days without drinking. These qualities made tribal migrations and eruptions out of the desert possible, and made the 'Bedouin' the lords of the peninsula. But the camel must have spread relatively quickly and simultaneously among all the tribes who were interested in acquiring it. Its adoption does not seem to have been linked with any other advance in military technique, so that the increased mobility of the camel nomads did not lead to the establishment of large empires, such as the adoption of the horse and war chariot had caused in the Near East at a slightly earlier period. In the sixteen hundred years or so within which the pre-Islamic history of North and Central Arabia can be traced back no state structure of any kind was set up by the native Bedouin on their own incentive except in the border regions, apart from the self-governing urban settlements.

The kingdom of the Nabataeans (incorporated into the Roman Empire in 106) and the city state of Palmyra (at its height about 260, liquidated by Aurelian in 272–273) do lie just within the geographical limits of the peninsula, but they are not Bedouin foundations. One might rather consider as such the three buffer states which were set up on Byzantine, Persian and Yemenite initiative in the fourth and fifth centuries of our era. The Ḍajā'ima established as a bulwark against incursions from the desert and Persian expansionism, and after 502 their more celebrated successors the Ghassānids—'Roman Arabs' in Byzantine service in contrast to the Lakhmids, the 'Persian Arabs'—were at pains to assert their claim to an independent history, but they had more success culturally than politically. Finally they had to accept direct control, Byzantine in 582, Persian in 602: changes which gave little joy to these sovereign states. The greater stability of their protectors gave the Ghassānids and Lakhmids a longer survival (and greater influence) than the state in Central Arabia which was set up under the south Arabian Kinda to control the interior of the peninsula for the Yemen. Less than ten years after the revolution which caused the collapse of the Yemenite royal house it had broken up into its separate tribes, whereupon the Kinda aristocracy moved back to its southern homeland. The project of a prince of the Kinda to re-establish the rule of his house with Byzantine help is attacked by the poet 'Abīd ibn al-Abraṣ, a son of one of the rebel tribes, who wrote these significant verses between 535 and 540:

'Hast thou declared thou wilt call on Caesar for help? Then wilt thou certainly go to thy grave a Syrian (i.e. an imperial subject).
We however refuse to put ourselves under any man's leadership, until we ourselves can lead men without a bridle.'

None of these state organizations, not even the Lakhmid princes of Ḥīra (which means 'army camp'), who from time to time emerged as representatives of Arabdom *vis-à-vis* the Persians, stood for any idea capable of weaning away the Bedouin from their anarchistic leanings.

It is quite noticeable how the waves of world politics and the great intellectual movements made an effective impact only on the established states, and among the urban settlements only on Mecca.

It is recounted in the histories that not long before the birth of the Prophet a man had almost risen to be king in Mecca, and again later the same thing was repeated of one of Muhammad's adversaries in Medina. The tone in which these affairs are reported indicates the hostility aroused everywhere on Arab soil by a despot, termed king (*malik*) or lord (*rabb*). A tribe might boast of rising to be master of other groups, but to have shaken off the yoke of the foreigner or even of the domestic tyrant was equally a subject for pride and indeed more congenial to the Arab temperament. Al-Quṭāmī in 700 describes with characteristic terseness the attitude of the Bedouin to authority: 'At one time we obey our amir, and then another time we disobey him; we do not feel ourselves bound to seek his counsel all the time.' The anarchy by which the Arab empire at a later date was to bleed to death could still seem a desirable condition while no idea was at stake in the political field; but it was without doubt to blame for the fact that in the century before the rise of Islam the tribes dissipated all their energies in trivial guerilla fighting, all against all. This is what reduced them to that pitch of malaise which alone explains the swift success of the Muslim evangel. South Arabian saga harbours dreams of world empire. In Islamic times these stood in the way of the growth of an historical sense, but they at least show a will to develop and organize their power and a certain understanding for the military mechanism necessary to found a state at that time. On the other hand the North Arab accounts of the 'battle days of the Arabs' are aesthetically much more attractive because they are more realistic and free of collective delusions of grandeur. They mirror an enclosed world of refined semi-barbarism, trying to compensate for the isolation of its existence by exaggerating the importance of the smallest episode.

Where kindred groups joined together for long periods in northern and central Arabia it happened under the protection of cult practices. The 'confederacies' which can be authenticated in Mecca at the end of the sixth century even seem to some extent to have set members of the same kindred groups against each other. In other parts of the peninsula, particularly on the borders of Mesopotamia, the oath of fraternization (*taḥāluf*) led sometimes to super-tribes; without managing to become a really united political force a super-tribe nevertheless felt itself held together in a close bond and called upon to carry out common action.

Economically the Bedouin, existing at a universally low level of material culture, were beset more by uncertainty than by poverty. They were understandably helpless before the caprices of the climate; their cattle population was considerable, as is manifest in the homicide dues; but the basis and manner of their life made it impossible to build up reserves. The markets were important both economically and culturally; they were protected by a relatively lengthy sacred truce, and this allowed the Bedouin to exchange goods. But it was only the contractors from the towns, who organized and kept a hold on long-distance trade, who enjoyed the relatively stable conditions that allowed them to make any notable profits. The stronger tribes could of course levy tolls from the merchants to whom they gave protection as they crossed their regions, and thus wrest some share for themselves from the evidently considerable income from transarabian trade. But on the whole, apart from migrating into Byzantium or Persia where they could for instance be sure of finding a living from the state as auxiliary soldiers, the only resource of the tribes was to plunder the sedentary peasants or to conduct a *ghazw* ('razzia') against another nomad group. In this way herds, often of great size, changed owners either directly or as prisoners' ransoms. The total wealth of the tribes taking part naturally did not increase, and basically all remained as before.

Here we should note that contrary to a widely held view, the first millennium of our era brought the peninsula a gradual increase in the amount of precipitation, though intermittently the rainfall declined, as for instance just between 591 and 640, during the foundation and first conquests of the Muslim community. For the rest the inhabitants of the steppe could only alleviate their distress by breaking into the areas of civilization when the governments of the latter were suffering from an onset of weakness. In other words the political factor seems to have played a larger part in these population movements than the climato-economic situation. Precise dates are only available for southern Arabia. There the exceptionally important and fabled dam of Ma'rib broke in 450; the kingdom was strong enough to call on the surrounding tribes to mend it without delay. When the disaster repeated itself in 542 the ruler had to engage in arduous negotiations with the local feudal lords to ensure voluntary collaboration to reconstruct it. A generation later political disintegration had reached such a point that the third break of the dam in 570 could not be repaired and the catastrophe resulted in a great loss of fertile land. It seems to be characteristic of the later sixth century, at least in the south, that the Bedouin reoccupied large tracts of land, and this of course brought an element of unrest, perhaps even of barbarism into the life of the whole peninsula. In this context it should be pointed out that even in periods of prosperity the ruling families of all the Arab princedoms were without exception of southern origin, that is to say they came to power in their territories by migration and 'colonization'.

This crisis of 'rebedouinization' is to be interpreted rather as a shift of power in favour of the nomads than as a return to nomadic life by large sections of the population. Apparently the urban settlements of the north-west were spared. Mecca is mentioned by Ptolemy, and the name he gives it allows us to identify it as a South Arabian foundation created round a sanctuary; in spite of this early reference it probably did not reach such importance as a market and centre of religious pilgrimage as is assigned to it by tradition until shortly before 500. At that time the tribe of the Quraish had seized it and made a working agreement with the Kināna Bedouin of the vicinity, who had perhaps only now lost their hegemony when supplanted by them. Lying at the crossing of the north-south trade route with that from the Red Sea to modern Iraq, in a hot, barren valley surrounded by inhospitable mountains, Mecca's existence originally became possible only because of the water supply provided by the well of Zemzem, later to be sanctified by the Muslim. The oligarchy of the Quraish clan leaders governed the city and also regulated the internal affairs of the clans. Military protection of the town was largely entrusted to the *Aḥābīsh,* originally Abyssinian mercenaries who seem later to have been reinforced by recruits from minor tribes camping in the neighbourhood of Mecca. Non-Quraish Arabs, aliens of all kinds, and particularly foreign slaves, probably constituted the majority of the population; the common interest in trade and the pilgrim traffic gave them what was for contemporary Arabia a strong cohesion, if not 'state-mindedness'. The main caravans, sent north one in summer time and one in winter, were communal undertakings, to which wide circles of the population contributed and from which they profited. They provided an enduring incentive to accept a certain political discipline, and to the formation of a class of leaders with a knowledge of the world outside Arabia founded on experience. This traffic gave them in addition some experience of a money economy; though barter still predominated Byzantine and Persian coins circulated in Mecca. The general level of education rose; involving of course some alienation from Arabian culture as a whole, and earning scorn for the Meccan merchants from the Bedouin who represented it. Above all people were now exposed to the intellectual—and at that time this meant religious—currents which had become dominant outside.

Added to this the city, because of its importance, inevitably became involved in the power game of the great powers, although the Meccans were sufficiently skilful—or perhaps unimportant—for them to remain aloof from active participation. Favoured by neutrality and by the cohesion and unity of its ruling class, Mecca avoided both the fate of the south and the internal struggles of its neighbour Yathrib 450 kilometres to the north, where in the last decades of the sixth century tribal quarrels broke out among the Arab settlers. These were complicated by their relations with a series of Jewish tribes also settled in the oasis and in the course of time they seriously threatened the survival of the city.

Since the middle of the third century the history of the Near East had been dominated by the conflict between first the Roman Empire, later its eastern half and finally its Byzantine successor, and Sasanid Iran with its capital at Ctesiphon in Semitic Mesopotamia. As is always the case in such situations the hostility spread into areas which intrinsically had little concern with the interests and cultures involved. The sphere of influence of the Persians in Arabia lay on the whole to the east of a line running from Palmyra to the eastern boundary of Hadhramaut, so that the trade routes through Sasanid Mesopotamia to the Persian Gulf and through Persia proper to Central Asia were under Persian control. This circumstance forced the Byzantines to use the sea route through the Red Sea; the entrance was in their hands and its eastern shore was not occupied by any power which could threaten them. The exit to the Indian Ocean however was controlled by the Yemenites, and on the western shore the empire of Axum, core of the later state of Abyssinia, made its interests felt.

It was therefore essential for Byzantium to ensure the goodwill of the Abyssinians and Yemenites, while the Persians seized every opportunity to disturb Byzantine understanding with these peoples. It should not be forgotten that South Arabia and Iraq had long kept in close contact over a much-used route. The kingdom in South Arabia seems to have declined slowly since the first century AD and to have shared its power increasingly with the local 'feudal' lords. As a consequence south-east Yemen fell under Abyssinian domination as early as the first half of the fourth century.

The conversion of Abyssinia to Monophysite Christianity emanating from Egypt began just at that time, but was not completed until the sixth century. It is very likely that because of this political connection Christianity was introduced at the same time in South Arabia. Their association with the hated 'blacks' was in any case injurious to the Christian mission and probably prejudiced the cause of the Monophysite preachers coming from Syria. The national reaction which drove out the Abyssinians towards the end of the century did not result in a renascence of native paganism, but led gradually to an impressive spread of Judaism, which during the fourth and fifth centuries found growing support from the Jews who had migrated into South Arabia after each of the two destructions of the temple in Jerusalem. Persian Mazdaism was too much a national phenomenon to spread at all in foreign parts; Byzantine intolerance of the Jews made them acceptable allies for the Sasanids.

Byzantium was prepared to make common cause with the Monophysites abroad. With her blessing the Abyssinians re-embarked on a policy of expansion at the beginning of the sixth century. Their first success forced the Yemenite king to flee into the interior and there to adopt the Jewish faith. But a change in the fortune of war brought fierce persecution on the Christians, though their cult centre in Najrān soon recovered. Renewed efforts by the Abyssinians culminated in 525 with the death of the Jewish king Dhū Nuwās and the transformation of his empire into an Abyssinian satrapy, which the legendary Abraha a little later built into an almost independent state under an Abyssinian ruling class. He encouraged Christianity and seems to have tried to get control of Mecca or at least to wrest it from the Persian sphere of influence, into which it had been brought by the sympathies of the leading circles in the city. This campaign must have happened at least ten years earlier than the date (560) traditionally ascribed to it. It failed and their repulse of the enemy strengthened the Meccans' 'national' pride.

Not much later the Yemenites rose against the Abyssinians whom they then expelled, with the sanction of the Persians. In 597 the Persians decided to put an end to the independence of the Yemen, since it was threatened by internal feuds. Persian rule converted the Yemenite Christians to Nestorianism. It was considered reliable by the Persians because of its irreconcilable hostility both to the Byzantine imperial church and to the Monophysitism which was strong in the Semitic borderlands and in Egypt. The Persians established it as a state religion of the second rank. Thus it was probably Nestorians who a generation later came to an agreement with Muhammad on the fate of the Christian town of Najrān.

The Christianization of the border lands meant that the areas that had remained pagan had a vague acquaintance with Christians and Christianity. This first, and secondly the penetration of Judaism into the peninsula were the two most important intellectual influences towards cultural change among the Arabs. The Greek church was for the most part harshly opposed to the heretical communities of the non-Greek subjects of the empire, and these in their turn forced out splinter groups into the furthest borderlands. Thus the Bedouin world learnt of Christianity mostly in a guise which differed considerably from our idea of the religion. Ancient Arab poetry does not convey the impression that dogmatic questions were of any interest; what made an impression were the hermits and the church processions. According to the evidence of the poetry the Christian pilgrimages were also a common pagan form of God- or saint-worship. Conversely Christians participated in the pilgrimage to the sanctuary at Mecca, whose lord was for them simply 'God'; refusal to join in this ritual subjected some tribes to the accusation of godlessness.

Only the Monophysites after their reorganization by Jacob Barde'ānā (Baradaeus, Bishop of Edessa, *c.* 542–578) seem to have applied themselves systematically to converting the Bedouin: bishops were appointed to the large camps. From the Monophysites, who sought to unite themselves after the middle of the sixth century, the Ghassānid princes adopted a new line of policy, which brought them into opposition with the central Byzantine government and ultimately hastened their end. But dehellenization was not a process that could be arrested, Greek gradually receded. When the Persians conquered Syria in the early seventh century they persecuted the Greeks but protected the Syrians; the Monophysite churches achieved their union in 610 under Persian aegis.

The advance of the Nestorians into Mesopotamia had resulted in the establishment of a see in Ḥīra, whose incumbent Hosea appears at a synod as early as 410. While the Monophysite Arabs continued their nomadic life the Nestorians of central Mesopotamia and chiefly of Ḥīra congregated into a community of 'servants of God' (*'ibād*) which tended to eliminate the sense of tribal differentiation. They put their mark on the culture of the Lakhmid state of the sixth century, although the dynasty itself, unlike the Ghassānids, did not adopt Christianity before its last ruler. The *'ibād* can be considered as a forerunner of the Islamic *umma*, 'community', for they represent the first known example of Arab speakers grouped by a common ideology, and this a group which, like the Muslim community in its first years, combined the organizational functions of the tribe with those of a religious fraternity. On the whole the contact of West and Central Arabia with the Lakhmid centre seems to have been stronger than with the Ghassānids. The stability of the court of Ḥīra towards the end of the pagan period attracted almost all the more important poets for a time; yet the development of Islam was not on that account more affected by influences from the eastern cultural centres than from the northern.

Be that as it may it was opposition to the Persians which led in 611 (some say 604) to the battle of Dhū Qār, in which the Banū Bakr and a few other tribes allied with them completely routed the Persians in alliance with other Arabs. This event had little immediate consequence, but in retrospect it appeared to the Arabs as the emergence of a national consciousness and as the trial of strength for a policy of conquest.

Although Christianity had touched and even been adopted by a number of different tribes, and Judaism too had been able to win proselytes, for instance in Yathrib, paganism suffered few losses in the northern zone of Arab culture. One cannot avoid the impression however that it continued rather from tradition and from the lack of organized opposition than because of any deep conviction. Of course the scholars to whom we owe the transmission of evidence of the pre-Islamic period have exercised a certain censorship in what they preserved and in the way they composed their information.

No monuments were built from whose remains we might now draw inferences; what was probably the only sanctuary erected in stone, the Kaʿba ('cube') of Mecca, was taken over by Islam. But it appears from literary sources that, particularly in the north of the peninsula, the religious atmosphere was fairly uniform: the same piety is mirrored in the 'red stone', the deity of the south Arabian city of Ghaimān, in the 'white stone' in the Kaʿba of al-ʿAbalāt (near Tabāla south of Mecca) and in the 'black stone' of Mecca itself; but equally in the conception and shape of the Kaʿba of Najrān, of al-ʿAbalāt and of Mecca. It can certainly be affirmed that the experience of divinity at that time was particularly associated with stone fetishes or was roused by mountains, special rock formations or trees of strange growth. This experience survives to this day; the sacred places of paganism still play their part as saints' or prophets' graves.

But it is certainly not the fault of the Islamic purveyors of tradition when they speak of the religion of the Jāhiliyya, the 'time of ignorance', as remarkably poor in myth, and can find no sign of an attempt to bring the numerous divinities together into a pantheon. The absence of a priestly class may be at least partly responsible. There were of course sanctuaries which were at the same time the property and cult estates of certain families—traces of such an order are to be found even in Mecca—but these families did not cohere over wide areas. Only once does a chief priest appear as the leader of a large group of tribes, the Rabīʿa, with the title *afkal;* the title is of Babylonian origin and has been mistakenly taken as a personal name. The nomads themselves who carried (and still carry) certain sacred objects or gods about with them had little to do with the local deities. The sky cult common to the Semites must also have been important in Arabia; the Koran gives a few indirect hints of this, for instance when it makes Abraham fight through to recognition of the true God by passing through a phase of star worship.

Fatalism and the star cult are closely connected throughout antiquity; in Arabia, even in the Koran, the Goddess of Fate appears together with Venus of the morning star and a third figure designated simply as 'The Goddess'. They are the 'daughters of Allah' favoured by the pagans. While in Arabic Manāt is the linguistic counterpart of Hellenistic Tyche, Dahr, fateful 'Time' who snatches men away and robs their existence of purpose and value, and who was the favourite of later pagan generations, particularly the poets, can be connected with the eternal Chronos of Mithraism and Zurvan theology the universal ruler and consumer of all things.

Another idea common to the Semitic peoples is that of the highest (local) divinity as a king. It can be found on Arab soil among the

Thamūdites, but seems later to have died away; at any rate *malik* does not occur among the divine names that have come down to us, although its transference to the One God of Islam has preserved it in Muslim names, for instance the Caliph 'Abd al-Malik, 'servant of the King'. Comparable to this is the term *Raḥmān* or *Raḥīm* for the High God, the 'Merciful' whom we meet in Safaitic, Palmyran and Sabaean; it has been preserved and given prominence by its transference to Allah. That the Islamic God received the most abstract of all possible names, *al-ilāh*, Allah, '*The* God' is certainly to a great extent due to the linguistic usage of Muhammad's environment, but it is to be ascribed too to its meaning, which is free of all associations, and to a certain resistance to an imported nomenclature. It seems quite a defensible suggestion that even before Muhammad the Ka'ba was first and foremost the holy place of Allah, and not that of the Hubal deriving from the Nabataean and the 359 other members of the astrological syncretic pantheon assembled there. Circumambulation (*ṭawāf*), standing in worship (*wuqūf*), bloodless and bloody sacrifice were the essential cult elements everywhere on the peninsula; equally universal among the Arabs was the piece of land (*ḥimà*) removed from profane use, the holy ground with right of asylum for all living things; the *ḥaram* surrounding the Meccan Ka'ba is no more than a particularly impressive example of it.

Within the consciousness of the Muslim community there lives a small class of seekers after God, one of whom was related to Muhammad's first wife and has been placed directly into the history of the foundation of Islam. Turning as alternatives to Judaism, Christianity or to an unorganised monotheism, these personages are to be understood, however much they may have been individualised by legend, not as distinct historical characters but as personified symbols of a current of unrest and spiritual experimentation. They seem to have singled themselves out from their environment, but evidently were not persecuted. They are all ascetics. Strangely enough not one of them is recorded as having ended his road by coming to rest in the Muslim community. Their contemporaries knew them as *ḥunafā'* (sing. *ḥanīf*), an Arabization of the Syrian *ḥanpā* 'pagan'. In church language the word was used for heretics, who were considered as hellenistic pagan renegades. Even the Manichaeans were damned as 'pagans'. The Arabic meaning—approximately: confessionally unaffiliated monotheist—is best understood if *ḥanpā* or *ḥanīf* be taken first and foremost to mean dissenter; and dissenters, individualists, the *ḥunafā'* remained. The sympathy for them felt both by contemporaries and by posterity throws light on the spreading dissatisfaction with inherited religion, whose preservation was impossible to combine with full integration into the Near Eastern cultural sphere.

Islamic prejudice against an outmoded stage of development, the relative backwardness of the peninsula—even of the Yemen—compared with Persian and Graeco-Roman culture and not least the later decline of the peninsula into political insignificance and backwardness compared with Muslim Egypt, Syria or Iraq have perhaps made us underestimate the level of civilization of ancient Arabia. Added to this is the one-sidedness of its cultural activity, which produced nothing in the artistic sphere and in the literary nothing worthy of mention except in a very narrow field. It is not mistaken to imagine the culture of the period as entirely oral in tradition; but this should not lead us to conclude that illiteracy was universal. There are inscriptions in North Arabic script dating from 512 and 568. Some knowledge of writing is evidenced in many Jahilite verses, and the Meccans must have used documents written in Arabic for their diplomatic and commercial dealings. At any rate it is certain that the Arab Jews had their holy books, although of course nothing can be said of the standard of their scholarship. The same is true of the Christians, though the question of the existence of a pre-Islamic translation of the Bible into Arabic is certainly to be answered in the negative; nor is the claim tenable that an Arabic Bible arose in the region of Ḥīra about 620. The psalms and the gospels were accessible in Arabic at the earliest in the eighth century, and a generally used definitive translation of the whole Bible was not available even in the tenth century. The Koran remains the first holy book in Arabic and at the same time—although the ordinances of customary law were highly developed—the first attempt at a codification of law. Science there was none, but poetry was highly cultivated. And poetic language and tradition (even these not as rigid as they were interpreted by posterity) created a cultural unity; the Meccan dialect seems to have played the role of a professional economic *lingua franca*, distinct from the language of the poets.

Nomadic life set very definite limits to cultural development. Not until the transition to sedentary life or the normative recognition of the ideology of settled peoples could these limits be transcended. Strangely enough the destructive tendencies of Bedouin life, its lack of discipline and its inability to make long term plans, so precisely analysed by later Muslims like Ibu Khaldūn (d. 1406), not only did not prevent the rise of the peninsula to the threshold of the transformation, but when given suitable leadership showed themselves capable of being channelled, if only for a short period, into actions of world historical significance.

Muhammad

In recent years Arab nationalists have taken exception to the custom of regarding the appearance of Muhammad as the starting point of Arab history; Persians too have shown a similar attitude and have protested against treating Islam as the beginning of a new epoch rather than a political and religious intrusion into an older cultural development. Despite all these quite legitimate shifts of accent in the service of a new self-confidence there are two related facts that cannot be denied: first that it was only the mission of the Prophet that made the Arabs capable of taking a positive initiative in world history, and second that the lines of development in the Near East were one and all, like rays through a lens, refracted through Islam, and even where they showed themselves resistant to its temptations and pressures they were deeply affected, if not radically changed, by being aligned into a new historical system of relationships.

History is so rich in events on so many different levels that every period can find valid answers in the past for the problems that occupy it in the present. But valuable though this retro-projection of present experience may be it is hardly likely to do justice to what was important to men in those times. For example there is no doubt that Muhammad was not in sympathy with economic and social conditions in Mecca; yet to represent him as a social reformer or even as a theoretical economist would totally misconstrue the forces at work and the way in which society operated in his time. Right up to the present day the social critics and politicians of the Islamic world have tried in vain to work out a concrete and coherent system of economic and social organization from the revelations of the Koran, not understanding that in religion it is only attitudes of mind and experience that can be presented in a binding way, since anything concrete relating to one period of time becomes obsolete and restrictive overnight. Much of the timeless effectiveness of Islam is in fact due precisely to the fact that it only referred at very few points to the learning of the seventh century, or to its achievement in the Arabian peninsula, and where it did so the conscience of the faithful has been severely tested to accommodate and reinterpret what are now outmoded data.

The essential significance of the appearance of Muhammad is the crystallization of a new experience of the divine, which welded all those who shared it into a new kind of community. The effect of this experience on contemporary relationships is evident and unmistakable in both language and art. Most important: if Muhammad's understanding of the divine had been inaccessible to his contemporaries he would have found no following, and both prophet and message would soon have fallen into oblivion, like the majority of the bringers of new tidings of God. But Muhammad and his work survived because he spoke, if one may be permitted so to express it, not only for God but for the Arabs, or, to put it more as he saw it, because he came as an Arab prophet to his people.

In a verse of Muhammad's middle period God bids him speak thus: 'See, my prayers and my devotion and my life and my death belong to Allah the Lord of the worlds. He has no companion and that is what I am bidden; for I am the first of the Muslims' (6, 163). These few words contain the essence of the new message that Muhammad had brought to his people. The rise from a primitive to a higher religion consists fundamentally in a limitation of the objects and ideas through which the divine is directly to be experienced. The passages between the natural and the supernatural become fewer, the distance between the visible and the invisible world becomes greater. It is no longer possible to endow spontaneously every element of one's surroundings with a spirit; the religious sources are concentrated in a single centre: the omnipotent God and Creator whose irresistible will, which sets no limits even for itself, becomes the principle of order that holds phenomena together and gives them the reason for their existence.

Some elements in Mecca and Yathrib, perhaps in the steppes as well, had begun to question as naive the aimlessness and arbitrariness of supernatural beings without full powers over the world. Muhammad had an answer to these questions. Its components were taken in detail almost exclusively from Judaism and Christianity, but as a whole his answer symbolized the awakening of a new conception of the world and a new perception of life.

Muḥammad ibn 'Abdallāh, a Quraish of the Hāshim clan, born into one of the noble families of Mecca, was orphaned early and was poor until his marriage, but he lived in close contact with the wealth and power of his native town. This class situation in other cases too has made men dissatisfied and more perspicacious than most of the world around them and has driven them to seek innovations. Tradition places his birth in the 'year of the elephant'. In this year Abraha, the Abyssinian ruler of the Yemen, attacked Mecca, probably in the Byzantine interest. He was forced by a miracle to retire. The year traditionally assigned to Muhammad's birth, 570, cannot be upheld, and with it the whole chronological structure of the Prophet's biography falls to the ground. Since, understandably, little attention was paid to the youthful history of one as yet obscure, legend has had an easy task in filling out the lacunae according to the taste of posterity and the Near Eastern idea of what is appropriate to a prophet.

Before and at his birth there are signs and wonders. Wherever the child dwells it brings blessings. Early in life he enters into contact with the supernatural world and from it come angels to cleanse his heart. A prophet guards the flocks; but a well-born Meccan goes into the caravan business. It is quite possible that Muhammad travelled with the caravans; he may well have reached Syria and, as legend tells, been discovered by a Christian hermit; but it can be stated with certainty that he had no close contact with the Christians there, nor did he attend a Christian service with any understanding, otherwise the factual errors about Christian teaching and customs would be inexplicable: there is for instance his portrayal of Holy Communion as a meal (Koran 5, 114). He married Khadīja, a rich merchant's widow fifteen years his senior (at her second marriage she had attained the 'round' age of forty so beloved in the orient: an age not made any more probable by the seven children whom she subsequently bore to Muhammad). The marriage came about on her initiative and gave him the freedom of movement and the leisure he needed for the development of his thought. Every year he spent a long time in solitude on the mountain of Ḥirā', at whose foot Mecca lies.

Tradition records that Muhammad received his call in the year 610 when he was about forty years old. It is curious that the early sources do not agree about this central fact of Islamic history. Both from other reports and from the Koran we gather that Muhammad had visions only at the beginning of his prophetic career, and then but seldom, and that on the whole his communication with the extra-sensory world was limited to acoustic experiences. There is much to suggest that Muhammad thought at first that he saw God himself, though he himself described it later as a nameless apparition. It was finally identified as Gabriel. When the heavenly messenger first ordered Muhammad to speak—the phrasing is reminiscent of Isaiah 40, 6—Muhammad refused; at the second command he asked what he should recite, and at the third he spoke the verses which appear as the 96th sura of the Koran:

Recite (*iqra'*)! in the name of thy Lord who created,
Who created man from congealed blood.
Recite for thy Lord is the most noble,

Who taught by the pen
Taught man what he did not know.

Qr', the root of the word claimed to be the first of the revelation, means both 'to recite' and 'to read', and from it the word *Qur'ān* (Koran) is derived on the Syrian model of *qeryānā*, *lectio*, 'reading of Scripture'; it refers both to single pronouncements and to the whole collection assembled in the Book.

After a cessation (*fatra*) of the visitations, a period of emptiness which he found very painful, experiencing the same abandonment by God felt by other visionaries, the revelations began again and did not cease until his death. His household and particularly Khadīja sustained him from the first with faith and encouragement. For three years he made known the tidings revealed to him to his intimate circle alone. Then at last he decided to present himself to the Meccans as the messenger of God.

What made him feel it his duty to warn his people was his certainty of the Last Judgment. This, together with his faith in the single Creator and Judge is the cornerstone of his message. In powerful, poignant utterances, with image piled upon image, he prophecies the end of the world. The dead will be awakened in the hideous despair of the Day of Judgment, each will be judged separately according to his deeds and will receive his deserts, being either condemned to eternal flames or vouchsafed eternal bliss in Paradise.

Although the vivid descriptions convey the impression that the crisis is near at hand, it is nowhere stated that the catastrophe will occur in the Prophet's lifetime. The Koran also differs from its compeers in the absence of any complacency or gloating or of any mythological speculation.

The certainty of the Day of Judgment determines the ethic and the emotional attitude. It is not enough to believe in it. The pious man is one who fears the Lord and trembles before the 'hour' (Koran 21, 50). Faith and works will be weighed at the end of time. Muhammad seems only gradually to have become conscious of the logical consequence of his experience of the divine: the helplessness of man before the divine decision, deriving from the unlimited omnipotence of Allah which—by earthly standards—subordinates divine justice to divine majesty. His warning, and he was a warner before he was a prophet, stood in direct contrast to the acquisitive worldly materialism of Mecca. The Meccans seem to have received Muhammad's preaching at first with a kindly indifference; possibly his word was more inflammatory to the Bedouin outside the town. At all events tradition insists that the conflict between Muhammad's small following, which was drawn from quite uninfluential circles, and the unconverted, only became acute when the Prophet made a direct attack on the divinities of the Meccans. It is said that at first he had recognized as the daughters of Allah the three great goddesses: al-Lāt, who was honoured in Ṭā'if, al-'Uzz'ā who was worshipped in Nakhla near Mecca, and Manāt, whose sanctuary lay in Qudaid between Mecca and Medina. This stand he now revoked and made a sharp distinction between the faithful and those who associated Allah with other gods. Intermediate beings who stand above men but below God can be legitimately accommodated with strict monotheism, and they were in fact sanctioned by Islam in the form of angels and of demons (*jinn*), so it seems likely that these goddesses were excluded along with others, some of whom are mentioned by name in the Koran, in order to concentrate the cult on the Ka'ba and eliminate the idea that there were other divine beings than Allah capable of independent activity and hence worthy of worship.

Tradition states that after two years of public activity the tensions between the Muslims, 'those who give themselves fully to God,' and their compatriots became such that Muhammad felt it necessary to send those of the faithful who were being directly molested to Christian Abyssinia as emigrants. Whereupon eighty-three male members of the Community, many of them with their families, settled for varying lengths of time across the Red Sea. If we can reckon the size of the early community by the number of those who went a few years later to Medina, then a considerable proportion of the converts must have been involved in this emigration. Probably this *hijra*, the emigration to Abyssinia, was motivated by an attempt to smooth out a split that was beginning inside the Community: perhaps between Muhammad and a group that from his point of view was hyperascetic. The date of 615 for the Abyssinian migration must be retained. Hence the first revelation must be placed before 610 or else the 'private' preaching must be reduced from the traditional three years.

In any case the numerical reduction of Muhammad's following did not lead to any mitigation of the conflict in Mecca. Religious resistance and devotion to the old gods and rites, ideological difficulties such as those arising from the teaching of the bodily resurrection of the dead (a folly to the Meccans as much as it had been to the Greeks), economic and social conditions which to us are no longer concretely tangible, though they still leave their traces today and were to lead a little later to the violent rejection of his message in Ṭā'if, finally political implications which Muhammad originally neither desired nor foresaw; all these factors made the relatively small community an alien body, troublesome and even dangerous.

There is no indication that Muhammad had any intention of taking power in Mecca. But in the nature of the situation, since he was the intellectual centre of a 'reform' group and for its members the highest, God-sent authority, he inevitably became a power factor whose incisive religious demands could not but encroach on the political sphere. Even Jesus had not been able to avoid a political construction being placed, rightly, it may be said, on his mission. It should be remembered that in the loose structure of 'city government' the personal recognition accorded to a prophet could all too easily create a quasi-official position. This may be one of the reasons why the Meccan pagans would not agree to recognize Muhammad as a messenger of God. Such recognition would have implied to the generality a recognition of his legitimate role as a leader. Moreover this prophet was not of a type calculated to impress the Meccans. To many the idea was unacceptable that God should have chosen so undistinguished a man to be his emissary. Allowing without hesitation that he possessed an intimate relationship with the supernatural world, it fitted with their philosophy to see him as one possessed by spirits (*majnūn*) or as a poet, who could be reckoned as a special kind of *majnūn*. The style of the revelations with its short sharp rhythms and the introductory oath-like asseverations is liable to create such a misunderstanding. In the most decisive tones God rejects such identifications: if the Prophet is not recognised as such his mission fails.

But unless they were prepared to undertake the physical annihilation of the Prophet and his followers the Meccans even then had lost any hope of prevailing against the new teaching. This was a result not so much of Muhammad's perseverance and cleverness, great as they were, or of the inflexibility of his sense of mission, or of the personal magnetism that radiates out of so many of the sources. What had become decisive was the fact that the Prophet possessed a system of ideas which drew its strength from an experience of God. This was clear even to his opponents, although they might not accept it. All the standard religious motifs which for centuries gone by had been echoing round the Near East were now present in his preaching, much altered and simplified, but in a certain sense complete, fulfilled. Where these motifs tended to punctuate religious history with a series of contradictory usages, Muhammad took a definitive stand.

His was the one God against the multiplicity of the pagan pantheon, but also against the two creators of Marcion and Mani, and against the trinitarian experience of the Christians. His was the

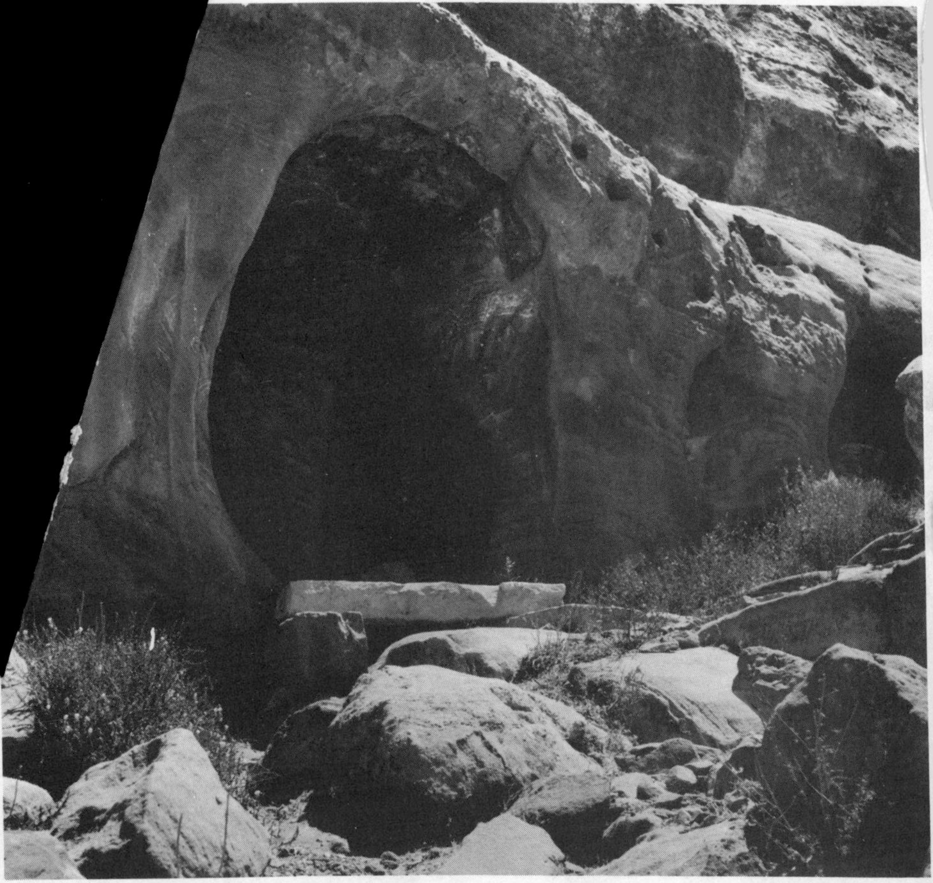

2 Cave on Mount Ḥirā' near Mecca, at the place where Muhammad received his calling. *Mme Frédérique Duran*

1 Horsemen hunting ostrich. Bedouin engraving on stone. Pre-Islamic period.
Department of Antiquities, Amman

human messenger of the Lord against the divine intermediaries clothed in human form. His too was the Book as testimony of the authenticity of the mission, the teaching of the Day of Judgment as an individual experience against the collective responsibility of a phase of Judaic development, to which the Islamic community indeed showed an inclination to return. With that he provided a moral turn to the concepts of paradise and hell, of reward and punishment, law and freedom—though this was primarily concerned in fact with the freedom of the omnipotent God. The separation of the creature from his creator, which many sought to reduce by deifying the living through gnosis and sanctification, was laid down as limitless and irrevocable; man was free of the corruption of original sin and only kept apart from truth and the right way by error and negligence—and on occasion by divine will.

During the early centuries an activating concept was the paradox, like that in Calvinism, of grace which does not exclude human responsibility. In the opposition of Mary and Martha Muhammad stood for Martha; the question of the value of this world was faced, and squarely, and though its supremacy was disallowed the idea that the world is absolutely wicked and repugnant to God was also rejected, so that limits were set to ascetism. The same realism shows in the concept of the individual, who in religion and morals is entirely dependent on himself, yet whose religious and moral task, above all the *jihād*, the 'endeavour on the path of God' or holy war, can only be achieved through and for the Community. Hence there was contemplation and periodic withdrawal from the world, but no monasticism. Muhammad's opposition to the pretensions and feck-lessness of the Bedouin does not actually belong in the doctrine, but it is plain in his intellectual attitude; his piety is entirely tailored to urban life.

No continuous pressure could be put on the Prophet and the early Community because their opponents had no corresponding organiza-tion, or better, because they were only inadequately capable of organizing themselves. Just as today the Communists in a liberal society are protected by the guarantees they are seeking to destroy, so the Muslims who set up their own Community in opposition to tribal society were protected by tribal ethic. Muhammad himself was safe from serious persecution because he was protected by his kin; the same was true of his followers who belonged by birth to Meccan society; intensive pressure was only possible within the clan. The Community could not be broken even when the rest of the Quraish carried out a prolonged boycott of the Hāshimites. But unfortunately towards the end of the boycott (619) occurred the death both of the head of Muhammad's clan, his uncle Abū Ṭālib, who had remained a pagan, and of Khadīja, whose support he evidently sorely missed. These two deaths affected him all the more in that Abū Ṭālib's brother and successor soon withdrew his protection from his nephew, allegedly because Muhammad had insisted that since Abū Ṭālib had died a pagan he was now in hell.

The Community does not seem to have suffered directly from this weakening of Muhammad's position. But it was becoming quite clear that in Mecca no community founded on a spiritual relationship could develop except within extremely narrow limits. However, what so frightened the Meccans, and no doubt the inhabitants of Ṭā'if as well with whom Muhammad at this time sought to make contact, namely the emergence of a new and potentially exceptionally strong power factor, appeared to the Arabs in Yathrib as the means of deliverance from the threat of self-destruction.

Mecca was organized as a homogeneous town. The oasis of Yathrib, a fertile area of about 55 square kilometres surrounded by steppe and desert, was divided into village-like settlements, some of them fortified with towers. In the middle of the sixth century it fell under the domination of the Banū Qaila, originally from South Arabia, whose sub-groups, the Aus and the Khazraj, had been in a continuous state of guerilla warfare against each other for generations. The name of Yathrib occurs early in inscriptions of Minaean traders from South Arabia; the name Medina, an Aramaic word for 'legal district, jurisdiction, city' certainly derives from the Jews but was given a new meaning by the Muslims as *Madīnat an-nabī*, 'the city of the Prophet'. The rest of the inhabitants, including three largish Jewish tribes, were drawn into the conflict. This came to a bloody climax in 617 in the 'Battle of Bu'āth', after which the protagonists were so exhausted that it gradually dwindled into an armistice, interrupted only by occasional acts of vengeance.

The smouldering crisis was damaging to husbandry, deprived the citizens of personal security and undermined the 'international' standing of the oasis. Nowhere can it be seen more clearly than in Yathrib how irrelevant was the tribal ethic to urban relationships, how impossible it was to combine the sovereignty of kindred units with the government of a complex region. It is difficult to imagine how even the ruthless supremacy of one tribe could have mastered the disorder: the defeated elements would have been latently hostile, every clan putting its own interests before the tribe as a whole, and stability impossible of achievement. The Muslim community on the other hand, with their Prophet and his God as foci, being accessible by personal decision and hence capable of unlimited expansion, embodied a principle of social and political order which could either fundamentally destroy the tribal organization or else embrace and absorb it. In either case the presence of the Muslims was bound to provide a stabilizing influence on the Arab tribes in their vain search for agreement.

The invitation to Muhammad to leave Mecca and settle in Yathrib naturally signified that he was recognized as a prophet, though it is not clear whether political rights were accorded him. After about two years of negotiations with representatives of an increasingly large group of converts, both individuals and sub-groups of the Aus and Khazraj who had gone over to Islam, Muhammad decided on the *hijra*, migration (also, breaking of old ties, leaving the tribal bond). In the summer of 622 some seventy members of his Community went ahead to Yathrib (Medina), so that he found a kind of bodyguard of *muhājirūn* (emigrants) when he arrived in the oasis about September 4, 622, with his friend and confidant, Abū Bakr. Sixteen years later this event, epoch-making in every sense, was taken to mark the year, starting by Arab reckoning on July 16, of the beginning of the Muslim era.

Muhammad left the choice of his dwelling-place to supernatural agency; the form followed pagan practice. Where his she-camel stopped he bought the place from its owners, two orphan boys, and erected a place for prayer; it is possible that it did not until later take on the style and form which the mosque (*masjid*) soon developed on the model of the Jewish synagogue. Beside it he built huts for his two wives, one of whom was 'Ā'isha, then only nine years old (born *c.* 614), the daughter of Abū Bakr. She has a place in history because she was his favourite and because of her political role after his death. Round her hut, the place where the Prophet died and was buried, arose later the world-famous pilgrimage mosque. In the course of time Muhammad's *dār* developed from these beginnings: a courtyard where the faithful could congregate, surrounded by dwellings, all built with the greatest simplicity of unbaked brick with beams of palm stems.

To accomplish his main task and unite a population torn asunder by dissension, Muhammad needed the harmonious co-operation of the *muhājirūn* with the Medinan 'helpers', *anṣār*. This in its turn required the economic independence of the immigrants. In the circumstances Muhammad had no other choice but to ensure this independence by raids on Meccan caravans. This procedure in no way scandalized his contemporaries morally, while its aggressiveness appealed to them politically. The first successful sally of this kind occurred during one of the sacred months; this weighed on the conscience of the members of the Community for a time, but was finally accepted as proper after the logic of economic necessity and the conscious break with pagan customs had made their full impact; this was confirmed in a revelation according to which the offence of the Meccans in their disbelief was graver than the sin of disturbing the peace at a holy time (Koran 2, 218).

The infringement made it desirable to hasten the inevitable military confrontation with the Meccans. The latter sent an army, or rather a number of armed troops amounting to about 950 men, to protect a specially rich caravan. After placing the caravan in safety at Badr, a little market village to the south-west of Medina, they fell upon the Muslims on March 15, 624 (or perhaps on the 13th or 17th). Their skill in strategy, their discipline, and their fervour in the cause of Islam bestowed an impressive victory on the something over three hundred followers of Muhammad (three-quarters of them Medinans) who defeated five or six hundred Meccans; about another three hundred had retired before the battle.

The small numbers involved should not lead us to underrate the importance of the battle. Among the fifty or so whom the Meccans left on the field were some of their most influential leaders; even more important was the fact that the young Community of Muhammad had put its strength to the proof; the political situation in Arabia began at once to take shape round the two poles of a decisive confrontation. The Muslims knew they had been supported by troops of angels, and felt exalted: what we should consider a denigration of human heroism by the appeal to miraculous help was more than compensated by the conviction that they were a chosen body and stood on God's side. 'Ye did not slay them (the Meccans), but it was God who slew them' came the revelation to Muhammad (Koran 8, 18). The mood of the faithful is mirrored horrifically in the verses of the dirge which begins:

'Let the enemy bewail his dead,
For they lie without hope of return;
Our brothers shall ye not bewail
For they are already in the heavenly spheres.'
(From the free translation by Goethe [Westöstlicher Divan, Chuld Nameh].)

Muhammed turned this wave of enthusiasm and increased prestige to account; using some trivial incident as a pretext he expelled the first of the three Jewish tribes, scarcely a month after Badr. After a short siege the Banū Qainuqā' were forced to leave Medina, abandoning their weapons and immovable property which were taken over by the *muhājirūn*. The Arab opposition to Muhammad, chiefly those nominal Muslims termed *munāfiqūn*, branded in the Koran as 'hypocrites' (lit. 'undecided, tepid'), allowed their cause to be weakened by this move, just as their opposition was destined in the future to be ineffective, mainly because they had no alternative to offer but absorption into the Muslim community which was becoming more universal each day. The Jews had shown themselves incapable of religious, and hence of political, assimilation, and since they denied Muhammad's role as the emissary of God they seemed even more dangerous than the Arab conservatives and malcontents.

The idea entertained by Muhammad about his mission was analogous at least, if not identical with the task with which a long series of God's messengers had been entrusted before him: to warn their people in their own language and show them the way to salvation. Once only does the Koran speak of Muhammad as the seal of the prophets, and therefore as the last in the series (33, 41). In detail Muhammad's view of himself has met with some alterations; but the inner logic of his position has been rather elaborated than erased by these changes. The Koranic revelation mentions a number of God's messengers by name, and stresses particularly Abraham, Moses and Jesus. It is quite evident that the messengers are all extraordinarily similar, in type and in their fate and in the content of their mission. Thus Muhammad might have expected the Jews in Medina to know him by his message and recognize him, particularly as he was certain he had been foretold in their holy scriptures. But this expectation was not justified in Jewish eyes. Although Muhammad tried to emphasize the real parallels of his teaching with the Judaic, and in the first stages at Medina imitated the Jewish service and addressed the prayers of the congregation towards Jerusalem, his teaching must have seemed to them fragmentary and twisted if not a positive caricature. The discrepancies, like those with Christianity of which he gradually became aware, the Prophet explained with the claim that the other religious communities had abandoned the original tradition through error or falsification, and that therefore he had the additional task of correcting error and confirming truth. According to him the Jews had turned aside from the monotheism defined in all its purity by their common ancestor Abraham, and Islam, seen aright, was returning to this unsullied original revelation whose cult-centre Muhammad declared to be Mecca. There Abraham had built the first Ka'ba with the help of his son Ismā'īl, who now emerges from the biblical shadows into the limelight, and there Abraham had practised the pure religion of the Ḥanīfs. What could be more natural than that henceforth prayers should be addressed towards Mecca? This completed the 'Arabization' of the revelation already inherent in its structure, and guaranteed the continuity of the Meccan tradition without infringing on the obligation to banish paganism from the holy precinct.

The idea of a truth repeatedly given to men corresponds to thoughts that had been constantly recurring since at least the first century AD, with basically unimportant variations. The prophet Elxai who preached in east Jordan at the time of Trajan proclaimed Christ as a being born many times in different people, who frequently speaks to humanity, not as himself, but through prophets. The pseudo-Clementines take up the dual motif of the Christ who is ever manifest anew but always in the service of the same eternal truth, and this motif was developed by a number of gnostic thinkers into the instrument which affords the spiritual unity of human history. Closer to Muhammad's experience is the modification of this conception whereby Mani (died 276) explained his own appearance: when he was 24 years old he was visited by an angel who announced to him that he had been chosen as a messenger of God. There had already been similar messengers before him who preached the wisdom of the Lord. Thus God had spoken in India through the Buddha, in Persia through Zarathustra and then through Christ to the west. But now, at the climax of the best generation, the office had come to the land of Babylon through Mani.

The accusation of falsification of Scripture has quite a venerable history; on many occasions the enemies of the Jews, the gnostics, and no less their antagonists made use of it with as much ardour as the Christian enemies of the Manichaeans; the argument as such is not particularly remarkable since it has always been the first to appear in any such polemic. More important, in fact crucial in its consequences, was the reduction to one level of all the teachings of all the 'People of the Book', arising inevitably from the identity of the divine message. Muhammad's defective knowledge of Christianity has often been pointed out. There was a number of factors making a theological agreement impossible from the start: the evanescence of the sacrificial death of Jesus, in whose place an apparition was fixed to the cross, as was believed by members of the docetic sects; the rejection of Jesus as the son of God; the repudiation of the Trinity (thought to be composed of God, Jesus, and Mary). At the same time, and almost unconsciously, characteristic eschatological ideas were adopted, even striking details like the view that the complexity of Jewish law was to be understood as a punishment. The Christian description of the Prophet as no better than an ambitious schismatic added one more impediment to an understanding.

Despite all this there is no doubt that the major part of the ideas and images that we meet in Muhammad's preaching are of Judaic or Christian origin. Yet this fact has little relevance to the question of the originality of Islam. Originality is not a religious value. Religious truth is experienced, and is 'rediscovered' because of its content; it has 'existed' unchanged since time began. The Prophet, in his own view and in the view of the Community, is not an originator of teachings but an awakener and a warner, and where necessary the creator of a form of life and community fitted to this newly acquired understanding of God, since this understanding can only be made concrete in the execution of commands and prohibitions, Understood thus Muhammad was a creative religious spirit and an emissary of God.

Even after the victory at Badr the survival of his revelation was still not secure. At bottom the victory for the young Community signified no more than a summons to battle. The Meccans, quite apart from the necessity of revenge, owed it to their prestige and to their foreign trade, the one dependent on the other, to keep Muhammad within bounds. So they brought together a carefully armed force of three thousand men, comprising every man available in the city and among the neighbouring Bedouin tribes. Shortly after the anniversary of Badr battle was joined on the north-west border of the settlement area of Medina. It is customary to name the battle after Uḥud, a mountain ridge where the Muslims took up their positions. Muhammad is reputed to have refused the help of the Jewish Banū Naḍīr; the leader of the 'hypocrites' retired with his people into the interior of the oasis before the battle began, perhaps to organise a second line of defence in case of a breakthrough. The sources are too much preoccupied with the fame and shame of the individual participants to give a clear idea of how the battle went; it is certain none the less that Muhammad was wounded, that the discipline of the faithful left much to be desired, and that in the end the Meccan cavalry carried the day. Taking Badr and Uḥud together, the losses of each party more or less cancel each other out. To many Meccans it may have seemed that the collective duty in the matter of vengeance had been adequately performed, and perhaps the army was more exhausted by the fight than the number of the casualties suggests; whatever the cause they left Medina alone and started on the homeward march without further hostilities.

The military success turned out to be a political mistake. The senselessness of a policy based on the *status quo* was made apparent when Muhammad managed to solve the theological problem posed by the misfortune. He laid responsibility for the defeat on the disobedience of a section of the troops, at the same time pointing out how God considered that any intervention in their favour would have involved the faithful in yet deeper disgrace. He was able to strengthen his position in Medina by forcing a second Jewish tribe, the Banū Naḍīr, to migrate to the Khaibar oasis to the north of Medina where the Naḍīr had a share of land. This he accomplished in August or September 625 by a siege, started on some trumpery pretext, and added to its effect by destroying part of their palm plantation. He intensified his policy, drastically followed ever since Badr, of winning the neutrals by intimidation. The Meccans on their side made systematic attempts to attract the tribes for a final campaign to put an end to the Muslim community, and organized a mass levy.

It took the Meccans two years to prepare. They then advanced on Medina with ten thousand men—though only seven and a half thousand of these can be vouched for with certainty. Muhammad was able to put only about three thousand against them. To protect the north-west frontier of the city's territory against the formidable Meccan cavalry Muhammad took the advice of a Persian slave convert and caused a ditch to be dug (*khandaq*), a stratagem apparently new to Arabia, which gave its name to the campaign. Although the ditch was quite shallow it brought the cavalry to a virtual standstill. The inclemency of the weather, the problem of supplies, and first and foremost the lack of cohesion among the attackers, only half of whom consisted of Meccans or their close allies, enabled Muhammad to create a breach in the enemy front by diplomatic means. The tribal contingents disintegrated, the attempt to persuade the neutral Banū Quraiẓa to open a front against the Medinans in the south was unsuccessful; a feeling of uselessness and apathy made the besiegers retire after two weeks; the sources report six deaths among the *anṣār* and three among the Meccans.

With the failure of the 'Battle of the Ditch' the old system was played out. The only question now was whether and when Muhammad would be able to assume the succession. Directly after the retreat of the allies the third and last of the politically important Jewish tribes, the Quraiẓa, was annihilated as a punishment for their ambiguous behaviour during the siege; about six hundred men were executed and the women and children sold into slavery. Medina was now virtually a homogeneous sovereign city of the Muslim *umma*.

The word *umma*, already employed by the pre-Islamic poet Nābigha in the sense of religious community, comes into use with the *hijra* to designate the Community; even in modern times there is no word for 'state': the word *daula*, in use since the eighth century, means dynasty or regime. The adjective *ummī* derived from the noun, corresponding to the Latin *gentilis*, was applied to Muhammad to identify him as the Prophet of the (pagan Arab) *gentes*. *Ummī* was now interpreted on dogmatic grounds as *vulgaris*, which is to say *incultus*, in order to protect the incomparable knowledge of human and divine things which the Prophet brought to light. The alteration of meaning has remained dogma to the present day, and has tended to prevent the emergence of Koranic source studies comparable with Biblical critique, or indeed of any kind of critical scholarship in Islamic studies.

It is worthy of note that the first and only document of its kind to provide information about the organization of Medina at the time of Muhammad, the so-called 'Covenant of the Community' of Medina, does not take account of the three great Jewish tribes, but only treats of small Jewish groups as members of the *umma*. It dates from before the battle of Badr but was completed in its present form after the elimination of the Quraiẓa, having been accommodated to the changing fortunes of the city. This community is characterized as *umma wāḥida min dūn an-nās*, 'a single community, separate from other men'. The tribes and clans are preserved within the *umma* and the mutual duties and rights are established by free agreement with the Prophet Muhammad. He emerges as a kind of tribal chief, deciding relations with the surrounding pagan world and acting in the way of a judge in the necessary dispositions for the various groups of the *umma*. He is also the leader in battle. *Dhimma*, God's guarantee of security, is valid for all the faithful; the Jews are expressly described as *umma ma' al-muslimīn*, a 'community with [or beside] the Muslims'. This formula separates the Jews from the *umma Muḥammadiyya*, and thus develops further the idea that faith gives access to the Community, a concept that has remained the basis of the Islamic interpretation of the state. Adherence to God and his Prophet makes the Muslim; Muslims live in the *umma*, even should they fortuitously dwell among the infidel; traditional right guaranteed the existence of various communities, which up to a point led an autonomous life based on a common spiritual descent. It did not take long for even the Meccan *mushrikūn*, the 'polytheists', to recognize the *umma* as a *sui generis* political entity.

After the Battle of the Ditch the Bedouin felt increasingly strongly the attraction and the pressure of the Prophet's power. Gradually they were drawn into the disputes between Mecca and Medina, and it is difficult to avoid the impression that though the quarrels of the nomads were still often trivial and amoral, they gained from this involvement a higher purpose and a higher worth. For the first time in living memory the victory or defeat of an idea was at stake, an idea affecting the ordering of society which was increasingly involving the whole of Central and North Arabia in its destiny. Thus it was in the logic of the development that from about 628 Muhammad insisted on the adoption of Islam by any party to a treaty, before making an alliance with them.

Muhammad seems to have tried deliberately to thwart the Meccans' trade with the north and so to weaken their economy. At this time it must have become apparent to him that if the *pax islamica* was to be maintained the only way to uphold the prohibition on fighting between Muslims was by continuous expansion. Economic intensification was impossible in Arabia, or at any rate it lay outside the contemporary range of vision. This explains why the campaigns northwards became more frequent in the years after the siege. In 629 an expedition of three thousand men came into contact with an imperial army at Mu'ta, apparently already considered to belong to Byzantium; yet although only eight or twelve men were lost it retired to Medina, apparently defeated. The reason for this undertaking and the details of its termination will probably always remain obscure. At this period Muhammad is supposed to have sent letters to six rulers of exceedingly varied importance—the Persian king, the Byzantine emperor, the Negus of Abyssinia, the regent (?) of Egypt, a Ghassānid prince and a chief of the Banū Ḥanīfa in South-East Arabia—with the demand that they adopt Islam; only the Persian king is said to have received the envoys unkindly; the others despatched them with encouraging words and valuable gifts. The historicity of these embassies cannot be seriously upheld. What the report demonstrates however is that Muhammad was successful in establishing relations with the outside world, and that his successors who devised the wording of the letters desired to provide documentary evidence that Muhammad had been sent to all peoples and not only to the Arabs.

Meanwhile the first months of the year 628 saw an episode in the conflict between Muhammad and the Meccans which I feel represents the climax of the Prophet's statesmanship. Inspired by a dream Muhammad suddenly decided to go with fifteen hundred volunteers, most of them Bedouin, on the 'little pilgrimage' (*'umra*) to Mecca. Only lightly armed, and taking with them the beasts for the concluding sacrifice, the Muslims drew towards the holy precinct. The Meccans feared their intentions and tried to bar Muhammad's way, but he reached the boundary of the *ḥaram* at al-Ḥudaibiya, whence he conducted negotiations which resulted in the pilgrimage being abandoned for that year. In return the Meccans promised to admit him for three days in the following year; during these days they were to clear the town. A treaty was drawn up which Muhammad, much to the annoyance of the Muslims, conducted in his own name and not as the Prophet, replacing the usual Muslim preface 'In the name of Allah, the Merciful, the Compassionate' by the conventional 'In Thy name, O God'. He guaranteed freedom of alliance for the Bedouin and undertook to return immediately any Meccan converts who came to Medina, without requiring reciprocal bail. The Prophet thereupon declared the pilgrimage to be at an end, ordered the sacrificial beasts to be slaughtered and set out for home.

The faithful were deeply disappointed; they felt humiliated and deceived in their faith in the Prophet to whom 'in homage pleasing to God' they had just recently given themselves for better or worse. Muhammad remained unmoved and it was not long before the advantages of this apparent retreat became noticeable. The treaty had recognized the political existence of the *umma* as a partner of equal importance with Mecca. The freedom of association for the Bedouin worked to the advantage of the *umma* since it alone could offer association to a growing system of power; Muhammad had no fear that they would choose to return to the confusion of the Meccan alliance, while the attractions of Islam could not be neutralized by a piece of paper. Increasing numbers of tribes sought to come to an understanding with Medina; the stream of deserters from Mecca never ceased. The leading circles in Mecca had seen that the game was lost and that they must save the status of the city, as far as that was still possible, by integration into the Muslim Community. Muhammad for his part needed the experience of the Meccan ruling class; the expansion of the *umma* and above all its fundamental organization could not be administered without the help of the men of the city.

The deferred 'little pilgrimage' was duly performed in 629. Muhammad had already secured the routes to the north by conquering the Jewish oasis of Khaibar. He allowed the inhabitants to stay on their land as a kind of tenant, without demanding their conversion to Islam, in return for the surrender of half the produce. Here he laid the foundations of a method often used later to incorporate non-believers into the empire of the *umma*. The Meccan who may still have harboured some doubts about the outcome thought better of it when he saw the army of pilgrims arrive. The leading lights in Mecca, such as the future conqueror of Egypt 'Amr ibn al-'Āṣ and the great General Khālid ibn al-Walīd, put themselves at Muhammad's disposal in Medina. Abū Sufyān, the first citizen of the city, was at pains as ambassador to remove any difficulties that might have arisen from the treaty of al-Ḥudaibiya. He did not succeed entirely, but he and his household were the Prophet's men before he returned. Al-'Abbās, an uncle of Muhammad and ancestor of the 'Abbāsid dynasty, though he played no outstanding role in Mecca at this time, seems now to have been converted to Islam.

The reason adduced by Muhammad for his decision to occupy Mecca was, as always in such cases, trivial. Mecca was undermined and ready to save what it could by incorporation into the *umma*. After a general amnesty had been declared for all who put themselves under the protection of Abū Sufyān or stayed in their houses, Muhammad appeared in the first days of January 630 with an army consisting largely of Bedouin allies. The resistance of a small group of Quraish was quickly dispelled and on January 11th he entered Mecca. The revolution was effected remarkably leniently. A handful of people who had infringed the law were put to death: not for the first time was Muhammad's sensitivity to ideological, or better propagandist, opposition, apparent; otherwise even the extremist leaders were shown mercy. Looting was forbidden; a few rich men were forced to make a contribution to compensate the poorer followers for having been deprived of booty. It is remarkable how little opposition was raised to the destruction of the sanctuaries outside Mecca and to the taking over of the Ka'ba for the new faith; even more striking perhaps is how many 'pagan' leaders pledged themselves fully to Muhammad, and served the *umma* as high officials or officers. In many cases they met a martyr's death in the expansionist wars of the next decade.

Mecca never quite won back its earlier importance after it adopted Islam; Medina remained the centre of the *umma*. This circumstance seemed to offer the tribes living round Mecca, the Hawāzin and the Thaqīf, the opportunity to acquire the control of the trade routes for the nomads. The Thaqīf also hoped to win back the supremacy in Ṭā'if which they had lost to the Quraish.

Under their chief Mālik the Hawāzin assembled an army of perhaps twenty thousand. As an incentive they took their women, children and herds with them into the field. Their aims are not entirely clear; but the fact that the Meccans even in their final affliction made no attempt to form an alliance with these Bedouin is an illuminating commentary on the depth of the contradictions inherent in the situation. In any case the decisive battle came hardly three weeks after the surrender of Mecca, at Ḥunain; its outcome secured the dominance of city culture and of a political organization based on cities. The siege of Ṭā'if, where the fugitive Hawāzin leader had fled, was raised by Muhammad after two weeks; the town surrendered voluntarily a few months later. In the distribution of the booty the new Meccan converts received more consideration than seemed justified to the veteran faithful; quite apart from a few transparent political practicalities, Muhammad must have been anxious to keep on the right side of the Meccan aristocracy; it was his strongest bulwark against the unruly nomads and the only class from which he could draw in any numbers for the personnel he needed for both military and civil tasks.

The conquest of Mecca was emotionally and ideologically the fulfilment of Muhammad's mission inside Arabia. It was the victory recorded in the beautiful one hundred and tenth surah of the Koran;

'Since Allah's help and victory have come
And thou seest men enter into Allah's religion in troops,
Then sing praises to thy Lord, and ask forgiveness of Him
For he turns not away."

But the dynamics of the political situation did not allow the Prophet to pause. It looked as though the *umma* could only survive if Muhammad succeeded in assembling the power of the Arab people further under the true faith. In the late summer of 630 he was already marching towards the Arab-Byzantine frontier at the head of a mighty army. Whether his aim was to subjugate the Christian Arabs who had taken their tents into Byzantine territory or, as a preparatory measure, to defeat the imperial troops, cannot be made out. What happened was that after ten days in the frontier oasis of Tabūk without any fighting the march homeward began, during which the Christian settlements ensured for themselves the protection of the Prophet and free exercise of their religion by undertaking to pay an annual tribute (and a Jewish settlement handed over weapons as well); the agreements created an important precedent. On his return Muhammad ordered the destruction of a mosque which, to judge from the character of its founder, had been built by an extreme seclusionist group in al-Qubā', a suburb of Mecca. This is one of the rare indications of religious dissension during the lifetime of the Prophet. Ideas that came to the fore in later internal disputes must of course already have had their supporters, particularly those of a kind which later provided the religious foundation for 'Alid legitimacy.

Even before the fall of Mecca Muhammad had made contacts to the south beyond the central Arabian cultural sphere; but he could not embark on effective incorporation of the Yemenite districts until the Meccan system of trade and traffic was entirely under Muslim control.

The murder of the Persian king Khusrau Parwēz in 628 had left the Persians in their Yemenite 'colony' entirely to their own devices; they and the *abnā'*, the children of Iranian fathers and Arab mothers, were not finding life there easy. Thus it is not surprising that, in the confused struggles for power, they along with a number of Arab tribes sought association with Muhammad. Muslim government officials and tax collectors arrived in the Yemen in the wake of small military expeditions, and it is due not least to the arrogant and inconsiderate behaviour of these tax collectors that after Muhammad's death there was a widespread falling off of support in the Yemen.

On the whole the pagans were prepared to join Islam, but not so the Christians and the Jews. An important treaty (*'ahd*) was drawn up between Muhammad and the Nestorian community of Najrān. It provided that the Nestorians, together with the Jews who had settled in the city, should be allowed to keep their faith and to be exempt from military service and other levies upon payment of a tax (*jizya*). A few years later 'Umar I forced them to resettle elsewhere, with compensation for their lost lands. Some went to Syria, some to the neighbourhood of Kūfa. But the tax remained. Until the end of the eighth century complaints of its severity were perpetually being brought before the Caliph.

During Muhammad's last years there gradually took shape the religious law of personal status: limited polygamy in the patriarchal family and a regulation of inheritance which took account of the new individualism. Religious custom was also in process of creating the image that to Muslim eyes was to seem characteristic of the new religion. At about the same time were introduced the prohibitions of various pagan customs, such as wine-drinking (2, 216) and the eating of pork (2, 174). The practice of circumcision, taken over from the pagan period without Koranic sanction, was affirmed. The latter two became the most important signs of adherence to the faith. But it was less these customs than the rites themselves which lent their rhythm to the Community, in particular the Koranic prohibition of the movable month, which had served the Arabs to adjust between their lunar calendar and the solar year, but had been handled it seems with little skill (Koran 9, 36–37). Apart from the inclination to disassociate from paganism, the new divisions of time established by God seem to have been inspired by a certain practicality of attitude to a measure which had previously made life exceedingly complicated.

The principal religious practice was, and is, the prescribed ritual prayer (*ṣalāt*); it is to be carefully distinguished from personal invocation (*du'ā'*).

The *ṣalāt* consists of a strict sequence of combined gestures and formulae to be performed five times in the day, where possible, in common and under a prayer leader (*imām*), though in Muhammad's lifetime the requirement of five sessions daily was not yet laid down. The Koran prescribes only two or three, and raising the number to five is probably the result of Jewish influence; it is worth noting that the Zarathustrians also prescribe five daily prayers. The basic connection of Islam with the older People of the Book gives rise to similar ritual prescriptions, though they are modified in practice: the solemn communal *ṣalāt* is performed on Friday (which is not a day of rest), the faithful are called to prayer by the voice of the *mu'adhdhin*, not by a bell or clapper. The required fasts consist of abstention from food from the first to the last glimmer of daylight for a whole month—as against the short total fasts of the Jews, the six weeks' Lent of the Christians and the forty days of the Manichees. But, unless it be classed simply as an ordinary pilgrimage, the *ḥajj* is an independent rite, combining and vitally transforming the most varied elements of pre-Islamic pilgrimages and weaving them into a complex chain of ceremonies which starts out from and returns to finish at the Ka'ba in Mecca.

The Prophet seems to have been much concerned in his last years with the revision of pagan customs; he himself performed the *ḥajj* in its final form in 632. The rites, not described in the Koran, created an easy transition to the new religion by sanctioning ancient practices like kissing the black stone, the circumambulations of the Ka'ba, the 'stoning of the (three hewn pillars known as) satans' at Minà and the animal sacrifice performed there; these archaic devotions together with the duty to undertake the *ḥajj* at least once in a lifetime gave Islam a spiritual ceremonial centre; it increased in functional significance as a focus of integration the more the circle of the faithful spread out beyond the Arab world. The universal facing towards the 'navel of the world' was to some extent a substitute for a church organization. The same effect was secured by Muhammad's decree to exclude non-Muslims from the pilgrimage; this was later understood as exclusion from Mecca and from the entire peninsula. The purification of the *ḥajj* and the commandment to fight the pagan without mercy signified in the circumstances of the age that Arabdom and Islam were to become synonymous; and indeed afterwards no large groups of Christian Arabs were tolerated except outside the peninsula, and even then only with reluctance.

It was felt as especially significant that this sharp dissociation from men of other faiths was finalized precisely in the preparation of the ultimate form of the pilgrimage. Only the Muslims shall (Koran 9, 18) visit the 'Mosques of Allah'. The idolators 'who place other Gods on a par with Allah' had been forbidden to marry true believers since al-Ḥudaibiya. They 'are unclean' and may not in future approach the Sacred Mosque in Mecca (9, 28).

And the earlier revelations speaking sympathetically of the People of the Book, particularly of the Christians (5, 85), whose teaching had indeed already been rejected, were now replaced by the general instruction: 'Fight those to whom the Book was given, who believe not in Allah and in the Last Judgment, and who forbid not what Allah and His apostle have forbidden and who do not practise the true religion, until they pay the tribute (*jizya*) as much as they are able (*'an yad*), and humbly. The Jews say Ezra is the son of God; and the Christians say that the Messiah is the son of God; that is what they say with their mouths, imitating the sayings of those who disbelieved before. Let God fight them! How they lie!' (Koran 9, 29–30).

The sharpening of the anti-Christian position went hand in hand with a more precise formulation of the Islamic message, and it corresponded to the expansion of Medina towards the Byzantine north. Hardly had he returned from pilgrimage before Muhammad was arming for a campaign into southern Palestine and east Jordan. But at this moment the Prophet was suddenly attacked by a fever from which he died, after a short illness, on June 8, 632, to the measureless dismay of the faithful.

He had made no provision for a successor. He was far from having consolidated his relations with the tribes, and there was much to be done about other religious movements similar to Islam which had spread on Arab soil. What Muhammad bequeathed to the bereaved Community was threefold: an organization erected on a universal principle of order, upheld by the authority of God; a long series of revelations, not yet systematically compiled, which gave a lead in every sphere of life and whose linguistic formulation exercised an aesthetic fascination that could not but lend support to the authority of their contents; lastly, the memory of a personality the like of which never before or since has appeared in Arabia: a thinker and judge, military leader and organizer, emissary of God and educator, comprehensible to his people in his virtues and his weaknesses, showing Arabdom the way to a religio-political destiny in which its greatness had scope to develop, although in the event it finally came to grief as the nation state of a *civitas Dei*, because of the excessive demands placed upon it.

External Power and Internal Division

FROM the classic Muslim point of view the climax of world history was over with the death of the Prophet. The unbroken *umma*, usually designated *jamā'a* since the last years of Muhammad, spread wider during the following decades and carried the partial realization of the order willed by God beyond the land of its inception, thus, in Muslim eyes, bestowing on the world an age of incomparable blessing. But the contradiction inherent in the message between theocracy and sovereignty, between the ideal of the 'best' community and the measures resulting from it, developed tensions which destroyed its spiritual as well as its political unity. After the middle of the century the joy in a turn of history which seemed to confirm the sense of election was attenuated by a sadness at the course of history and a suffering which is only too discernible even today in the Muslim's image of himself. All the more deeply should the believer examine that time of origin when the break between norm and reality had not poisoned men's hearts; all the more carefully should those born later filter out the directions for living provided by this short epoch. For while it may be an exaggeration to say that in those first days life was lived in every way as a model for ever, it is the life of that period which, together with the Koranic judgments and commandments, provides the outlines of correct existence and shows the categories by the help of which the problems of the successors are to be understood and solved.

The Muslim feels himself driven to glorify the deeds of the Prophet in order to ensure himself a flawless basis of life. We find this as alien as we feel embarrassing the question of his subjective sincerity. It is not easy to accept a 'revelation' as one of a series running into hundreds. But in a society for whom the trance has the character of a supernatural source of understanding the line separating the conscious from the subconscious doubtless runs at a different level from where we would draw it. It is at all events certain that doubt was never cast on the possibility of such an inspiration; all that was disputed in the early days was the person and the sources. Apparently too the appearance of Muhammad set precedents: towards the end of his life 'the prophet' was regarded as the political leader 'par excellence' in East and South Arabia, and would have remained so for a long period, had not the victory of Islam rendered the spontaneous continuation of this type of personality impossible.

As a charismatic leader Muhammad was irreplaceable; but for the administrator of the Community the *muhājira* and the *anṣār* each wanted to see one of their own people. The *anṣār*, 'Helpers', were unquestionably in the majority. The *muhājira*, 'Companions of the Flight', were mainly Meccans of various dates of conversion, though the title of *muhājir* was bestowed on converts attracted from other tribes; it seems likely that the Prophet had distinguished a *bai'a 'arabiyya*, simple adherence to the Community, from a *bai'at al-hijra* which involved the migration to Medina as well. It is not without a certain interest that the word *anṣār* has an adjective formed from it and has been included after the manner of a tribal or local affiliation in the names of numerous individuals, whereas this has not happened with *muhājir*, in spite of the high esteem and close fraternity of the Companions of the Flight. At a stormy session the *anṣār* were finally persuaded not to insist on the succession going to one of their own members nor on the double rule of a Companion and a Helper, and partly under pressure from the Bedouin who were streaming into the city, they agreed to do homage to Abū Bakr, one of the Prophet's oldest adherents, and thus to a representative of the religious aristocracy, who was born a member of one of the smaller Quraish clans.

Abū Bakr had been entrusted by Muhammad to represent him at communal prayer during his last illness. And it was as 'representative' of the emissary of God, *Khalīfat rasūl Allāh* (soon simplified to *Khalīfa*, caliph) that Abū Bakr saw himself in his office. In the view of the gradually developing Islamic law the succession of Abū Bakr had been established by election and made legitimate by *bai'a*, homage through shaking hands, at which those present also pledged the absent. Abū Bakr's conception of his office probably explains why he refused to be dissuaded from the northward campaign planned by Muhammad, though the political situation had changed to the disadvantage of the Medinans meanwhile, and with the constant threat to Muslim communal life the campaign caused a sensible worsening of military security. The troops returned after two months. No significant result of the campaign has been recorded.

Upon the announcement of Muhammad's death the political structure erected by him began everywhere to totter. A number of the most important tribes considered themselves released from their treaty obligations by the death of the Prophet, drove out the tax collector and returned to their old ways. It is worth noting that this falling away (*ridda*) was not accompanied by any reanimation of the pagan religion. The rebellious Bedouin simply left, by unilateral declaration, the alliance that had secured to the Medinans a dominating influence over the greater part of the peninsula. Muhammad's state was in no way a political unity; like the Roman Empire and its hellenistic predecessors it had been an aggregate of territories or populations, each with its own peculiar dependence on the *umma*, or, in their own view, on the Prophet. Only here and there had a region been included directly within the sovereign sphere of Medina; in particular there was Mecca, which Muhammad had put under the control of a governor. Collective entry into Islam, involving obligations of prayer and tax, preceded actual religious conversion. Muhammad himself was quite aware that the Bedouin had been only superficially won over. 'The Arabs (i.e. the Bedouin) say "We have adopted the Faith (*āmannā*)". Say (to them): "Faith ye have not. Rather say: We have become Muslim (*aslamnā*). For faith has not yet entered your hearts" ' (Koran 49, 15).

Perhaps the most important phase of the *ridda*, although it was not entirely part of it, is the emergence of Maslama, scornfully called Musailima, small or miserable Maslama, by the Muslims. He had already been recognized as a prophet by the Banū Ḥanīfa in the Yamāma in Muhammad's lifetime. Like Muhammad he received revelations which he rendered in rhyming prose; he also preached monotheism and only differed from Muhammad in his extreme asceticism. That Maslama appeared earlier than Muhammad, as is sometimes suggested, is extremely unlikely; the other prophets of these restless days are certainly later: 'Aihala al-Aswad in the Yemen who was particularly concerned with the solution of local political questions and whose proceedings have an archaic flavour; Ṭalḥa (Ṭulaiḥa to the Muslims) among the Asad; and the woman Sajāḥ who was active among the Tamīm for a short time before the Muslim army made her retire once more to Mesopotamia. Musailima alone offered any opposition worthy of mention, and for this reason the Ḥanīfa, who were associated with the Tamīm for a time through a [symbolic?] marriage of their respective prophets, were cruelly suppressed. Al-Aswad had already been murdered before Muhammad's death. In little more than a year after Abū Bakr took office the *ridda* was defeated; tribal separatism had failed as a principle of state; further theocratic experiments, again serving particularist interests, were no more than imitations doomed to failure. Although the required new organization of Arabia and of the *umma* was to be undertaken from Medina it took place in a geographical and political context that Abū Bakr could not have foreseen.

The Sasanid war against Byzantium brought the Persians to

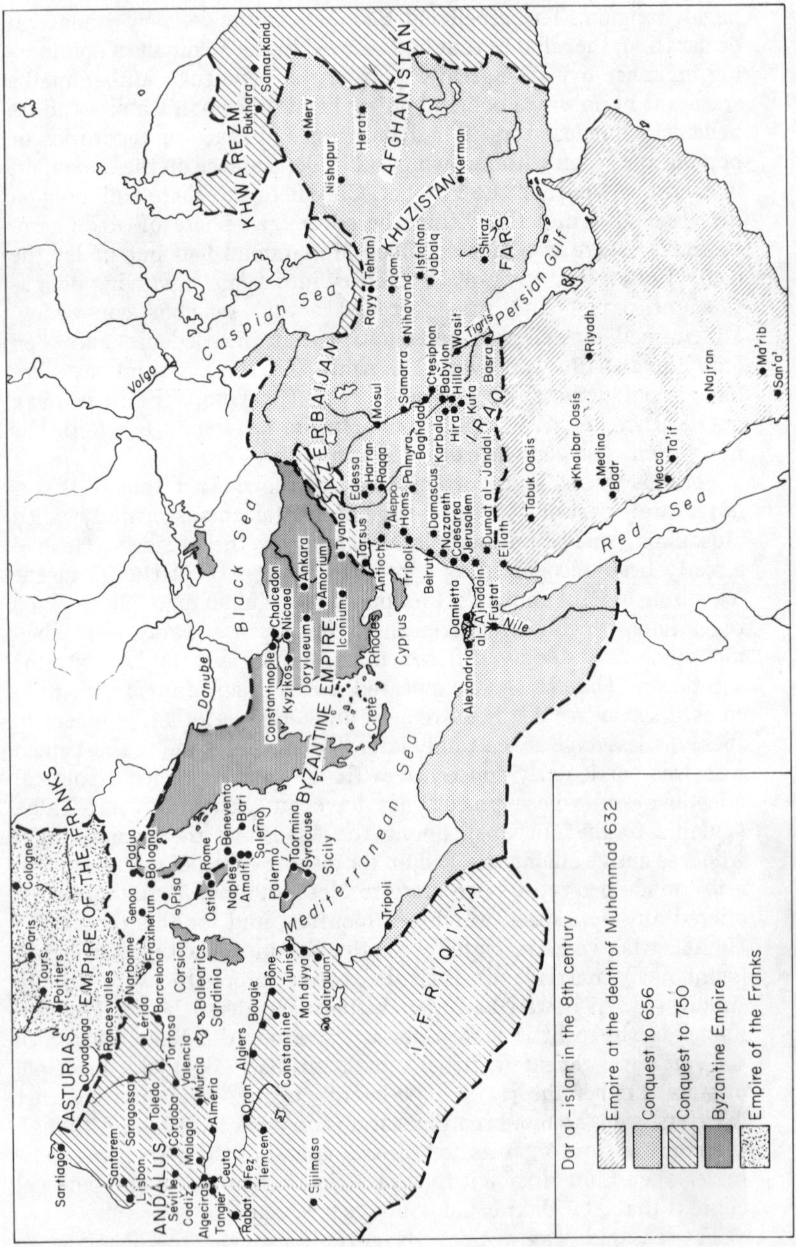
Dar al-islam in the 8th century
Empire at the death of Muhammad 632
Conquest to 656
Conquest to 750
Byzantine Empire
Empire of the Franks
ASTURIAS
EMPIRE OF THE FRANKS
ANDALUS
I'FRIQIYA
BYZANTINE EMPIRE
AZERBAIJAN
KHWAREZM
AFGHANISTAN
KHUZISTAN
FARS
'IRAQ
Mediterranean Sea
Black Sea
Caspian Sea
Persian Gulf
Red Sea
Danube
Volga
Tigris
Nile
Santiago
Covadonga
Roncesvalles
Poitiers
Tours
Paris
Cologne
Narbonne
Fraxinetum
Genoa
Padua
Bologna
Pisa
Rome
Ostia
Naples
Amalfi
Salerno
Benevento
Bari
Palermo
Taormina
Syracuse
Sicily
Corsica
Sardinia
Balearics
Barcelona
Lerida
Tortosa
Valencia
Murcia
Almeria
Toledo
Saragossa
Santarem
Lisbon
Cordoba
Malaga
Seville
Cadiz
Algeciras
Tangier
Ceuta
Rabat
Fez
Tlemcen
Oran
Algiers
Bougie
Constantine
Bône
Tunis
Mahdiyya
Qairawan
Sijilmasa
Tripoli
Constantinople
Kyzikos
Chalcedon
Nicaea
Dorylaeum
Ankara
Amorium
Iconium
Tyana
Tarsus
Antioch
Rhodes
Crete
Cyprus
Aleppo
Edessa
Harran
Raqqa
Homs
Palmyra
Tripoli
Beirut
Damascus
Nazareth
Caesarea
Jerusalem
Damietta
Alexandria
al-Ajnadain
Fustat
Eilath
Dumat al-Jandal
Tabuk Oasis
Khaibar Oasis
Medina
Badr
Mecca
Ta'if
Najran
Riyadh
Ma'rib
San'a'
Mosul
Samarra
Baghdad
Karbala
Hira
Kufa
Hilla
Babylon
Ctesiphon
Wasit
Basra
Nihavand
Rayy (Tehran)
Qom
Isfahan
Jabalq
Shiraz
Kerman
Nishapur
Herat
Merv
Bukhara
Samarkand

Jerusalem in 615, to Egypt in 619 and culminated in a final effort before the gates of Constantinople in 626. But internal crisis in Persia aggravated by the recent reorganization of the Byzantine army turned the promise of victory to a crushing defeat, and the war was over. Sensing the incipient disintegration of the Sasanid frontier defences al-Muthannà ibn Ḥāritha, a chieftain of the Banū Shaibān, took it upon himself to invade the Sawād, the fertile region of Central Mesopotamia, in 633. Significantly, he embraced Islam before setting out, though it did not bring him any support from Medina until after the lapse of several months. The great general Khālid ibn al-Walīd then appeared with a small troop of *anṣār*; but by this time the predominantly Arab city of Ḥīra had fallen. Persia only gradually assembled herself in defence, and meanwhile Medina undertook a simultaneous attack on Byzantine Syria.

To follow the course of the campaigns in detail makes them seem more difficult and the opposition stronger than the speed of the successes would lead one to assume. A number of factors contributed to the extraordinary success of the Arabs: the mobility of the Arabs fighting on an inner line, and using the camel which allowed them to move rapidly from front to front; the inadequate co-ordination of the Persian defence, led by independent and isolated marcher lords; and in the Byzantine Empire the alienation of the Greek orthodox population from the Semitic Monophysites, of the coastal towns with their Greek culture from the (re)orientalized rural interior, and everywhere the indifference to the old ruling class of a subject population accustomed to foreign domination. Equally, if not more, important was the drive towards existence as a great state, initiated and directed from Medina by the Muslim community identifiable with the Arabs. It derived its moral justification from the Koran, in the summons to fight the unbeliever. What is often forgotten, too, is that the Arabs had at their disposal what amounted to a people under arms, that every Muslim was a soldier, whereas the Byzantines and Persians went into battle with a professional army strengthened by conscription, and this meant that the conduct of war was slowed down and made more expensive. Of course religion is not to be underrated as a factor in the indomitability of the Muslim armies; but their offensives were less in the nature of an endeavour to force the true evangel on to foreign peoples—no one gave a thought to the conversion of non-Arabs—than the outcome of a desire to make the totality of the Arab people as Muslims the lords of the ancient civilized lands on their borders. This would of course make Islam, the religion of the new overlords, the dominant religion. But the concept of an extension of *dār al-islām*, the Islamic sphere of dominion, as a logical consequence of Muslim universality, comparable with the *dilatatio imperii Christiani* of the German empire under the Ottonians only arose later, although in retrospect even the earliest wars of conquest seem to have this character.

At all events the expansion made gigantic progress. Southern Palestine fell at the same time as Ḥīra (633), and the victory of al-Ajnādain (July 634) opened up the rest of the province. Damascus surrendered in September 635 after a siege of six months, the defeat of the imperial army on the river Yarmūk (August 636) decided the fate of Syria for centuries; Jerusalem held out for two, hellenized Caesarea for four years longer. In 639 'Amr ibn al-'Āṣ crossed the Egyptian border, and the Byzantines were decisively beaten in July 640 outside Babylon (Old Cairo), to the north-west of the modern city; the fortress itself held out until the following year. In Babylon the Patriarch Cyrus made an agreement whereby Alexandria, the key to Byzantine control of Egypt, was evacuated in September 642. The imperial troops re-occupied the city for a few months once again by a coup, but its second fall spelt the end of the Byzantine presence in Egypt. The legend that the library in Alexandria was burnt at the order of the Caliph first makes its appearance in the thirteenth century, in the work of an Arab writer; its origin is not clear; it probably preserves the memory of the collection of books destroyed at the fall of Caesarea.

Meanwhile the battle of Qādisiyya to the south-west of Ḥīra in 636 and the occupation of the capital city of Ctesiphon (al-Madā'in) gave the non-Iranian provinces of the Sasanids into the hands of the Muslims. Two years after the conquest of Upper Mesopotamia, or the Jazīra, had been accomplished from Syria, the offensive reached Persia itself, with the victory of Nihāvand in 642. This victorious Muslim campaign demonstrated once again that the heartland of Persia with its scanty economic power and the separatist interests of its provinces was capable of serving as the basis for an empire only under very favourable circumstances. This was not the first time that it had collapsed before the onslaughts of a relatively small army or a culturally backward people. The defeat at Nihāvand led to a new outbreak of Persian separatism, driving the last of the Sasanids, Yazdgard III, to retreat ever further north-eastwards, where in the end he was murdered, in Merv in 651. His son tried to set up the Sasanid empire once more from the periphery, with help from the Turks of Central Asia and even from the Chinese, but his efforts were unavailing.

These momentous events had taken place under the caliphate of 'Umar ibn al-Khaṭṭāb, the successor appointed by Abū Bakr on his deathbed. 'Umar was without doubt the greatest ruler of his time; like his predecessor he belonged to the 'Islamic aristocracy' and to one of the less influential Quraish families. He added the title *amīr al-mu'minīn*, 'Commander of the Faithful' (*amīr* lies somewhere between 'prince' and 'general') to that of caliph. 'Umar did more than any other caliph to formulate a system of government; it might be described as an Arab-Muslim theocracy. It was conducted from Medina, which was its moral and administrative centre, but it allowed considerable independence to the provincial authorities. The population was divided into two 'classes', the ruling Muslims and the subject peoples of other faiths.

The young state was a theocracy to the extent that its aims, its structure, its conditions of admission and the elements of its technique of authority were all based on divine revelation or on precedent set by the Apostle of God. In the last resort it was the religious integrity of the *umma* that had to be ensured, but from the very beginning this was not easily distinguishable from its political integrity. Muhammad had decreed that there was to be no *ḥilf* in Islam, no federation of genealogico-political structures among believers. Even so the tribes and clans remained the real units of social life, so that contradictions of serious consequence arose between two ethico-political principles, each of which brooked no less than a man's full loyalty. The conquests drew men's attention to other matters however, and made these tensions irrelevant for the time being.

The tribes were encouraged to emigrate into the new provinces with their goods and chattels; but they were not to assimilate themselves as landlords to the population already settled in the villages. They were brought together in *amṣār* (approximately: military centres, provincial capitals). The caliph nominated the governor, who both commanded the army and was responsible for internal order. At the end of the century it became the custom for a judge (*qāḍī*) appointed by the governor to relieve him of the burden of jurisdiction. In places a financial officer was appointed to stand beside the governor, and it was his task to see to the despatch of the surpluses to Medina. In the early days the Community was maintained by the spoils of war, of which a fifth was due to the Prophet, which is to say the state, or in the language of the time, to Allah; to this were added *ṣadaqāt*, sometimes also called *zakāt*. These at first were voluntary contributions and later when Bedouins joined the Community they were settled by contract. During the lifetime of the Prophet *zakāt* probably meant tribute in the form of the basic means of subsistence, but after his death it signified 'statutory alms' or 'poor tax', and was levied annually on the basis of about 2½ per cent of property (not of income). In a conquered country of course it was the subject population that paid. Public law as it gradually developed distinguishes carefully between territories that had become Muslim peaceably, that is to say by voluntary surrender (*ṣulḥan*) and those that had been acquired by force (*'anwatan*). The former retained their property and paid a collective levy which could not be arbitrarily increased by the government—hence the many not always genuine documents of contract conveying this status on a town—the latter had forfeited their property rights but held their land against payment of a tax assessed by the government.

In practice the difference was not as great as might be imagined; the conquered peasantry suffered no more nor less than under its previous rulers. Strictly speaking, the conquered land should have been divided among its conquerors, that is to say the occupying army, in which case of course the Islamic Community as an entity would soon have perished. So the state lands of the defeated power and any private property freed by the flight of its owners were made over directly to the *umma*, and the monies deriving from them flowed, generally via the provincial chest, into the treasury at Medina, the *māl Allāh*. Like the Persian and Byzantine provinces, those of the Muslims were only connected one with another through official channels by way of the central government. Conquests by the troops of a province as a rule became a part of that province, to be administered and exploited by it. Hence the close association of Khorāsān with Baṣra and of the Jazīra with Syria.

The Arabs in so far as they belonged to the active host were classed as 'fighters' (*muqātila*) or 'emigrants' (*muhājira*, into the Muslim provinces!) or else, following 'Umar's decree of 636, they were numbered among the 'Islamic aristocracy', because of their early conversion, or because they had participated in the battles of the heroic period like Badr or Uḥud, or else because they were related to the Prophet. They received graded pensions according to (religious) merit, defrayed from the income deriving from the land tax and the *jizya*. Hence they were of course in a certain sense dependent on the state, and they must have become more aware of this as income from direct booty diminished because of the extent and consolidation of the *dār al-islām*. Claims to pensions were based on the proven covenants of a tribe with the Prophet. For this reason historians attach great importance to the *wufūd* (delegations) which poured in to Medina from all sides towards the end of Muhammad's life, in order to effect the inclusion of their tribes into the system of the *umma*.

Hence it was necessary for the newly converted to find some tribe entitled to a pension which would accept them, so that they could—usually as a 'client' (*maulà*)—acquire full citizenship, meaning in fact inclusion into the lists of state pensioners.

This system, understandably enough, could only function as long as the privileged Muslims retained their identity as a military caste and kept aloof from the conquered population. The Prophet is reputed to have said: 'The survival of my Community rests on the hoofs of its horses and the points of its lances; as long as they keep from tilling the fields; once they begin to do that they will become as other men.' This is also the context of the alleged saying of 'Umar: 'Study your (tribal) genealogies and do not become like the Nabataeans of the Mesopotamian plain. If any of them is asked his origin he answers: "(I come) from such or such a village".' It would however be mistaken to conclude that the Arabs were prevented from acquiring landed property outside the peninsula. The conquerors often interposed themselves as landlords between government and peasantry just as earlier landlords had done; it is interesting that most of the Byzantine owners abandoned their lands as the Arabs advanced, while the Persian gentry managed by and large to stay on. The caliphs assumed the right (and it was never challenged) to reward the deserving by bestowing on them state domains as *qaṭā'i'*, which then meant allod and not as later, estate in fee; in this way the close companions of the Prophet, for instance, like 'Alī, Ṭalḥa and Zubair, came into considerable estates. The one essential difference from Byzantine legal practice was that the Islamic landlord possessed no public rights, such as minor judicial powers, and the officials of the government had access to his property at any time in the course of official duty. On Persian soil the position of the great landowners gradually improved because of the *talji'a*, whereby smaller proprietors tended to abandon their rights of possession against the lord's guardianship and protection, in a manner reminiscent of the *commendatio* of mediaeval feudalism.

It is easy to see why, as booty began to run dry, there were vociferous efforts to increase the *māl al-muslimīn*, the incomes flowing direct to the Muslims, at the expense of the *māl Allāh*, the Community coffer. This tendency was bound to increase the already strong particularism of the provinces and tribes to the disadvantage of the *umma* and the empire as a whole. Two things should be remembered here. First, a great empire in classical and mediaeval times could never be a centralized state in the modern sense, because of the technical level of its communications. It is hardly an exaggeration to say that its stability presupposed the existence of provinces that were self-governing and hence potentially autonomous units. The governor, often a self-appointed dynast even in Islam (though not perhaps at the beginning), had to be capable of maintaining order and security in normal times from his own resources, and when circumstances required it himself taking the lead in securing conquests. When things were going well the legality of the caliph shone down upon the governor, control from the central power brought opportune financial and military help and above all strengthened his sense that he had a firm place in the Islamic *jamā'a*. But situations could arise when the large provinces with traditional boundaries continued on their own despite a refusal from the caliphate; no one considered that the unity of the *jamā'a* implied a single administration, quite the contrary. Regionalism was justified by alleged sayings of the Prophet, who had more or less declared himself in its favour by allowing each country to keep its own coinage and weights.

Second, particularism was strengthened by the new grouping of the tribes who had been settled in the new garrison towns—Kūfa and Baṣra in Iraq, Fusṭāṭ (Old Cairo) in Egypt, later Qairawān in present-day Tunisia—in their own quarters. Separated from their fellow-tribesmen who had migrated into other regions they adhered more and more closely to other Arabs belonging to the same genealogical units set over the individual tribes. In this way there grew up a feeling of community within the 'super-tribes' of Tamīm, Rabī'a, Muḍar or Quḍā'a, associated with a certain local pride as Kūfans or Baṣrans, though this adherence only overlay and did not supplant the primary tribal loyalties. In any case it was not long before the Kūfans or Baṣrans acquired political status as townsmen. It was a general consequence of the expansion that military and therefore political power moved quickly from the centre to the periphery. The continuous *hijra* of the Bedouin not only rendered the peninsula politically insignificant after a few decades but left it to sink below the level of the last phase of the pagan period, demographically and economically.

None of this was foreseeable in 644, however, when 'Umar was stabbed to death by the private vengeance of a Persian slave. He had lived long enough to establish a *shūrà*, an elective committee which consisted of the six most distinguished members of the Islamic aristocracy, who in fact were all Quraish. They agreed on one of their members as his successor, 'Uthmān ibn 'Affān who was a son-in-law of the Prophet, and much advanced in years; perhaps he was considered the weakest of the possible candidates. The latent tensions within the *jamā'a* came out in open rift during his office, and have never been fully healed since.

'Uthmān was a member of the family from which had come the last and most obstinate leaders of the Meccan heathens against the Prophet. He has been repeatedly accused of placing family interests before those of the Muslim commonwealth, since he conferred all the key posts of government on his relatives. Many of these men quite cynically and openly exploited these appointments to their own advantage. This provided the Islamic aristocracy with a focus round which their propaganda against the worldly 'heathen' aristocracy could crystallize. Relations were strained within the Islamic aristocracy itself between the Quraish, whose kinship with Muhammad gave them a precedence within the *umma* that they were only too willing to utilize, and the *anṣār* (Companions), who not entirely without justification considered that it was they who had saved the situation at the really crucial moment, even though under Quraish leaders. But this rift was temporarily submerged under common opposition to the 'secularized' regime. The Medinans did not see that real power was moving with every year more and more to the provinces and that their own supremacy would depend more on the prestige of the central government than on memories of the Prophet. They were also blind to the fact that the caliph had no other means of curbing the independence of the provinces than to send out officials who were under obligation to serve the general interest of the Community.

The provinces for their part, particularly Kūfa and Egypt, felt themselves imposed upon and saw no necessity for giving the empire impartial administration. Thus there was great protest when 'Uthmān had all the revelations of the Prophet collected and put in order by a commission, and in 653 officially issued an authorized edition, declaring that previous collections were to be suppressed or destroyed. At this time were first heard those complaints, subsequently frequent, that the state was hindering the implementation of the 'Word'; that 'power', *sulṭān* (an Aramaic expression appearing already in Thamūdic inscriptions, which only later acquired the meaning of 'ruler') was setting itself up against Allah. This was an expression of the moral absolutism of the religion, inevitably disappointed each time an attempt was made to put it into concrete practice; no less was it an expression of its inability to reconcile the principles of tribal autonomy with the sovereignty of the state.

The rebellion broke out, fostered by the ambitions of consequential Companions of the Prophet and of cold-blooded politicians, but carried through too by the pious in Medina and the *muqātila* of Kūfa and Egypt who had nothing to occupy them during the temporary cessation of wars of conquest. In 655 it broke out in Kūfa, where it was put down, and in 656 in Egypt. In Holy War against the internal enemy an army only 500 strong laid siege to Medina. The population was sympathetic, but preferred to leave it to the outsiders to stain themselves with the blood of the Caliph (June 17, 656). The picture of the aged 'Uthmān receiving the death blow as he was bending over the Koran, was one which remained indelibly imprinted on the memory of the Community. The great 'Companions' had repudiated the movement, but without coming to the help of 'Uthmān and, like the extremely influential 'Ā'isha, the favourite wife of Muhammad, had left for Mecca before the catastrophe occurred. Only 'Alī remained, and received homage on the very day of 'Uthmān's death.

Revolutionary fervour in Medina changed to uneasiness. The whole of 'Alī's reign is pervaded with a mood of disillusion and uncertainty of conscience. The Companions Ṭalḥa and Zubair who had departed to Mecca joined with 'Ā'isha against 'Alī, the 'murderer of 'Uthmān'. It may be surmised that this transparent change of front contributed to the success of 'Alī in the 'Battle of the Camel' fought near Baṣra (December 9, 656). The two claimants Ṭalḥa and Zubair fell; 'Ā'isha, whose camel, according to ancient tradition, had been the mascot and centre of the army, lived on in retirement until 678. 'Alī now took up the reins of government. Medina's role as the capital city was played out. 'Alī chose Kūfa from which to rule the whole empire—with the exception of Syria, whose governor Mu'āwiya ibn abī Sufyān, appointed by 'Umar in 636, refused him recognition. Without claiming the caliphate for himself Mu'āwiya called for vengeance for 'Uthmān in the name of legitimacy. After long delay the inevitable battle took place, on the Syrian border near Ṣiffīn on the right bank of the Euphrates; it seemed to be turning in favour of 'Alī when the Syrians spiked copies of the Koran on to the points of their lances and called out that the Holy Book should be the arbiter and not war. 'Alī was forced to accept arbitration: his followers were averse to bloodshed within the *jamā'a*.

As they returned home from the battle, some began to see that a mistake had been made, but it was too late. Those who felt most responsible wanted 'Alī to revoke his agreement at once. When, understandably, he refused, they left him; hence their name *Khawārij* (Khārijites), 'Seceders', rebels. Their slogan was the now famous *lā taḥkīm illā lillāh*, 'Decision is with God alone'. 'Alī managed to win over the majority of the rebels after lengthy negotiations. His final break with the extremists came when 'Alī really sent his representatives to Dūmat al-Jandal (or Adhruḥ?) on the day of the arbitration. About 4,000 men assembled in Nahrawān, on the left bank of the Tigris, under their caliph. Meanwhile the tribunal had reached a decision unacceptable to 'Alī and he called on the Khārijites to rally round him and defeat the common enemy. They hesitated, and were laid low by the Kūfan army, only eight of them surviving (July 17, 658). The Kūfans however lost heart for further fighting and Mu'āwiya had no difficulty in taking Egypt, helped by the decision of the tribunal, which had indirectly strengthened his political position.

The debate in Dūma was factually over the person of the rightful caliph, but juridically the question was whether 'Uthmān's blood had been justly shed. Naturally when the answer was negative there was a proposal that a new *shūrà* should appoint the rightful caliph. The impressive story of how 'Alī's plenipotentiary declared himself for the deposition of both adversaries, while Mu'āwiya's envoy only proposed that of 'Alī, cannot be correct, because Mu'āwiya did not assume the title of caliph until two years later, in Jerusalem. None the less the foundations of 'Alī's legitimacy were tottering. This, together with the Iraqis' lack of unanimity and indiscipline would certainly have turned events in favour of Mu'āwiya even had 'Alī not been murdered by a Khārijite on January 24, 661. His son Ḥasan (d. 669) agreed to abandon his right to the throne in favour of Mu'āwiya in return for financial compensation, and the civil war came to an end a few months later.

It is surprising how little the subjugated peoples used this rift to shake off Arab rule; there was unrest only in Iran and in Baḥrain. Of course the *jamā'a* itself was now formally reunited, but beneath the surface the division into parties was irrevocable. The *shī'at 'Alī*, the 'Party of 'Alī' at this time found its support in Iraqi local patriotism, while the Umayyads who were now to occupy the caliphate for almost a century were for the most part upheld by the Syrians. But these parties were no less bound and entangled in religion than the Khārijites; the burning question was always to decide who was the legitimate caliph, never what the caliph was or what he should be in relation to the Muslim Community and its empire. Each party in its own way was trying to interpret the principles laid down by precedent or statement of the Prophet, and the civil war took on the character of a moral trial or test, ***fitna***, under which name it was recorded in Islamic history. Every believer shared responsibility for the Community. It was unforgivable to shed the blood of a fellow believer; yet to refrain from taking sides contradicted the fundamental duty of a Muslim, to acknowledge the Truth and secure its triumph.

The Khārijites took in earnest the Koranic principle that personal piety is the only criterium of the rank of an individual within the

Community. The ethics of individual and state were the same. Leadership of the *umma* appertained to the best Muslim; the state of grace of the individual was to be seen in his behaviour; the masses in their indifference were no better than heathens; their rejection of the Khārijite conception of Islam excluded them from the true Community and justified their being killed. But even the Khārijite, if he sinned badly, was excluded from the Community. Descent was of no avail. At first this only meant that the prerogative of the Quraish to the caliphate was denied; the caliphs chosen by the Khārijites came from a great variety of tribes. The equation of moral absolutism with the right to rule made it a duty to depose a caliph who had fallen into grave sin and did not publicly repent; this of course provided a foundation in dogma for internal dissent and division into sects, in short for the impossibility of building a state. Soon the Khārijites came to declare the moral equality and hence the political equality of Arabs and non-Arabs in Islam: they are the first *Shu'ūbites,* champions of the equality of all those who follow the Prophet and the Book of God; this reasoning constantly attracted support among the oppressed and disappointed. As perpetual revolutionaries, incapable and perhaps unwilling to build a world-wide Community, they were ready to 'sell' their lives to gain paradise. They provided a rallying point for all those who felt it more important to destroy political and social injustice by breaking through the narrow mesh of reality in the name of a never fully thought-out divine law, than to preserve the all-embracing *umma,* whose universality they yet confirmed with their concept of the equality of all believers.

The Community which as time went on became predominant in Islam as the 'Sunnite' was probably most clearly represented in the Syrians. The Community was to hold sway over a single unified state; political and social superiority was vested in adherence to the Community; religious data were considered as they affected the realization and universality of the Community; exclusion of the non-Arabs from government was axiomatic and at this time hardly even discussed. Such tenets culminated in the faith, anchored in ancient Arab sentiment, that it was the Quraish, the tribe of the Prophet, who had the right to the caliphate. This attitude, derived from the general ideology, was later adopted by the overwhelming majority of non-Arab Muslims. It may be interpreted as a timidly formalistic element of centralism in the *jamā'a,* which indeed never assumed the character of a church organization. In relation to the Umayyads the *Shī'a* saw itself increasingly required to provide a theological prop for the naive legitimism taken over from Persia, which would reserve the caliphate exclusively for the descendants of the close family of the Prophet. This idea found little support in Arab tradition. Themes foreign to Islam had to be imported, such as the transmission by inheritance of a divine element from Adam to Muhammad and 'Alī and his successors, and so provide a justification which would enable the influence of the Shī'a to spread across Iraq and take root among the Syrians.

But every party, then as later, held fast to the fundamental and binding revelation of the Koran and its embodiment (though at the time of the *fitna* it had of course hardly begun) in the *sharī'a*, the concrete working out of the law. This gave that religious colouring to political confrontations which has endured throughout history, and turned history itself into a theological problem, to a much greater extent than in any other great religion. Impartiality in the quarrel between 'Uthmān and 'Alī meant postponement (*irjā'*, hence the Murji'ites) of judgment—even postponement of judgment of the faithful who had been sinners, until the Last Judgment. It became the theologico-political confession of the Umayyad-dominated *jamā'a*; while taking sides for 'Alī meant the recognition of an individual and collective obligation to rebel in the service of the 'just' *imām*, who is the symbol of the 'just' ordering of the Community in conformity with divine law.

The Umayyads

THE Umayyad period (661–750) can be generally described as the Mediterranean epoch of the caliphate, the period of the second great expansion of the *dār al-islām*. It became clear during this period what intellectual and organizational furniture was needed to preserve the caliphate and to give it substance; it can also be termed the period of the self-destruction of the Arabs as a nation-state.

Arabs and arabized Muslims carefully subjected themselves to scrutiny and self-analysis during these events, not without allowing themselves in retrospect all kinds of politically motivated postures. There is even a kind of myth-building whose documents, as it were fragments of a prose epic which never comes to an end, are not too difficult to disentangle from real history. Some are poems set in the mouths of heroes, another, a chronological description of the conquests, purporting to be a serious report, according to which the Oxus and Indus were reached by 640 and Spain was defeated under 'Uthmān. Yet on the whole the Arab chroniclers are far ahead of contemporary western historians in the wealth of their content and their narrative technique (Einhard's *Life of Charlemagne* perhaps excepted).

The islamization of the subject peoples progressed very slowly everywhere; only in Arabia was a (not entirely wholehearted) attempt made under 'Umar to expel the non-Muslims. But in the provinces previously belonging to Byzantium relations between the ruling Arabs and their subjects were better than elsewhere. This should not lead us to imagine that the Syrian Christian population had been in a decline. Quite on the contrary, the seventh century was a period of lively intellectual activity. The Muslims did not interfere in the cultural doings of the Christians; the government came forward against religious customs only sporadically, as apparently in 690 in Egypt against an excessively obtrusive adulation of the cross and, a generation later in Syria itself, against the cult use of images. But these attacks were lacking in systematic intent. The intellectual life of the Christians in Syria, Egypt and in Mesopotamia was isolated from the centres of Christian thought and excluded from Muslim imperial policies, though not from imperial administration. The natural consequence was that it was gradually squeezed out of the broad intellectual currents as well. Even so the bare fact of its existence, of its greater maturity and complexity,

3 The Ka'ba in Mecca. *Mme Frédérique Duran*

4 The Dome of the Rock (Mosque of ‘Umar) in Jerusalem. Built by ‘Abd al-Malik in 691. *Mme Frédérique Duran*

accelerated the irresistible process of development and systemization of the Muslim articles of faith.

At any rate the government did not need to concern itself with protecting a rear in Syria, although it had been involved in frequent battles with Byzantium, the leading Christian power, ever since 'Uthmān, whose generals had succeeded in 646 in bringing Armenia under the much-disputed sovereignty of Medina. An advance beyond the western frontier of Egypt had led in 647 to a first occupation of Cyrenaica; in 649 followed the conquest of Cyprus; in 654 the Muslim fleet consisting mostly of Egyptian ships defeated the Byzantine fleet off the southern coast of Asia Minor. The deficiencies in the Byzantine defences even in well-circumscribed and loyal regions, so characteristic of the whole of mediaeval history, allowed Islam to reach the capital three times in little more than fifteen years. In 667 the Arabs occupied Chalcedon, threatened Constantinople, and overran Sicily for the first time; between 674 and 680 Constantinople was under threat from Kyzikos, but the defeat of the army on land and 'Greek fire' at sea put to naught the hopes raised high by the advanced position of the fleet. Meanwhile Crete and Rhodes had changed rulers several times. The final and most highly organised attempt to bring the Byzantine empire to an end by capturing its capital city was undertaken in 716–717, but it was foiled by the defensive genius of the Byzantine engineers, and by the complexities of a foreign policy whereby Bulgars appear on the scene to repulse the Arabs.

By this time the last traces of Byzantine suzerainty over North Africa had long since disappeared. 'Uqba ibn Nāfi', who as Sidi Okba was to become one of the greatest of North Africa's saints, had established Qairawān in 670 as a base for operations against the Berbers; it soon grew, comparable to the Iraqi garrison towns of Kūfa and Baṣra, not only in population but as a cultural centre. (The new inland headquarters of Fusṭāṭ and Qairawān show the caliphate as a land power, in contrast to the sea ports of Alexandria and Carthage.) But it was not 'Uqba, who lost his life in 683 on a campaign near Biskra in present day Algeria, but the less celebrated Ḥassān ibn an-Nu'mān al-Ghassānī who finally drove the Byzantines out of Carthage in 698. (It was at this juncture that the remains of St Augustine were brought to Padua by emigrants.) He broke the resistance of the Berbers under their 'Prophetess' Kāhina sufficiently to allow the Arabs to continue their advance to the coast; considerable contingents of Berbers attached themselves to the Arab armies. Yet enmity continued, for the Berbers had every reason to feel themselves slighted by the Arabs within the Muslim army.

The Latin patina of the coastal cities disappeared remarkably quickly; the Berbers had not been seriously affected by classical culture; the bearers of Latin Christian culture mostly emigrated, and the native Christians were soon submerged in Islam. Ḥassān's successor Mūsà ibn Nuṣair no longer took orders from the Governor of Egypt, but was himself directly responsible to the caliph as governor of a province which he extended along the coast as far as Tangier. This opened the way for a crossing to Europe. In 711 one of Mūsà's officers, his Berber 'client' Ṭāriq, undertook a raid into southern Spain which was, as will be told later, to lead to the conquest of about four-fifths of the country within a few years. The impetus of the combined Arab and Berber forces was not yet exhausted, however; the Pyrenees were circumvented and Narbonne incorporated into the Muslim empire. But expansion to the north was blocked by Charles Martel near Poitiers, probably in 733 (and not, as is usually supposed, in 732). This setback may have been important from the European point of view, but for the Muslims at that time, who saw no master plan imperilled thereby, it had no further significance. In the east, to the north of the Caucasus it was the Khazar state which performed this same function of arresting the advance of the Muslims. Between 650 and 975 it extended from the steppes to the north of the Caspian Sea to the Sea of Azov. The fight was less dramatic but equally effective, and for almost a century, though most intensively between 722 and 737, they made it impossible for the Arabs to acquire a basis for operations beyond the Pass of Passes, Bāb al-abwāb (Derbend). It may be surmised that had there been no Khazar resistance the Arabs would certainly have at least attempted an invasion of the plains of the Don and Dnieper.

On both frontiers with Christendom, that in Asia Minor and Syria against Byzantium and that in northern Spain against the 'rump' princedoms of Asturias and Cantabria, war, or rather summer campaigns (*ṣā'ifa*), became the norm. In Byzantium as in Islam there grew up a new population of frontiersmen, military settlers who were there to maintain the status quo—the boundary of the Taurus mountains. They were bravos to whom legend has lent more than human stature, and who managed to combine their professional enmity with peaceable relations and mutual consideration, even connubiality. These soldiers were professionals, and very different from the fighters for the Faith in the frontier fortresses (*ribāṭ*). The latter were ascetics and evangelists to a man, they preached the Holy War and were in fact the instruments of islamization, and, although often themselves not of Arab origin, of arabization also.

Islamic occupation of the southern shores of the Mediterranean destroyed the old unity founded on classical antiquity (Henri Pirenne). This is a view which has been losing ground, mainly from the results of research into commercial history. But in fact freedom of trade within a more or less united zone of government had indeed come to an end. After the victorious expansion of the *dār al-islām* three similar and mutually dependent cultural spheres took shape in the Mediterranean basin; they each led autonomous lives and were shut off from each other by both political hostility and linguistic barriers. The cultural rift between the European and the Egypto-Syrian shore (and the direct hinterlands) which was already apparent towards the end of classical antiquity was heightened by the recession of Europe and the flowering of Islamic culture in the early centuries after Muhammad's death; despite the persistence of mutual influences the factual and psychological line of demarcation deepened after 750 as a consequence of the easterly and north-easterly orientation of the policy of the caliphate.

This trend had begun with the failure of the last siege of Constantinople. Hishām (724–743), the last statesman of the Damascene Umayyads, seems—judging by the change in the symbolic language of court art—to have renounced the idea that the caliph was due to take possession of the emperor's inheritance and to have begun to revive Persian traditions of sovereignty. The influence of the caliphs had for long been felt all over Iran itself. In 664 the army reached Kabul in what is now Afghanistan, ten years later it crossed the Oxus to Bukhārā whence the victor brought a bodyguard of two thousand archers, first to Baṣra and shortly afterwards to Samarkand. These conquests and the consequent Arab settlement of Khorāsān then were extended further with Baṣra as their base. They brought the Muslims into contact with a highly cultivated world of relatively small city states, basically Sogdian in speech and culture, bordering on the west with the Khwārezmians (who were also related to the Iranians) of modern Khiwa, and all interspersed with Turkish tribes who often furnished the ruling families.

This plethora of peoples created a colourful juxtaposition of religions. The heathen shamanism of the Turks, the Nestorian version of Christianity, even Buddhism in the great temple centre of Balkh (Baktra) (the family of the Barmakid Vizirs, later to become so famous, acquired its name from the office of *parmak* or principal [Sanskrit *pramukha*] of the Buddhist monastery of Nava Vihāra [Naubahār] which was held by its ancestors), and in the monastery (*vihāra*) to which Bukhārā owes its name, not to mention the Zarathustrians and the Manichaeans, all seem to have lived side by side without serious friction. The wealth of the land depended in part on the fertility of the oases which must have been more densely populated than now, but mainly on transit trade. This was not noticeably affected by the perpetual skirmishes between Turks and Iranians, between steppe-dwellers and peasantry. The Sogdians were not defeated nor the cultural centres islamicized until the campaigns of Qutaiba ibn Muslim (705–715); then Arab garrisons were set up in Khwārezm, Bukhārā, and Samarkand, as they had been earlier in Khorāsān at Merv, Nīshāpūr and Herāt. The local petty princes remained in many places for some time as allies or as the instruments of indirect rule.

The extension of Islamic rule in Sindh went on at the same time (711/712). A reconnaissance expedition had already reached there under 'Umar. The port of Daibul (now Karachi) and Nīrūn (now Hyderabad) with its statue of the Buddha 'forty ells high' fell into the hands of Muḥammad ibn al-Qāsim, who like Qutaiba was despatched by the governor of Iraq. Although various poets and scholars of Sindhi origin are met with in Islam in the eighth century, the province as a whole exerted no influence worthy of mention on intellectual life. In Khwārezm and Transoxiana it was different. The decimation of the Sogdian and even more of the Khwārezmian élites was followed by a 'colonization' which turned these territories into mission centres, and Bukhārā and Samarkand especially developed an individual and highly intensive Islamic intellectual life. In the Iranian territory the Arabs were a small minority. According to Arab sources the Arab population of Khorāsān was calculated at two hundred thousand, of which about 40,000 were fit for military service. Hence it is understandable that the native converts to Islam, who had also taken over the Arab language, should become of more importance, and sooner, than they were for instance in Syria. By about 700 Iranian officers were already beginning to play a role, and their importance grew from decade to decade. Qutaiba himself contemplated building up a Persian army whose first loyalty would be to him personally.

From the point of view of the Iranians, especially in Khorāsān, the main task of the Arabs was to protect them against the Turks, a task which on the whole they performed with greater success than the Iranian petty princes, and even than the Sasanids. It is true that the bastion erected by the Arabs was not vouchsafed a long life. With the crumbling of the power of the caliphate the defensive strength of the empire waned, and the Turks, themselves now largely within the *dār al-islām*, soon won back their supremacy. Even so Islam grew in strength as a spiritually productive religion, unprejudiced by the changeable political circumstances of its position. The intellectual and political orientation eastwards towards China which had previously been dominant now gave way to one turned southwards towards the Islamic world. The battle on the Talas (July 751) in which Western Turks and Arabs inflicted a crushing defeat on the last Chinese army sent out to central Asia, signifies the end of direct Chinese influence, and at the same time of Sogdian hopes of a political recovery.

Although the Arabs were unable to maintain their rule in every outpost they had established in lands of an alien culture, their expansion in the eighth century is all the more remarkable in that it took place in a period of almost uninterrupted internal dissension. Mu'āwiya (661–680) and later 'Abd al-Malik (685–705) were able to purchase peace with Byzantium during periods of crisis at the price of annual payments, but internal peace was not to be bought with material means. Mu'āwiya was universally recognized as caliph, but the pious nursed the suspicion that his rule was more Arab than Islamic, and that he, to use their own words, was lowering the office of caliphate to no more than an ordinary kingship. The Iraqis repeatedly accused him of leaning on the Syrians, and behaved in such a way that he indeed saw himself driven increasingly to rely on this heart land. The Khārijites as the champions of anarchy served as a focus for the resentments of all those who harboured social grievances or who objected to the 'unislamic' behaviour of the authorities, and it was impossible to eradicate them. More and more the cause of 'Alid legitimacy attracted non-Arab malcontents; and the Arab tribes themselves were incapable of coming to terms with a situation in which the power of their state turned out to be so far-reaching that it limited their own freedom of action. The century of the Arab empire did not create among the Arabs a sense of their common political interests—it was really only the Syrian government which seemed to understand what they were—instead it restored the pre-Islamic relations of the peninsula on the new immensely larger stage of the *dār al-islām*. Tribal rivalries sharpened, now that more was at stake; the tribes amalgamated; or better: the genealogical units which traditionally were superposed over the single tribes became politically important power groups, and gradually in spite of their fragility they took up firm attitudes against each other. Everywhere in the caliphal territory the Rabī'a and the Azd held together against the Tamīm and the Bakr. This hostility in time developed into hostility between north and south Arabs, between the Qais and the Kalb, and it was conducted with a bitterness we now find hard to understand. These tensions were no legacy of time immemorial nor do they reflect racial differences; they are the consequence of transferring primitive pre-Islamic concepts of the state and judiciary customs to the government of a world empire.

Lulled into security by their relatively easy initial successes and unwilling to endanger their monopoly of power by the full admission of foreign Muslims, at the same time blind to the weakness of their own position as a minority, the Arabs behaved as though no fratricidal wars, no massacres, no rebellions could jeopardize their hegemony. The closer the Umayyad period neared its end, the more impossible became the prospect of a regime above parties. Whoever the Qais supported was *ipso facto* opposed by the Kalb. The strength of the Quraish lay in their belonging to neither of the two groups, the suitability of many an official was decided by the unimportance or traditional neutrality of his tribe; a number of the most prominent imperial office-holders belonged to the Thaqīf; although they were connected with the Qais they had specialized in a kind of 'supranational' position.

Under Mu'āwiya matters were relatively peaceful. He managed to find the right tone for handling the heads of the tribes, left the Byzantine and Persian state apparatus undisturbed and relied on the sterling loyalty of his Syrians, sparing no pains to foster their devotion to the dynasty. The exhaustion that followed the civil war and the incipient economic prosperity stimulated by welding together enormous territories allowed him to keep the irreconcilables in check for a time without undue exercise of force. The lack of discipline among the Baṣrans, who were motivated primarily by tribal interests, and among the Kūfans who were split into political parties, weakened the strength of the opposition, without at first damaging the interests of the empire. In Baṣra (and later in Kūfa as well) sat his adopted half-brother Ziyād ibn Abīhi (d. 673). His accession speech has become famous on account of the perfection of its Arabic; it reflects above all the atmosphere of Iraq and the governmental style acquired with the help of a newly organized police force (*shurṭa* from *cohors* through the late Greek *khorte*). It shows with incomparable succinctness what a province might expect from the government, and it shows also the attitude which made an ordered relationship so very difficult.

Without a word of introduction Ziyād is said to have begun: 'You allow kinship to prevail and put religion second; you excuse and hide your transgressors and tear down the orders which Islam has sanctified for your protection. Take care not to creep about in the night; I will kill every man found on the streets after dark. Take care not to appeal to your kin; I will cut off the tongue of every man who raises that call . . . I rule you with the omnipotence of God and maintain you with God's wealth (i.e. the state's); I demand obedience from you, and you can demand uprightness from me. However much I may lag behind my aims I will not fail in three things: I will at all times be there for every man to speak to me, I will always pay your pensions punctually and I will not send you into the field for too long a time or too far away. Do not be carried away by your hatred and anger against me, it would go ill with you. I see many heads rolling; let each man see that his own head stays upon his shoulders!' (From the German translation by Wellhausen.)

Nevertheless there was a strong ferment beneath the surface. Whatever the government did the pious in Medina considered Mu'āwiya to be a usurper, the Iraqi Shī'a remained irreconcilable, and the religious individualism of the Khārijites was perpetually on the point of erupting. Mu'āwiya had tried to have his son Yazīd recognized as heir to the throne, contrary to Arab practice; the provinces swore allegiance to him, but not the most distinguished representatives of the 'Islamic aristocracy'. Thus Mu'āwiya's death gave the signal for uprisings which ultimately led to the establishment of a counter-government in Mecca.

The opponents of Yazīd (680–683) have given him an evil reputation. He had the misfortune to have to suppress a rebellion by Ḥusain ibn 'Alī provoked by the Kūfan Shī'a, in which the grandson of the Prophet was killed in a battle of negligible military importance, at Karbalā', about 40 kilometres north west of Kūfa, on October 10, 680. Within a few years this had provided the Shī'a with a human hero of metaphysical significance, around whose martyrdom the emotional life of the movement has remained crystallized until our own time. In Ḥusain was revived the motif of the suffering intercessor, of the super-human human who becomes a voluntary sacrifice for the community. In rallying round his descendants the Shī'a did not of course discover the unity of a political programme, but it found the unity of an uncompromising attitude by which the basic teaching of Islam was experienced differently from the *jamā'a*. The Imām as the true charismatic ruler—even without political power—and as intercessor, interpreted by extremists as partly of divine substance and as a kind of prophet figure, is strictly speaking no more to be reconciled with Koranic prophetology than with the Sunnite concept of the caliph.

It was not long before the heightened Shī'ite excitement assumed political form. Al-Mukhtār, a distinguished Thaqafite, rose up in the name of the only surviving son of 'Alī, Muḥammad ibn al-Ḥanafiyya, and came forward as his representative. He preached the 'Hidden

Imām' who would at the end of time reveal himself as 'Mahdī' and set up the kingdom of righteousness, whereby the movement (in the long run) would become largely independent of the vicissitudes of the present moment. Mukhtār fought with the slogan 'Vengeance for Ḥusain' and maintained himself for two years (685–687) in Kūfa, supported by the enthusiasm of chiliasts, Persian and Arab. It fell to the lot of the Zubairid Muṣ'ab to fight him: as Yazīd after conquering Medina was within an ace of bringing Mecca once more under his authority and making an end of the 'pious' anti-caliphate of 'Abdallāh ibn az-Zubair (a son of the Companion of the Prophet who was killed in the Battle of the Camel), he died. The confusion that broke out over the succession developed in Syria into tribal feuds and jeopardized the continuance of the dynasty. The Qaisites who had turned aside from the Umayyads to Ibn az-Zubair were defeated at Marj Rāhiṭ in 684. They in their turn would not renounce blood vengeance on the Kalbites for their losses—the war of succession and tribal feud thus remained undifferentiated—and this proved the final blow to Arabdom in its increasing weakness. That the Arab state survived at all is only because even after the Umayyad restoration under 'Abd al-Malik the regional interests in the leadership of the Islamic empire and a certain loyalty towards the dynasty held the destructive tendencies in balance. There was also the fact that only in Syria was a professional army developed which took no sides in the tribal conflicts, at least before the death of Hishām.

'Abd al-Malik took trouble to ensure the religious autarchy of Syria; he completed the building of the Dome of the Rock in Jerusalem (691) and encouraged pilgrimage there as a substitute for the *ḥajj* to Mecca. But the unity of the empire could only be re-established after the Thaqafite al-Ḥajjāj ibn Yūsuf had stormed Mecca in 692 and the anti-caliph had found his death in the holy precinct. Ḥajjāj was then transferred to Iraq as viceroy and soon afterwards entrusted with the governorship of Khorāsān; he put the rebels to flight after having to deal with a further uprising which came near to setting the whole of the east alight. Ḥajjāj has gone down in history as the bugbear of the pious and of the Iraqi particularists. The writers no more forgave him his lack of consideration for the tribes than his intolerance of the pious ideologists who were in fact a danger to the empire; this in spite of the great conquests of his generals and the economic prosperity which his administration brought to Iraq. It is a telling reflection on the atmosphere even in 'pacified' Iraq that he found it necessary to move his residence to the military town of Wāsiṭ, about half way between Kūfa and Baṣra on the west bank of the Tigris, and that he needed to rely in the first place on the Syrian troops stationed there, whom he kept apart as much as possible from the settled Arabs.

A large part of the unrest that was spreading there and in the Persian districts, especially in Khorāsān, is certainly to be ascribed not to the conflict of the tribes but to the Arabic structure of government. Formulated at its simplest, the Arab-Muslim ruling class, who were state pensioners inasmuch as they belonged to the military, and frequently landowners, were maintained by the non-Muslims. In this respect the Arab empire only continued what had always been the custom; but the exploitation of the *contribuens plebs* was, it seems, more tolerable than before. The Byzantine upper class had for the most part left the land, but the Persians remained and rose gradually into the Muslim upper class. Although they were on the whole unmolested, and indeed officiated as intermediary between government and population, the *dihqāns* (the lower nobility) were threatened by a slow decline in their prestige, and this together with their desire to intervene in the political control of their own destiny, increasingly promoted islamization. But it was just this islamization and above all of course the conversion of the much more numerous non-noble Iranians that sharpened the contradiction between the political exclusivity of Arabism and the egalitarian Islamic religion as it was understood not only by the new converts but by the 'pious' order as well, although it was hardly ever implemented outside the Khawārij.

Conversion brought the *maulà* (plural *mawālī*) neither social nor economic equality although the 'democracy' of the Prophet's message had seemed to give them this right. The *mawālī* troops received maintenance pay and a share of booty, but no pension; they often served on foot, while the Arabs were mounted; neither did Islam free them of land tax, *kharāj*, or if it did it imposed a tithe, *'ushr*, on the harvest instead. The relatively numerous middle class of *mawālī* of good education and considerable wealth enjoyed high respect in the circles of the pious; for example the legal profession was open to them before 700. This together with the circumstance that their social position in no way corresponded to their contribution sharpened the explosive potential of their grievance; at the same time the conflict among the tribes could only encourage the rise of the non-Arabs.

The consolidation of the imperial frontiers and the consequent diminution of war booty, the swelling of the pension lists and the internal strife which absorbed enormous sums would have made it difficult even for the most 'pious' government to do without the *kharāj* of the new converts. The inadequacy of the administration, sometimes simply its mismanagement, meant that the converts were not even regularly freed of the poll tax imposed on the non-Muslims; it was considered degrading, as it was in the Roman-Byzantine realm, where the corresponding levy was even called *iniuria*. To avoid it the converts streamed into the towns from the villages, thereby injuring the state as well as their former coreligionists whom they had left behind and who were held collectively responsible for the tax. The drastic measure of Ḥajjāj is recorded, when he had the immigrants returned to their villages by force and the name of their village branded on their hands to prevent a repetition of their evasion.

These measures of force were accompanied indeed by vigorous efforts to improve the productivity of the land that had declined in the troubles of the civil wars. In Iraq this meant setting in order and enlarging the neglected canal system to provide more land for agriculture. The population saw the increase of fertile land with mixed feelings, for in this way, often with the help of the private capital of the caliph or governor, there arose new large estates which were not to their advantage. The personal enrichment that went with it led under the last great Umayyad governor of Iraq, Khālid al-Qasrī (724–739), to such dissension that the caliph Yazīd III (744) felt it incumbent on him to promise, in his speech of accession, that he would build no new canals (and also start no buildings). The floruit of the towns, especially in the Iranian language sphere, falls mainly in the 'Abbāsid period, but it was already adding strength to the economy of the empire under the Umayyads and was beneficial to *mawālī* and non-Muslims as well.

Attempts to reconcile the tax on the subject population with the precepts of Islam were undertaken more than once towards the end of the Umayyad period. The model was provided by the pious caliph 'Umar (II) ibn 'Abd al-'Azīz (717–720): converts would be freed of poll tax but must pay land tax, although they had forfeited their possession of the land with their conversion; the new Muslim was to continue on the land as a tenant. This system did not go into operation right away—the caliph died after ruling for less than three years—but it laid down the principles which were gradually to become standard. The accusation that 'Umar's reforms placed the interests of Islam before the necessities of the empire and would provoke a financial catastrophe is certainly an exaggeration; a tax on urban capital or on trade could easily have offset the loss on rural taxes. Lastly, as islamization spread there were increasingly large sections of the population who considered intolerable a system of taxation based on the exploitation of the non-Arab subjects, whether or not reform might prove injurious to the 'Arab' state.

However, while this weakened the Arab state a compensating force was at work in the arabization of the administrative system. This is particularly true of the reform of the coinage. The conquests had left untouched the circulation of Byzantine and Persian money; only occasionally would a Koranic phrase be stamped over figures of the Persian rulers or over Christian symbols. The *dirham*, the silver coin, resembled the Sasanian *drahm* (from the Greek *drachma*) in form, and the *dīnār*, the gold coin, the Roman-Byzantine *denarius*. Sporadic minting under Mu'āwiya was followed under 'Abd al-Malik by a period of experimentation, resulting in 698/699 in purely epigraphical coins. Not until the second and third centuries of the *hijra* (eighth and ninth centuries) were the names of the issuing caliph or governor added. *Dirhams* were minted principally in territory previously Sasanian; Wāsiṭ seems to have been the centre of production. The *dīnār* type coin struck in Damascus did not displace the bilingual (Latin-Arabic) gold coins in the west of the empire until about 720; Umayyad Spain, though independent of the caliph, only struck its own gold *dīnārs* after the assumption of the title of caliph by the princes of Córdoba in 929.

Contemporary with the introduction of Arabic coinage was that of Arabic as the official language. A bilingual Greek-Arabic document appears in Egypt as early as 643, but Greek and Coptic remained the languages of the administration; in Iraq, Pahlavī, the 'Middle Persian' governmental language, was taken over together with Persian methods of administration. The assimilation of the foreign speaking clerks, perhaps also the recruitment of Arabic-speaking staff and the increasing self-consciousness of the public service made the linguistic reform necessary and possible. That non-Arab and bilingual documents still occur after the official introduction of Arabic (in Damascus in the year 705) is not surprising in view of the viability of Greek, and particularly of Coptic in Egypt. It fits in with the picture of these reforms that the vulgate form of Arabic commonly called 'Middle Arabic' should be traceable in towns like Alexandria by about 700; in other words, Arabic had by this time already become the business language; the idiom of town life had begun to separate sharply from the language of the literati and scholars. The penetration of Arabic into the non-Muslim communities led to small differentiations among the regional dialects. The at least partial arabization of the non-Muslims was by 700 the indispensable condition for cooperation in the Islamic empire and clearly also for any cultural exchange.

It is in the nature of things that a community built on (racialized) religious affiliation should not find it possible to draw people of other faiths into collaboration on an equal footing. When in addition this community is a minority and finds itself dependent on the dissenters both culturally and economically, then full integration becomes an impossibility if only because of maintaining their identity. But the Islamic world found a solution for the problem of a number of different religious communities living together. The individuality of the 'People of the Book', firstly the Jews and Christians, then also the Zarathustrians, was respected on condition that they raised no claim to participate in the government, especially in the executive. Jurisprudence confirmed the inferiority of the non-Muslim in the most explicit manner; the weregeld due for him amounted to only half that demanded for a Muslim, his evidence had no weight against that of a believer, and he had, as we have seen, to pay a poll tax.

The non-Muslim would observe these restrictions, which changed in detail, but which always stressed his social weakness; in return the legal fiction guaranteed him *dhimma*, a bond of protection, life and property, free exercise of his religion and the autonomy of his religious community. It also laid down the rights and duties of the individual. As in the Germanic world of the migration period, and indeed as it was to a great extent in antiquity and in the early Middle Ages, rights in Islam were personal and not, as in modern times, territorial. To this period it was self evident that men of different faiths and rites, even when they were subject to the same government, should be accorded differing legal status; one might defend oneself against particular constraints, but the principle of differentiation was accepted as natural. It would hardly be appropriate to talk of tolerance or intolerance. This only has a meaning in connection with the readiness of the rulers to allow foreign communities their differences. And here we must establish that the Muslim in the Middle Ages was on the whole more ready to do this than his European or Byzantine contemporaries, and even fitted in the alien ways constructively, as long as they did not aspire to upset social customs, which were easily identified with divine order.

The contracts that regulated the relations of the Muslims with Jews and Christians, *'ahd*, were often dated to the time of the first 'Umar, but in general they reflect the later, often post-Umayyad conditions. We may perhaps allow ourselves the generalization that the position of one of the People of the Book, particularly in high society, was the more favoured, and the readiness to include him in civilizing collaboration was the greater, the surer the Muslims themselves felt of their cultural and political stability. Hence the relative prominence of the *dhimmī* in the intellectual and administrative life of the ninth and tenth centuries, and hence the oppression of dissenter and unbeliever when the great crisis of Sunnite Islam arose in the eleventh century.

Hishām saw that reform was necessary; but a satisfactory result would only have been reached if the non-Muslim subjects had been treated like the Muslim, and in order not to lose all support the Umayyads would have had to make a drastic change in the law by which they themselves had come to power. There was in Hishām's last years a Khārijite uprising of the Berbers, who in spite of their participation in the *jihād*, the Holy War, saw themselves treated almost like heathens; they even had to pay the Arabs a child tribute, the measure being apparently provoked by the irritation and bitterness to which the incurable political unreliability of the Berbers had given rise. The habit—following the Islamic concept of the state rather than necessity—of giving a religious garb to political demands and complaints, introduced into the quarrels an element of irreconcilability and an absence of compromise, which even surpassed the obstinacy of tribal enmities. With the accession of Hishām's poetically highly gifted but politically totally inadequate nephew Walīd II the Umayyad family, which until now had preserved at least an outward semblance of unity, fell apart; three caliphs followed each other in little more than a year, and only after a long struggle, in which the Syrian basis of the dynasty was shattered, did Marwān II, a professional soldier (he is credited with creating a modern order of battle) succeed in re-establishing the nominal unity of the caliphate. This he did in 747, after putting down an extremely dangerous Khārijite uprising in Iraq. But at the very moment when peace became likely in the centre a conspiracy broke out in Khorāsān, and for the moment Marwān had no adequate force to oppose to it; on June 9, 747, the Shī'ites in Sikādang unfurled the black banner of the 'Abbāsids.

The extreme Shī'a had adopted Mukhtār's teaching of the return of the prophetic spark in 'Alī and his descendants in the line of Muḥammad ibn al-Ḥanafiyya, and had for some time been loosely grouped round a series of imams, with conspiratorial intent; like all religious opposition they found support in Iraq. Soon after the death of the imam Abū Hāshim 'Abdallāh (698–716) it was spread abroad that he had bequeathed his function to Muḥammed ibn 'Alī (d. 743), a great great grandson of Muḥammad's uncle al-'Abbās. In fact his partisans did attach themselves to Muḥammad ibn 'Alī; he intensified anti-Umayyad propaganda and after about 720 began sending off proselytizers to Khorāsān. But the real centre remained Kūfa; the active agents in Khorāsān were merchants, the leaders of the sect in Merv were craftsmen and again merchants and almost all of them Iranian *mawālī*; though some were Arab Shī'ites. The parties were primarily concerned in overthrowing Arab monopoly of the State, or in other words Arab nationalism, and instituting instead a theocracy under a scion of the house of the Prophet; Islam, not Arab birth, was to provide the right to participate in the theocratic state.

To undermine the Umayyad government Abū Hāshim had settled earlier in Ḥumaima, a small village south of the Dead Sea, whence he could deploy the activity of his family, strangely enough almost without hindrance. Not until 748 did Marwān step in against the imam of the time, Ibrāhīm, and deported him shortly before his death to Ḥarrān, which, much to the injury of his popularity, the caliph had made his capital instead of Damascus.

Independently of the 'Abbāsids the Fāṭimid (the descendant of 'Ali and Fāṭima, Muhammad's daughter) Zaid ibn 'Alī prepared an uprising in Kūfa which was to restore the Book of God and the tradition, *sunna*, of the Prophet to their rightful status (and also to distribute all the state revenues). Discovered by the government, Zaid had to act prematurely on January 5, 740. The rebellion was suppressed within a few days. His son Yaḥyà fled to Khorāsān but was discovered under Walīd II and killed. The Zaidites themselves who, oddly enough, rejected the Iranian neo-Platonic speculations on the imam, were able later to make their political mark on the borders of the *dār al-islām*; a Zaidite state arose on the southern shore of the Caspian Sea (864–928), a region not fully islamized previously, and another was founded in 897 in the Yemen, which has survived to the present day. The most important direct result of Zaid's and Yaḥyà's 'martyrdom' was that it deepened the alienation of the Iraqi Arabs from the Umayyads and provided Abū Muslim with an effective rallying-cry for vengeance.

The great achievement of Abū Muslim, whom Ibrāhīm sent to Khorāsān as representative of the *ahl al-bait*, the 'Family of the Prophet', was to co-ordinate the various groups of the Shī'ite opposition and to lull the non-Shī'ite Arabs into security until it was too late for them to organize an effective resistance. The last Umayyad governor of Khorāsān saw through the game, it is true, but was unable to accomplish anything without support from the caliph, and he was fully occupied in the interior of the empire on his own account. In verses which have become famous he called on the Arabs of Khorāsān to unite, and appealed to Syria for solidarity, prophesying the end of Arab rule if he should be defeated. '(The rebels) have a religion which does not derive from the Messenger of God and is not in the holy books; and if any one asks me about the root of their religion—(to him I say) their religion stems from the injunction to kill the Arabs.' But the Arabs did not listen to him. Abū Muslim, an Iranian *maulà* adopted by the family of the Prophet and a Shī'ite 'extremist', rode into Merv as arbitrator and in June 748 occupied Nīshāpūr. Naṣr ibn Sayyār, who had been forced to abandon Khorāsān, died at the decisive battle of Jabalq near Iṣfahān (March 18, 749) which freed the way through Nihāvand into Iraq for the *musawwida*, the 'black robed ones': black, used by the earlier opponents of the Umayyads, evoked messianic associations. On September 2nd the Khorāsānian troops occupied Kūfa, where the 'Abbāsids also appeared a month later. The leader of the movement in Iraq, Abū Salama, was not pleased to see them; his intention was to pass the government to the 'Alids—so at least was the report disseminated after his murder —if he had not been prevented from doing so by Abū Muslim. On November 28, 749, Abu 'l-'Abbās, the eldest son of Muḥammad ibn 'Alī, took homage in the Chief Mosque of Kūfa.

To understand the situation we must remember that Abū Muslim had taken an oath of fidelity from his army in Merv for a future caliph; the soldiers were only bound 'to that man from the family of the Prophet of God upon whom they would agree'. The speech from the throne of Abu 'l-'Abbās founded the claim of the 'Abbāsids on the Koran; it was directed against all those who wished to grant the right to the throne to the 'Alids as the nearest relatives of the Prophet, and declared Iraq the centre of the new regime. But this regime was not secure until Marwān himself had been decisively beaten on January 25, 750, on the Great Zāb. Even before Marwān was killed in Upper Egypt in the August of the same year together with a few loyal followers, the 'Abbāsids (ostensibly as avengers of the 'Alids since they themselves had suffered nothing) had begun to exterminate the Umayyads and their high officials with cruel thoroughness. Even to the caliphs who had died (except for Mu'āwiya and 'Umar II) they granted no rest. The Syrians, whose lack of unity had hastened the débâcle, made a belated uprising in 751, which was of course a failure. Their traditional adherence to the fallen dynasty survived, however, although it could not longer stir up any concrete trouble, and in Syria 150 years later it was strong enough to cause concern to the 'Abbāsids; it was concentrated in the eschatological hope in the Sufyānī, who would bring in the final empire of righteousness as an Umayyad Mahdī. 'Abbāsid historical writing however has been at great pains to convince its contemporaries and posterity of the godlessness of the fallen dynasty.

The 'Abbāsids

The Legacy of Greece and The Rise of Persia

THE victory of the 'Abbāsids signified a pushing back, but not the elimination of the Arabs. Regional differences became more marked as time went on; in the transition to national states the importance of the Arabs as a racial and military unity declined visibly. The dissemination of Arabic as a cultural medium, the adoption of Arab nomenclature by the islamized non-Arabs and not least the Arab origin of the dynasty were all factors tending to conceal the gradual disappearance of Arab preponderance in the 'Abbāsid central administration. Pensions were gradually retrenched, until in 831 the *muqātila* as an independent corps was dissolved. Pensions were no longer paid to all Arabs liable for military service, only to Hāshimites and 'Alids, the Islamic 'aristocracy' of the descendants of the Prophet. But although the political influence of the Arabs was reduced, their social or socio-religious prestige remained. The Persians and even more the Khorāsānīs, of whom a not inconsiderable number had been taken into the 'Abbāsid family as 'sons', formed the military core of the empire at the beginning of 'Abbāsid rule. The 'Abbāsids had not taken power as protagonists of the Iranians, however, but as bearers of the law of religion and of the Islamic form of life and government.

The difference between Arabs and *mawālī* therefore lost the basis of its significance. The faithful were all set at the same distance from the ruler who no longer functioned as *primus inter pares* (*protosýmboulos*, as the Byzantine historians express it) by virtue of his rank as a member of the Arab aristocracy, but administered the rule of religion from above to his subjects, like a god-king, from a hieratic distance and isolation, as the representative of revealed order. This alteration in the position of the caliph also put an end to his previous connections with the Arab aristocracy. No one was of equal rank with the 'Abbāsids; for this reason they only married slaves; after 800 not a single caliph was born the son of a free mother. The personal licentiousness of many of the caliphs made no difference to the fact that for the people he was 'the shadow of God on earth', 'the Caliph of God' and not of the Prophet; which formula, however, was naturally rejected by the pious as blasphemous. What held the empire together was no longer the 'Arab nation', the Arabs in leading positions, but the dynasty as the administrator of Islamic unity,

5 Courtyard of the Umayyad mosque in Damascus, 705. *H. W. Silvester*

6 Courtyard of the Aḥmad ibn Ṭūlūn mosque in Cairo, 877–879. *Freda Unger*

7 Page of a tenth-century Persian manuscript of the Koran, Sūra 30, 22–23.
London, Victoria and Albert Museum

8 Hall in the residence of ʻAbd ar-Raḥmān III near Córdoba, late tenth century.
Mas, Barcelona

ultimately therefore Islam itself. It fulfilled these tasks as long as, and to the extent to which, the free survival of the religious Community seemed to be associated with the legitimate state power vested in the caliphate. What the great writer Jāḥiẓ (d. 869) said of the Khārijites in a famous passage can rightfully be said of the Community as a whole, or of the Islamic state: 'When we see the people of Sijistān, of the Jazīra, of Yemen, the Maghreb and 'Umān, the Azraqī, the Najdī, the Ibāḍī and the Ṣufrī (four Khārijite sects), *maulà* and Arab, Persian and nomad, slaves and women, weavers and peasants, despite their various origins and their different homelands all fighting on the same side, we understand that it is religion which creates this unity between them and reconciles their conflicts.' (Translated by W. M. Watt.) Here it is religion that lies open to all and, like the idea of the state in Rome, guarantees the universality of the spiritual and the political structure.

Naturally this state of affairs led to increased sensitivity to the political significance of religious opinions and debates. Conventicles and religious speculation had already become widespread under the Umayyads, particularly in Southern Iraq and in Iran; in many contexts pre- and extra-Islamic ideas found an entry; the further a religious party deviated from the Community, the more unbridled became the theologemes and the greater the tendency to yet further ruptures and fragmentation. These sects had little with which to damage the Umayyads, particularly as they developed in circles which were already opposition-minded. The Umayyads only made the occasional attack, for instance under Hishām when the first systematic theological 'school' made itself felt: the 'Qadarites', who propagated the idea of free will in opposition to predestination (*qadar*), among the Sunnites, who were the majority of the Community, and on principle loyal to the authorities. They called on the example of the Prophet and rejected both the narrow legitimism of the Shī'ites and the faith in works of the Khārijites. In their efforts to be recognized as willed by God and predestined, the 'Abbasids were continuously forced to take up a position in relation to religious trends and disputes. They had risen by means of the Shī'a, at first indeed they appeared as 'extreme Shī'ites'. But they soon understood that this extremism, which among many went as far as deifying the 'Abbāsid ruler, would irretrievably alienate the *umma*. The murder of Abū Muslim, one of the first deeds of al-Manṣūr (754–775), the second and probably the greatest 'Abbāsid, was perhaps not so much an attempt to free himself from the patronage of the powerful Khorāsānī leader as a rupture of the bond which joined the dynasty with the radical Shī'a. The 'moderate' Shī'a thereupon felt itself betrayed and began encouraging a series of uprisings in favour of 'Alid pretenders.

The turn to the *jamā'a*, to the Community of the majority, was therefore indicated as politically inevitable; but it had to be effected; the 'Abbāsids did it so skilfully that they first neutralized and then won over the pious opposition which had given the Umayyads so much trouble.

Strangely enough the feeling of the sinfulness of power increased under the 'Abbāsids, and the desire to withdraw from collaboration in guiding the Community. Although the pious were the 'salt' of the *umma*, on whose behalf the state was permitted *ex professo* to arise, they gave in to a parasitic attitude which combated or withdrew from the political structure on which their very existence depended. The insistence that everything needed for the good of all was exhaustively regulated in the 'rightly understood' Koran and the 'rightly understood' *sunna* of the Prophet has haunted many a government in Muslim countries until the present day. It is not only the 'pious' of Islam who have confused the required attitude with the stated precept, the immutable validity of the revelation with the desires of the interpreter, the complex with the sinful, who have made an adjustment to the timeless which all too often misconstrues the immediate. But since the secular and the spiritual concerns are undifferentiated in the *umma*, subject as it is to one indivisible divine decree, these confusions can hardly be removed as they are in the Christian world, by a compromise in our day-to-day existence. Ultimately they are only to be endured if the religious community draws in on itself and passively accepts the state.

In Islam too the lack of a church organization means that the representation of specifically religious interests is left to the consensus of the Community, though in fact to the advocacy of respected theologians. The Community as a religious association is thus never forced to face reality, so that the fulfilment of the ethical obligation of faith can be seen in the debate of abstract principles, and at the same time peace can be concluded with whatever state order is in force. The lack of a church does not of course mean that there is no clergy; but we can expect no priesthood distinguished sacramentally from the laity as an intercessor with God. The '*ulamā*', who by that time knew of no stratification by hierarchy but only by personal distinction, possess the specialized knowledge without which Islam could not carry on; as jurists they hand on and develop the order of the *umma* which as normative self-representation offers it its true basis of existence and which is at the same time its greatest intellectual achievement: the *sharī'a* laid down in the *fiqh*, the Road, the Law hallowed by origin and purpose.

But the development of the *sharī'a* neither brought a centralization of the exercise of law and administration, nor, curiously, did the absolutism of the caliph seriously try to establish such a centralization. What happened, and fully corresponded to the 'Abbāsid conception of law and state, was the underpinning of local legal practice with the prophetic tradition, the possession of which was the boast of Medina, the city of the pious and of the leisured Islamic aristocracy. This signified in practice that every positive legal maxim was found a sanction through the testimony of the Prophet or by contemporary reports of his behaviour. This certainly made for a unified foundation of law, but in the provinces there was no supplanting of customary procedure. A further consolidation of the legal structure which did not result in the levelling of regional differences either, was the systemization of the legal sources and the collection of their contents, undertaken by ash-Shāfi'ī (d. 820 in Egypt), a Palestinian educated in Medina.

Superficially the law schools are all preponderatingly in agreement. Koran and *sunna*, analogy and independent development of the established pronouncements of the schools are, whether avowedly or not, recognized everywhere as the sources or 'roots' of jurisprudence, although the Ḥanbalites, named after Aḥmad ibn Ḥanbal (d. 855), tried to gloss over the contributions of certain school representatives rather more carefully than for instance the followers of the Iraqi school of Abū Ḥanīfa (d. 767); Koranic and prophetic evidence, too, was not everywhere advanced with the same exclusivity. The Ẓāhirites who established themselves towards the end of the ninth century carefully avoided deducing their maxims, composing themselves to the recognition of unambiguous authority. The frequent practice of antedating contemporary situations and inventing prophetic decisions did not of course help to create a unitary legal system. Ultimately the *ijmā'*, the consensus of the jurists, comparable to the *consensus prudentum* in Rome, was the true foundation of the *fiqh*. Recognized by every school, normative through taking cognizance of legal usage, given authority by the pronouncement of the Prophet that God's Community could never agree on an error, the *ijmā'* lent to religious law the flexibility without which it would soon have become an antiquarian collection of curiosities. The *ijmā'* legalized regional differences; what was law in Baghdad did not have to be enforced in Fez.

Thus the *fiqh* gives no systematic codification of positive law on the basis of a few axiomatic principles; it is built on need and custom and embraces both the cult and the relations between men. The common concept of the nature of the *fiqh* therefore gave and gives unity to Islamic law and Islamic life, and not agreement on individual rulings. On close examination however the decisions of the schools allow us to recognize the sociological conditions which they were in court to satisfy. The practice of jurisdiction fell only gradually (and especially under the first 'Abbāsids) into the hands of the jurists educated in the schools. The ruler was free to restrict the powers of the judge in point of space, time and range; following the example of the first caliphs and the ancient traditions of the orient, he could reserve certain fields of jurisdiction for himself.

The same spirit, its principal aim being to maintain and strengthen the Community, underlies the political theory of the *sunna*, which is little more than a rationalization of history, a rendering absolute of that which has happened, and which is understood as having always existed. Interpretation was fundamentally only concerned with a subsequent justification of the cases of precedent ratified by the *ijmā'*. Since what had already happened in history was of supreme importance as the manifestation of the divine will and the nature of the charismatic Community, any working out of the central concepts of political thought simply took the form of a typology derived from an analysis of the past. In practice it was chiefly the idea of the caliphate from whose development the ideological orientation of the Muslim community can be deduced.

The caliph—discussion usually ranges round the person, not the institution—must be untarnished in behaviour and understanding; fundamentally the legitimacy of his administration is not affected by the manner of his assumption of office. The quality of a *mujtahid*, one versed in the law, is expected of him, though the formulation and elaboration of the teaching are not necessarily his affair. More precisely, the caliph is a *muftī*, one qualified to render legal opinions, such as for instance a *sharī'a* judge, a *qāḍī*, could invoke for support, and of course the highest authority in the political sphere. Hence later even a usurper could lay his 'case' before the caliph and the latter could legitimize him, and allow him to exercise government on certain conditions.

The unity of the caliphate corresponds to the single rule of God and symbolizes the unity of the *umma*. Thus it was difficult for theory to take into account the actual plurality of the bearers of the title of caliph (after 929 even within the Sunnite community itself). The required direct kinship with the Prophet is the problem on which minds were divided, the ultralegitimists being again divided among themselves on whether this relationship transmitted a 'divine spark' and with it the continuity of the Prophet's function as intercessor.

In fact the 'Abbāsid caliph claimed responsibility for the cure of souls; he protected the religion from error and degeneration. Although the concept (or legal picture) of sanction by election is preserved, the authority of the caliph does not stem from the Community. The caliph is unconditional and necessary, he is provided for in the law, and hence unlimited in his executive power as long as the law sets him no bounds—an ambiguity which theory never managed to master. Even less did it succeed in evolving a right of succession. Even in a question which was of such practical import it did no more than the *ijmā'* in general, which was to establish and classify the *faits accomplis*. It was never in a position, and did not even try, to serve the interests of the *umma* by preventing those appointments to the throne, so injurious to the peace of the realm, by the various caliphs, such as the choice of their next two or three successors among their sons, brothers or uncles; nor those divisions of the empire that recurred repeatedly, in spite of their disastrous consequences.

With the change in the basis of rule the style of rule also changed. The ancient oriental court ceremonial was started up in a Sasanid guise. The caliph cut himself off from his subjects, access to him was controlled by chamberlains (*ḥājib*); the generality was seen by the caliph only in public audiences, which were frequently legal sessions at the same time—the caliph was the final court of appeal—and on certain ceremonial occasions. The court, the family of the caliph, his household servants, guards and administrators were the centre of the empire; the standing with the ruler determines rank and influence. His favour raises the menial from nothing, his disfavour plunges him back into nothing. With a sudden entrance the caliph appears and shatters his enemy, sometimes on the spot in public execution in the throne room. 'As soon as one is suspect in their eyes, he is no longer guiltless' (Racine).

The religiously founded moral sermon would be accepted in public, but not—and this entirely in keeping with the style of the times—necessarily followed in the palace. Thus Hārūn ar-Rashīd allowed himself to be taken to task by Sufyān ibn 'Uyaina for using a spoon, on a very subjective interpretation of a verse of the Koran; and the same ruler praised another holy man who extricated himself from the leading question of whether the Umayyads or the 'Abbāsids were the better caliphs by answering 'The Umayyads did more for the people; you are more conscientious in holding prayers'.

The strength of the jurists and of all the representatives of religious life in the early 'Abbāsid period lay primarily in their close contact with the population among whom they worked; the judges were often notables of their region and besides had to belong to the dominant school of their jurisdiction. This link with local interests was also maintained in the administration of the pious foundations (*auqāf*, singular *waqf*) of the 'diocese', and usually delegated to the *qāḍī*; it clearly distinguished the class of the scholars in law and religion from the officials of imperial government. The administrative authorities (*dīwān*) are more or less to be equated with modern state chancelleries or ministries; they developed on the Sasanian model in the imperial capital, which after 762 was the newly founded Baghdad, and in the provincial capitals as well. In them it was the *kuttāb*, the 'scribes', who ruled. These were not schooled in the *sharī'a* and, what was decisive, they were creatures of the ruler: mostly Iranians whose families had been *mawālī* for some time, and there were also Christians among them; in short representatives of the traditional techniques of government. They were not necessarily anti-Islamic in attitude, for they had to deal as it were with the side of official life unconnected with religion, but they tended to stand to some extent in contrast to the *fuqahā'*, the representatives of the *umma*. More free-minded perhaps than the latter, certainly with a more literary and humanist education, the *kuttāb* soon formed a kind of caste which lived relatively isolated from the population and hence could not expect any support from them in time of need. Nevertheless, or rather therefore, it was on the *kuttāb* that the caliphs founded the cohesion of the empire, in conjunction with the armed forces. The decentralization of jurisdiction, of 'manners and customs' and the independence of the governors, unavoidable in view of the means of communication, were to be balanced by the centralized administration.

Only gradually did the *wazīr*, generally drawn from the *kuttāb*, become the first minister and *alter ego* of the prince—and thereby the head of the administrative *maẓālim* (literally : torts) jurisdiction which complemented the *sharī'a* jurisdiction and often supplanted it, being more effectual. His is an office which has most deeply impressed itself on Western consciousness because of literary reminiscences. Both in function and in title the *wazīr* is of Arab origin. First he was the helper and representative of the caliph who had to see to justice on all sides, and then he took over one or other government office. In the early 'Abbāsid period, when the ruler still kept a firm grip on the reins, he finally became the omnipotent minister, an ideal of the Sasanian period (in which many contemporary aspirations were mirrored). In this role the great vizirs of the late ninth and early tenth century became involved in perpetual strife with the military. The famous vizirs of the Barmakid family, who ruled the empire under Mahdī (775–785) and Hārūn ar-Rashīd (786–809), and the equally celebrated Faḍl ibn Sahl who played a similar role in the early years of Ma'mūn (813–833) had, in conjunction with the governorship of Khorāsān, the superintendence over all the most important offices of the central government, and thus at times exercised complete control without being in charge *ex officio* of the administration of every department.

The dichotomy of mentalities which can legitimately be illustrated in the difference between the *fuqahā'* and *kuttāb* corresponds to the two forms of education which were soon to come into conflict: the Arabic-grammatical style which concerned itself both with the study of Writ and with the Bedouin tradition—especially its classical poetry, and the Persian- (or Indo-Persian-) inspired style which, cultivating an elegant contemporary town Arabic, drew primarily from Iranian legendary history, and took pleasure in finding new forms of refined love motifs of a sentimental 'platonic' stamp. The tension between these spheres, which roughly speaking mirrors the extent of their roots in Islam (and the measure of their arabization) was concentrated in the ninth century into a clear division which, particularly within the *kuttāb*, and generally among the intellectuals, set Arabs and non-Arabs against each other in support of their inherited cultural traditions. Despite the rather childish character of its arguments the *shu'ūbiyya*, 'folk (ethnic, national) consciousness', movement had great importance because it sought to break the monopoly of the Arabs over culture, now that their political monopoly had been destroyed for over half a century since the change in dynasty. Both parties remained within the framework of Islam and used Arabic. Not even the Persians, nor the Nabataeans, Copts, Berbers and Abyssinians who followed their example, gave themselves out as political revolutionaries; they saw themselves as no more than champions and protectors of their own position within the *umma*. There is no evidence that the Iranian *shu'ūbī* cultivated the Persian language, although in the ninth century the Iranian provinces had in many cases extricated themselves from the direct control of the central government and consciously cultivated and displayed their special character.

Nor is there any sign of a connection between the Shu'ūbite *kuttāb* and the anti-Islamic movements which were time and again springing up in Iran. They were indubitably loyal to the empire of the caliph, although they introduced into it the propagation of Persian ideas and Persian state and private ethics which constituted a threat to the unity of state and Community. Probably his desire to meet the Persian infiltration with superior intellectual weapons was one of the incentives which made the caliph Ma'mūn support in grand style the gradually expanding work of translating Greek philosophy and science. He founded the *dār al-ḥikma*, a translation centre with library and observatory. The rise of prose writing, connected chiefly with the name of the great man of letters and publicist Jāḥiẓ, and the codification of Iranian history and legends by Ibn Qutaiba (d. 889)—both consciously in the service of the Arab (counter) *shu'ūbiyya*—provided a curb on further Persian influence: the works of the Persian renaissance of the tenth and eleventh centuries remained virtually unknown in the Arab-speaking regions, and hence without effect on Islam as a whole. They did however become the basis of a second great cultural unit within the *umma Muḥammadiyya*.

Support for the 'Hellenists' was less a reaction to the Iranian *shu'ūbiyya* than the result of considerations arising out of the religious situation. Religion, too, was the motivation of the uprisings which repeatedly convulsed the empire. Even under the first 'Abbāsids, who really held power firmly, not a year passed without rebellions of some kind, large or small. But in the first hundred years these conflicts did not affect the reputation of the caliph abroad or the great cultural upsurge; on the whole they disturbed even political life less than might be expected. The energy of cultural life, the wealth of the main provinces of Iraq and of the Iranian cities allowed the internal disintegration and the crumbling away of a few territories to go unnoticed at first. To an increasing degree even the 'loyal' Sunnites gave themselves to every possible school and opinion. Without a church organization no binding orthodoxy had been able to form, and this made the penetration of un-Islamic ideas and associations of ideas all too easy in a population intellectually unschooled and by its origins far from homogeneous.

Whether animated by Zarathustrian orthodoxy, by the Mazdakite movement which could never be completely stamped out (though frequently suppressed because of its communist tendencies), or by a combination of Islamic and traditional Iranian and Near Eastern motifs, prophetic or mahdistic revival of Persian teachings created a following for a series of anti-'Abbāsid insurrectionists, all the way to Transoxiana; it was repeatedly defeated but always ready to fight again. The Zarathustrian church, which did not lose ground materially until the tenth century, found itself on the side of the caliphs in its efforts to achieve political unity and internal religious peace.

Particularly significant for this religious attitude is the uprising of al-Muqanna', the 'Veiled One' (the radiance of his holy power [*baraka*] would have made the sight of his face overpowering) who organised his followers in a secret society with grades of initiation, taught the transmigration of souls and conceived of himself as an embodiment of the same divine substance which had already seen incarnation in Adam, Abraham, Moses, Jesus, Muhammad, 'Alī and Abū Muslim. The Turks supported him. Like the extreme Khārijites, he declared it permissible to spill the blood of the Muslims because they were stiff-necked unbelievers. His self-chosen death on the funeral pile in the year 783–4 put an end to the effectiveness of his 'white robed ones' (*mubayyiḍa*), but it did not destroy the sect's viability; for five hundred years it held together under the shield of an outward adherence to Islamic usages.

The Mazdakite Bābak from Azerbaijān managed to defy the might of the caliph for more than twenty years (816–838) deep into western Persia. Even the victory of the imperial troops under Afshīn, who was an iranized Transoxianan princeling whose great grandfather still bore the Turkish name of Kharabogha, did not prevent the century-long survival of his 'Reds' (*muḥammira*). It is not without significance that Afshīn, the celebrated saviour of the empire, fell shortly afterwards, a victim to a political trial where the charges mirror the endurance of pre-Islamic religions in the Sogdian cultural sphere.

Ḥasan Āzarak is another of the numerous 'secessionist' leaders; he maintained himself for many years (795–828) in Sijistān and in the south-west of present-day Afghanistan. They found militant support under the early 'Abbāsids in Iraq as well as in the Jazīra, in 'Umān (where the Khārijites are dominant to this day), as well as in the Arabian peninsula, and indeed in Syria and even in Khorāsān itself. In the Maghreb the identification of the Berbers with Khārijism, though the Spanish Berbers did not join in, gave the movement an attraction which was virtually irresistible. At times the Khārijites even occupied Qairawān; and though the 'Abbāsid army managed for the time being to restore the *status quo* of the Umayyad period after a long campaign, they were unable to prevent the establishment of independent Khārijite states in Tāhert, modern Tiarat in Algeria, in 777, in Sijilmāsa (757) on the road leading into the Niger area, and in Tlemcen (taken from the Idrīsids in 786). In 787 the 'Abbāsid governor in Qairawān made his peace with the Persian-born imam of Tāhert, implying recognition of his political existence as a separate power. The Shī'ite Idrīsids in Central Morocco belong in this context too, since they were foreign born organizers of Berber tribes. Their second ruler founded Fez in 808, later to become an influential centre of Islamic life.

But the greatest danger in the eyes of the 'Abbāsids was the 'Alids, because their influence was so extensive precisely in the key regions of the caliphate. The second 'Abbāsid, Abū Ja'far (he started the tradition followed by all later rulers in his family of adopting a theophorous throne name: al-Manṣūr (bi'llāh), 'supported (by God) with victory') had to clear the field of two important Ḥasanid 'Alids, Muḥammad ibn 'Abdallāh (d. 762) celebrated as 'the pure soul' *an-Nafs az-zakiyya* and his brother Ibrāhīm (d. 763) to whom not only Baṣra and southern Persia but the holy cities of Mecca and Medina had rallied. The rebels claimed to be obeying the injunctions of the Koran in their methods of fighting—one is reminded of the 'war scroll' of the community of Qumrān—thus it was probably not too difficult to defeat them in the field; but it was impossible to eradicate latent 'Alid legitimism. At the least opportunity 'Alid pretenders rose up or were put forward if, unlike the Berber Shākiya in Spain, the revolutionaries were themselves unable to advance a credible 'Alid genealogy.

In the memory of the Community the government of Hārūn ar-Rashīd (786–809) constitutes the golden age of the caliphate. We may concur in this evaluation without styling him a great ruler, for he lacked both the brutal energy of Manṣūr and the intellectual finesse of Ma'mūn. We, like his contemporaries, must also gloss over two facts: first it was in his reign that the Aghlabid governor of Ifrīqiya (Tunisia) severed his relations with the central government; second, the lengthy insurrection of Transoxiana was not brought under control until after his death and remained a painful reminder of the impossibility of governing the remote borderlands from Baghdad. It took the Caliph seventeen years from his accession to achieve full power, after which time he executed his foster brother Ja'far and expelled the other Barmakids from the most important government offices and imprisoned them. Seven years before his death (802) he wrote his will and divided the empire among his sons; what was in his mind remains a mystery. The eldest son, Muḥammad al-Amīn, whose mother was an Arab, received the caliphate and the Arab lands; the son of a Persian slave, Ma'mūn, the Persian territories. Perhaps his intention was to legalize a split already apparent. The division of authority soon proved intolerable, however.

As at the end of the Umayyad domination a Khorāsānī army marched into Iraq; but in contrast to the days of Abū Muslim the cause of the conflict was this time openly the antagonism between the Iranians and Arabs. Amīn's attempt to arm the lower classes during the siege of Baghdad was effective, but it certainly hastened his downfall. At his death (813) the Arabs were played out as a political factor. Ma'mūn tried to administer the caliphate from Merv and nominated 'Alī Riḍā, an 'Alid, as his successor, in the hope of reconciling 'Alids and 'Abbāsids. Both experiments failed. In Baghdad one of Ma'mūn's uncles, Ibrāhīm ibn al-Mahdī, much celebrated as a singer and bon viveur, received homage as anti-caliph. Ma'mūn himself marched on Baghdad and it quickly capitulated; 'Alī Riḍā had already died, it is said from poison; his grave became the famous Shī'ite pilgrimage town of Meshed. Not until he had received homage did Ma'mūn exchange the green of the 'Alids once more for the black of his own house.

A family of the islamized aristocracy took over the reins of government in Khorāsān: the Ṭāhirids became practically independent in their province while at the same time one of their family was appointed the prefect of police in the imperial capital. It was a Ṭāhirid also who retrieved Alexandria for Baghdad in 827 after it had been occupied for eleven years by Muslim refugees from Spain.

Even disregarding the fact that the 'Abbāsids owed the throne to a religious slogan, the intense religious excitability of the times alone would have made religion into a public concern and with it philosophy, then beginning its development; there was an inherent need to interpret social grievances as religious deficiencies and to seek the means to abolish them in religion and eschatology. On the other hand it was characteristic of the Islamic world of the time—and it has hardly altered to this day—that theologico-philosophical investigations and trends were wont to start from political situations or problems.

A typical instance is the school responsible through agreement and conflict for the formulation of the articles of faith: the 'Mu'tazilites', 'Those who hold back', 'The Abstainers'. They received their name towards the end of the Umayyad period by refusing to recognize either party to the rift in the *jamā'a* as free from guilt. The very fact of association with this abomination was tainting; yet this sin neither involved exclusion from the Community nor did it excuse the use of force against the guilty government, for this would only have brought injury to the Community as a whole. Nevertheless in Baṣra, which remained well into the ninth century the most active intellectual centre of the Islamic world, the sympathies of the early Mu'tazilites lay rather with the 'Alid and later with the 'Abbāsid side, and the 'Abbāsids (with the exception of Hārūn ar-Rashīd) maintained good relations with them for a century. This attitude of the caliphs was in the last resort because the Mu'tazilites alone were in a position to undertake the disciplining of theological and religious reasoning which had become so necessary through the uncontrolled growth of different sects, and to protect Islam in this way against rival faiths or modes of thought.

The later attacks of 'orthodoxy' against them should not disguise the fact that the Mu'tazilites stood firmly on the ground of the Muslim revelation. They were concerned with the absolute unity and righteousness of God demonstrable from the Koran. They were in no way freethinkers or men of the enlightenment, they disciplined the methods of thought, concerned themselves with clear theological concepts and, one might say, humanized the teaching in that they raised up *ratio* (*'aql*) to the decisive criterium of truth as an element which joined God and man in a kind of pre-stabilized harmony. Like Plato in the Euthyphron, though independently of him, they conceive of what is morally good and what is reasonable as set up by God in conformity with their own essence; they do not just become good or reasonable by divine ordinance. Thanks to the reason common to God and men, man has an insight into the motive of creation and moral judgment and with it—without prejudice to the divine knowledge of the totality of being—freedom of decision and moral responsibility. Evil exists only in the human sphere, as a result of free will; on the cosmic level God can only will good. The separation of creator and creature is absolute, the Koranic anthropomorphisms are to be understood allegorically. Such traditions and *ijmā'* as seem to support their literal sense are spurious and without authority; not *consensus* but *ratio* is the touchstone. The believer has a duty to assist in the triumph of right and to eliminate wrong—an attitude indeed common to almost all Muslim movements—though this does not imply any duty to rebel, but justifies the alliance with state power in order to make secure and pursue the true faith.

To 'orthodoxy' the Mu'tazilite position was distressing on two scores: first their attempt to circumscribe and define the religious experience; second their restriction of the omnipotence of God, the 'humanism' which conceives of Allah as bound by his own moral laws and ordering of nature, and sees the key to God's actions and motives in the reason common in essence to both God and man.

But at first the Mu'tazilites were successful in their 'mission' in all parts of the empire, though they never formed a united school. They even served orthodoxy as useful campaigners against a dualist movement which was gaining ground among the intelligentsia and the upper reaches of society influenced by Iran. The belief in a double creation which frees the 'good' God from any responsibility for evil and assigns to man his role in the universe is common to the Zarathustrians and the Manichaeans, and in spite of persecutions it found constant support in mediaeval Christendom along with the extreme asceticism peculiar to the Manichaeans. How far the government tried to stamp out Manichaeism, which had increased towards the end of the Sasanid oppression, and how far it was merely anxious to prevent the public reversion of islamized circles is not clear. At any rate al-Mahdī felt it necessary to intervene against the Manichaeans (*zindīq*) in a series of trials which even led to executions. The concept of *zandaqa* went beyond actual 'dualism', it characterized an independent attitude to revealed religion which subjectively and frivolously rejected the reference to definite teachings. That an undertone of political dissonance vibrated in sympathy hardly needs saying, in the Islamic context.

The arsenal of intellectual weapons to use against the Manichaeans, and the means whereby the Muslim revelation could be brought into a form suitable to the day were only available in one place: the heritage of antiquity. This had already rendered Christian theology the service now required of it by Islam. The material was to hand. The Alexandrine academy never ceased to study Aristotle until it closed, and it had reached Baghdad by way of Antioch and Ḥarrān (the seat of a tenacious Hellenistic star cult); the Christians there (mostly Nestorians) were acquainted with Greek philosophy and science in the original or in earlier Syriac translations; and the interest of the educated class of Muslims was exceptionally great, though indeed only in so far as the classical texts were suitable to give support to the Faith with their philosophy, and to make scientific, principally medical, facts accessible. Fine literature and history awoke no echo, partly because of the totally different background which would have been necessary to make them comprehensible.

In addition there was an attractive and highly prized native tradition in poetry, and an independent historiography was quickly developing which dealt with the appearance of the Prophet and the rise of the Islamic empire. Lastly a personal and political ethic had already been created from Persian sources. Many classical influences also reached Arabic through Middle Persian. In contrast the Roman tradition remained quite unheeded because of the remote position of Spain and the low cultural level of the romance-speaking world at the time of the Arab conquest. For Islam the classical world was the Greeks, and in the first place the neo-platonic interpretations of Plato and Aristotle.

The translations, performed with admirable scholarship and for the period with exceptional philological perspicuity, reached their zenith under the Nestorian Ḥunain ibn Isḥāq (d. 873), though they were continued into the eleventh century in response to great public interest. The formation of an Arabic terminology for the philosophical sciences and the extension of available knowledge was in its effects perhaps less important than the possibility afforded by the new concepts not only to express ideas but to be able to conceive them at all: in some ways analogous to the intellectual development in Europe between the sixteenth and eighteenth century, when the development of vernacular languages made it possible to extend thought as well. In 1654 Pascal could still complain that it was impossible to formulate a mathematical problem in French. We will only note in the margin, but none the less with gratitude, that the Arabian translators preserved a highly important heritage for the West.

The tension between the 'rationalists' and the pious masses who remained untouched by the movement came to a climax on a specially sensitive issue. To the Mu'tazilites, whose fundamental tenet was the immaculate unity of God (*tauḥīd*), His Word appeared—like His Knowledge—as ancillary and in this sense not coeval with the Divine Substance and thus not eternal *a parte ante*. Any other conception implied the deification of the Word and hence the association (*shirk*) of a second divine being and the destruction of the Islamic idea of God. The reverence of the mass of believers for the Word of God, the *kalām Allāh*, was too great for them not to feel injured by the doubtless conceptually correct position of the Mu'tazilites; they could not accept, so to speak, that the word of God should be made into a 'Logos'.

The combat was conducted under the battle cries of the Created or Uncreated Koran. Official opinion was in time won over to the 'Created Koran' (*khalq al-Qur'ān*). In 827 Ma'mūn decreed the *miḥna* (often translated 'inquisition', more correctly *test* of faith); the theologians and jurists had to acknowledge in writing the 'Created Koran'. The majority of theologians acquiesced, but in their hearts remained on the side of the uncompromising Aḥmad ibn Ḥanbal, whom the government in this case, unlike some others, did not dare to put to death. The anthropomorphism of many verses in the Koran was less distressing than subtilizing over the Word of God; the Hellenizing systemization seemed an alienation from living piety. Ma'mūn's third successor al-Mutawakkil (847–861) tried to win over the *jamā'a* in his efforts to strengthen the authority of the caliphate and in 849 he declared himself publicly for the 'Uncreated Koran', abolished the *miḥna* and dismissed the Mu'tazilite chief judge. At the same time, characteristically, he attacked the cult of Ḥusain in

Karbalāʾ, and had his tomb mosque razed to the ground, while he intensified the external marks of inferiority attaching to Jews and Christians.

The true significance of the conflict and its outcome did not reside in the fall of the Muʿtazila, which survived as a school and even more as an attitude of mind, but in the understanding between government and *umma* that both Islam and the caliphate would be best served if the public authority limited its interference in religious life to guaranteeing its external conditions. The result was that politics were disassociated from religion and the universal *umma*, now increasingly independent of a government committed to the affairs of the moment, took on a new momentum.

This independence forced theology to reassure the self-confidence of the faithful by the reliability of its reasoning. This happened in two ways. On the one hand the concepts and methods of thought of the critics had to be accepted, often unwillingly, and thus to some extent the problems the theologians had to solve were prescribed: freedom of will and predestination, the nature and attributes of God, the sense of the anthropomorphic epithets of Allah in the revelation, the *visio dei*, the question of the Logos. Secondly the attitude to the prophetic tradition was changed; since it was the only conclusive criterion it was inevitable that each party should invent it anew to support the aims of the day as circumstance dictated: a practice often censured but never really condemned.

By the ninth century the traditional material had swollen beyond all manageable proportions and a critical sifting became essential. The nature of the case dictated, and the insufficiently developed sense of anachronism too, that no selection of the words of the Prophet by content was possible. Hence investigations centred round the chain of witnesses, round the process of tradition which led back to the Prophet or his contemporaries. Only too often it became apparent that a tradition was attested only once, or only from unreliable witnesses. Thus it is typical of the aims of this new science that the first great collections were compiled by men who are remembered by posterity chiefly as the founders of law schools: Mālik ibn Anas (d. 795) and Aḥmad ibn Ḥanbal. With the transition from arrangements by persons—the authorities standing closest to the Prophet in the chain of transmitters—to systemization by subject matter, criticism also was appreciably refined. This circumstance created enormous authority for the collections of such men as Bukhārī (d. 870) and Muslim (d. 875). The other four collections to achieve equal canonical validity also derive from the late ninth century.

The laconic notes on the transmitters of tradition gave rise to the biography so characteristic of mediaeval Islam. There is nothing in the West until well into the sixteenth century remotely comparable to the comprehensive lexika which treated of poets, scholars and the eminent in all walks of life. These biographical collections, perhaps even more than the historical writings, have provided Islamic civilization with its own portrait.

Hellenization went apace. Before the end of the ninth century the caliph al-Mu'taḍid was again supporting scholars and attracting them into his palace. Receptivity for Greek thought grew remarkably quickly even outside theology. While al-Mu'taṣim was still reigning (833–842) the 'first Arab philosopher' Ya'qūb al-Kindī from Baṣra began his work on a synthesis of Greek thought acceptable to Islamic premisses. In it the Platonic element shows to greater effect than the Aristotelian. An occasional lack of skill in handling the new concepts and a certain insensitivity to the contradictions between Greek and Islamic axioms is compensated by the seriousness and proud confidence of a great searcher after truth. 'The truth never degrades him who seeks it, but ennobles all. . . . It must be taken wherever it is to be found, whether it be in the past or among strange peoples. To me it appears right first to produce in its entirety what the ancients have said on a subject, and thereafter to complete what they omitted to say according to (our) way of speaking and the customs of our time.' (Trans. R. Walzer.) Kindī's voracious openness to knowledge and truth becomes the hallmark of the next generation—not only among 'Hellenists' but among those concerned with the Arab tradition alone like that astoundingly encyclopaedic anti-shu'ūbī, Ibn Qutaiba (d. 889), outstanding as traditionist, linguistic praeceptor, historian and theoretician of literature.

Kindī worked for the 'men of our tongue' *ahl lisāni-nā*, important evidence for the emergence of a new consciousness of a common culture balancing, at least in many circles, the religious separatism. This cultural consciousness is documented in the great Muslim philosophers, al-Fārābī (d. 950) and Ibn Sīnā (Avicenna; d. 1037) who, one of Turkish, the other of Persian extraction, found themselves working together in a common philosophical idiom. Jewry too made its first pervasive contact with the Greeks through the intermediary of Islam. Throughout the whole Hellenistic period it had obstinately turned away from it all, apart from Philon. Greek thought at that time was irresistible; it pervaded all intellectual endeavour to such an extent that even the Zarathustrians of the ninth and tenth centuries were seized by Aristotelian scholasticism. The leading spirits of mediaeval Islam never lost the sense that intellectually they belonged to the Greek West.

9 Arab Astrolabe. Chased brasswork from Toledo, 1029

ته وعوارف سنية وعطايا هنية وتقرر بحكم السلطنة في مناصب الثبات واستقرت قلوب الخواطر والعوام وأوسع والشريف على مطاوعته

10   The bestowal of a robe of honour on Maḥmūd ibn Subuktegin, and his death.
     Miniatures in a Persian manuscript, *c.* 1314.   *Edinburgh University Library*

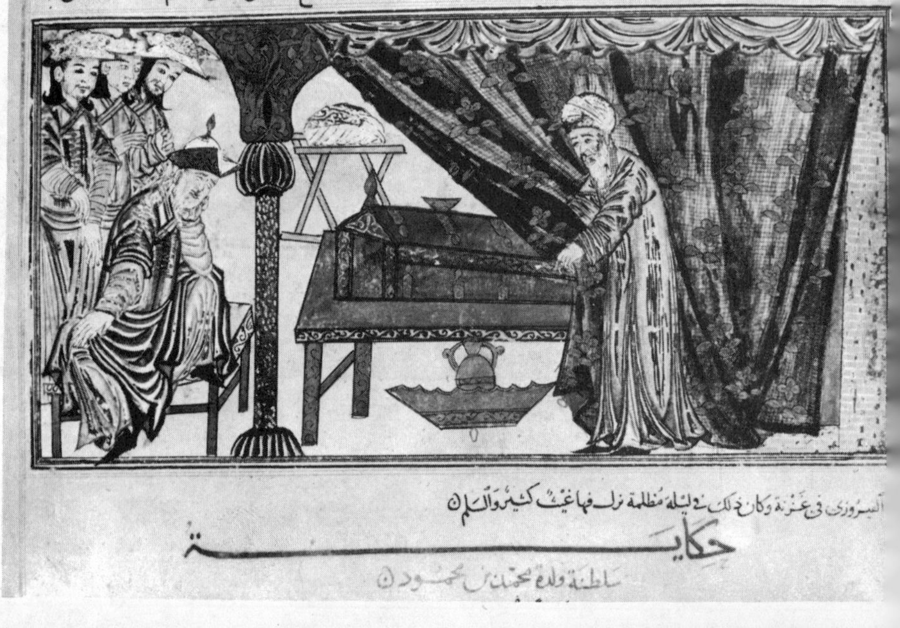

But while this intellectual life was turning towards Hellenism the caliphate moved its political fulcrum from the Mediterranean where it had for so long been centred, into central Iraq, with its interests oriented towards the Asiatic north and east. This of course did not mean that peace had descended on the Byzantine frontier. The unstable balance of forces had tended to swing in favour of the Muslims between 750 and 850 but it did not allow the *jihād*, the 'battle on the path of God' to rest in its duty to incorporate the unconquered 'war region' (*dār al-ḥarb*) of the unbeliever into the *dār al-islām*. Guerilla warfare, apart from several larger expeditions, continued without interruption. Hārūn ar-Rashīd defeated the Emperor Nikephoros at Dorylaeum, conquered Tyana in 806 and reached Ankyra (Ankara); Ma'mūn died in 833 in the military camp at Tarsus; al-Muʿtaṣim took Amorium in 838 and was preparing a fresh siege of Constantinople, but had to abandon the plan when a storm destroyed the Arab fleet. In 838 the same caliph deported the Zuṭṭ or Jaṭṭ to Cilicia, thus rendering them innocuous after their three years' rebellion. These were ancestors of the gypsies, who had migrated into the region of the lower Tigris from India before the Islamic period. Yet in general the status quo was maintained, and more important, cultural relations were unaffected and unbroken by political tensions. Just as the Byzantine emperor disregarding all hostilities had placed craftsmen and artists at the disposal of the Umayyad 'Abd al-Malik for building the Dome of the Rock in Jerusalem (691), so now Byzantium assisted the Arabs in the collection of Greek manuscripts.

Spain had officially outgrown subjection to Baghdad; Egypt stood in the background within the imperial union; Ma'mūn only visited the province in connection with the great Copt uprising of 829–830. Although the oriental sources are silent on this point, there is no reason to doubt that relations existed between Hārūn ar-Rashīd and Charlemagne. There is no trace in Greek sources either of the indubitably historic visit of the Buddhist missions sent by King Aśoka to the Hellenistic courts in 255 BC. The elephant sent to the Emperor from the Caliph aroused a great sensation; and the 'right of patronage' which was apparently conceded to Charles for the pilgrims to the Holy Land occupied the imagination of the contemporary West intensively. Notker Balbulus (d. 912) still makes Hārūn consider the argument against his envisaged donation of Palestine (thus the monk of St Gallen viewed the right of protection) that it would be difficult for Charles to defend the country should Hārūn in his *magnanimitas* bestow it. Even the weakened caliphate of the tenth century seemed important enough to European courts to warrant establishing diplomatic relations with it; we have only to remember the 'embassy' of Bertha of Tuscany to the caliph al-Muktafī in 906, an occasion for celebrations of every kind.

The defeat of Amīn (813) had finally given the Arabs a minor status and removed them from the imperial army. Even so Arab troops, especially Bedouin, continued to figure largely, particularly in local struggles for power. To the Caliph Ma'mūn it seemed as impossible as it was impracticable to rely entirely on the people of Khorāsān. Increasingly the half civilized or half islamized border populations, Kurds, Dailamites, Christian Armenians and above all central Asiatic Turks—the only people to be easily approachable and sufficiently numerous—were recruited into the professional army of the caliph. Inevitably this evoked tensions in Baghdad and an extraordinarily rapid growth of Turkish influence at court. In order to avoid the continuous troubles between Turks and the native population in Baghdad al-Mu'taṣim in 838 moved his seat of government to Samarra, a city constructed on an exceptionally grandiose plan and situated about one hundred kilometres to the north. As was only to be expected, the Caliph in his isolation became more and more the puppet of the Turkish officers; their self-seeking tyranny remained impervious even to such a bold political manoeuvre as the religious policy of Mutawakkil. The other troops of the guard were not equal to them in military ability. Al-Mutawakkil himself was murdered by them in 861 and the same fate hastened the end of three of his four successors whom the soldiers placed on the throne during the following nine years. Al-Mu'tazz (866–869) attempted to use an African guard as a counterweight to the Turks so hated by the Iraqi population, but he failed. Meanwhile the larger part of the Persian-speaking territory had become independent to all practical purposes, completing the picture of political decline. It was however counterbalanced by exceptional vigour in the religious and cultural sphere.

Islamic Society and Social-Religious Movements

The empire and its culture were carried on the shoulders of the peasants, but dominated by the townsmen; the countryside was organized from the town and exploited by princes, burghers and mercenaries. The Islamic East, from the intrusion of the Turks in the ninth century to the fall of Baghdad (1258), is the history of the victory of a predominantly Turkish military landowning aristocracy over the landowning but primarily mercantile Arab or Arabizing aristocracy dominant in civil government. But both classes, like all the ruling classes in the Islamic world, were town dwellers. The Fāṭimids managed to hold back this development in Egypt, but even there the two leading classes succeeded in establishing the same division of power which had now become typical in the East. Only in the West, in North Africa and Spain, was the state able to assert itself without the Turks; there the repression of the mercantile Arabized aristocracy by the politico-military executive took on other forms, certainly more favourable to the native population. Yet there too the town was the real centre of power.

This opposition of town and country was so extensive that our sources ignore the country almost entirely—for the townee officials and historians it simply does not exist—it found no echo in the law either. The *sharī'a* recognizes no exceptions, no privileges which might distinguish one area (or one class) in the Community of the Faithful or would exonerate it on principle from taxes and contributions. Even so the lawyers were concerned sporadically with urban questions. The Muslim town therefore, although from the beginning and everywhere the centre of political power, is not politically autonomous like the Greek city and possessed of an area of countryside belonging to it; the countryside 'belongs' to the state, whose seat of power is the town, or to its inhabitants as private individuals, but not to the town, which has no juridical personality. In this way it differs from the towns of mediaeval Europe, called into being by rulers who lived in the country and possessing a precisely defined position within the sovereign area. The Islamic town is perhaps, as Claude Cahen has suggested, to be compared with the Byzantine town of the late classical period, which, deprived of any sovereignty over the surrounding country and over itself, was wholly incorporated into the centralist state. Yet though the town acquired enormous importance both in Byzantium and in Islam, in many provinces, for example in the Jazīra (Mesopotamia) and Egypt, the towns are very sparse.

The reference to late classical Byzantine towns is relevant from other points of view. When it was laid out as a new foundation at least, the hellenistic town was planned on the chess-board pattern with numerous through roads and rectangular squares; the Muslim town on the other hand was typically a built up medley of winding narrow streets, few of them through roads, and the different districts were shut against each other with gates, each with its own market and mosque and to some extent self-sufficient. The main mosque formed the nucleus of the urban complex, beside which generally rose the house of the governor or prince, unless he resided in the fortress (*qaṣaba*). The cloth hall (*qaiṣariyya*), most precious part of the buildings because of its stock, also lay in the centre and was easily guarded. The small producers, who were at the same time petty merchants, had their stalls in streets according to their trade. The confusion of the layout seems incomprehensible if one regards the Islamic town simply as the successor to the Hellenistic and forgets that in the centuries immediately preceding the Arab occupation the Greek towns had become to a large extent orientalized in population and therefore in manner of living, so that Arab-Islamic urbanism in fact derives organically from the preceding period.

History is extremely vague on the sizes of populations. Probably Baghdad had about three hundred thousand inhabitants when at its zenith in the ninth century, thus far surpassing Constantinople and of course the western towns, even of the late Middle Ages; Paris in 1380 had about 58,000, Cologne in the thirteenth century 45,000, Bologna in 1206 about 64,000, Rome at the same time some 35,000 inhabitants. The Spanish Arab capital of Córdoba together with its suburbs never reached more than 100,000 inhabitants, even at the height of its prosperity round the year 1000.

The craftsmen and merchants were assembled in 'guilds' (*ṣinf*); these had juridical personality and could for example claim and receive the compensation due to an under-age heir for the murder of his father. In this respect the guild corresponded to the tribe, which it also resembled in that the *nisba* (designation of origin or affiliation) in an earner's name was customarily derived from his profession, where in the traditional kinship group it was derived from the tribe. The head of the guild was a member chosen by consensus and confirmed by the state. Economic activity was supervised by an official nominated by the government; his original title of Master of the

Market (*ṣāḥib as-sūq*) betrays its derivation from the Byzantine *agoranomos*. About 700 it was changed into *muḥtasib* (Spanish *almotacén*) indicating the islamization of the office. At the same time the sphere of his duties was widened; he was put in charge of rectitude of practice with summary authority (*ḥisba*), extending the traditional supervision of weights and measures, methods of production and quality, sometimes also of prices, into a moral and religious duty. The manuals compiled for the *muḥtasib*—the oldest one surviving is from the ninth century—are far from exhausted as a source for cultural history in the widest sense. In spite of all the differences, particularly those consequent on islamization, the connection between the late classical state-ordained and state-supervised *collegia* (and their Sasanid counterparts) is clear. That the corporations do not appear in Ifrīqiya until about the eleventh century gives added support to the validity of this connection. Crafts tended to be inherited, again a late classical tradition, though it was indeed general in the ancient orient.

The amount of slave labour was not inconsiderable. The slave worked directly for his master or else was 'hired out'. But he could also work on his own account; sums which he earned over and above the daily due to his owner were his own property (not heritable), and if occasion arose he could use them towards buying his freedom. Muslims could not be enslaved, but were often born slaves. The decreasing opportunities for acquiring slaves, consequent on the growing pacification of the *dār al-islām*, gradually reduced the supply to Slavs (the designation is, however, used for all Europeans), Negroes (all Africans, the Zanj) and Turks. They, as has already been mentioned, were primarily trained as soldiers. Slave armies such as were stationed on Roman *latifundia* only existed in southern Iraq.

There is no doubt that free hired labour predominated both in the countryside and in the town. In the first centuries of the 'Abbāsid period there developed simultaneously a propertyless working class and a wealthy burgher stratum. A process of industrialization began, craft techniques, particularly in the textile and weapons industries, were improved and new fields of production developed, such as paper, which spread between 751 and the eleventh century—i.e. very slowly, by modern standards—from Samarkand as far as Spain and in the tenth century brought the Egyptian papyrus industry to an end.

There is also no mistaking the rise of a relatively numerous 'internationally minded' middle class in the cultural sphere. The expansion of long-distance trade went hand in hand with that of banking. The scale of activity and the magnitude of the capital sums accumulated can be deduced from the relations of several bankers with the 'Abbāsid government, and again from records of confiscations. Profits were invested in land, though to avoid the ever-present threat of the government's seizure there was always a certain amount of hoarding and depositing with friends and clients.

The Islamic theory of taxation made legal distraint on urban income difficult. Tolls, taxes on sales and other levies were strictly speaking unlawful. 'State credit' was unknown, and therefore in times of crisis it was practically impossible to avoid forcible encroachments on private property, particularly as these pressures were mostly exercised against officials who, it was generally considered, could only have acquired their wealth by illegal means. In accordance with the technical possibilities of the time the administration was severely restricted, and the state was thus obliged to farm out taxes, a recourse which did not weigh lightly on the population. Not only had they to discharge the customary taxes which were very arbitrarily reckoned because land surveying had deteriorated since late classical times (a problem which also beset the Byzantine administration), but also to provide the profit for the tax farmer. *Vis-à-vis* the tax collector the townsman was more favoured than the peasant, to whom incidentally the land did not generally belong; he farmed it in *muzāra'a*, receiving the working capital from the owner and in return paying him a fixed, often very high percentage, of the harvest. Taxes were carefully assessed according to the nature of the land—whether artificially or naturally watered, whether well watered, garden or agricultural land—and according to the crop.

But the growing need of the state and the military rulers for money only too often cut across the intentions of the lawgiver. With the transition to a military government the ownership of land in the provinces fell more and more into the hands of absentee officers who were not of course interested in long term plans. Often enough they managed to convert their tax liability from *kharāj* to *'ushr*, whereby the difference, about four-fifths of the amount of the *kharāj*, returned to them. Starting in the late ninth century this development inflicted considerable harm both on the productivity of the land and on the state treasury. About 920 military expenditure must have already accounted for at least a third of state income, to judge from a caliphal budget which survives for 918/919, and various data about the soldiers' pay: the infantryman received approximately three times, and the cavalry soldier six times as much as an unskilled labourer. In consequence perhaps of the extremely lavish court expenditure the outgoings on public works, such as maintenance of the streets and frontier fortifications, were infinitesimally small.

The caliphate had at first a double currency: gold standard in the Byzantine west, silver standard in the Sasanid east; the relation of the *dīnār* to the *dirham* was 10 : 1, later usually 12 : 1, but the value of silver sometimes sank to a twentieth (and even a fiftieth) of the price of gold. By about 900 the gold standard won; the stability of the *dīnār* abroad was as remarkable as that of the Byzantine solidus. The influence of Islamic currency can be traced right into the Carolingian period; its standing is reflected in coin hoards, found as far afield as Scandinavia. The adoption of the gold standard did not take place without some damage to the eastern provinces however; they were bled economically to benefit those of the centre, a consequence of the fragmentation of the caliphate. Nevertheless in return Baghdad retained the advantages of united imperial rule and bore by and large the expenses of army and administration. But the more the caliph's power crumbled the more the other provinces were burdened. The vicious circle can be imagined: the increasing unreliability of the provinces made it necessary to increase the army, and that was only to be financed from higher taxes, which necessarily aggravated the separatism of the provinces. Added to this was the reduction in income from the government estates and state-administered industries—the best known being luxury textiles, which were a state monopoly—which particularly in Egypt had enormous economic importance: whether because of a rebellion, or whether, as more often in the tenth century, a province was abandoned to a governor general who undertook to maintain his army out of local income.

Burghers and 'scribes' (*kātib*) were natural allies against the soldiery. Yet one can question how far the interests of these two classes were bound up with the existence of the centralized empire. The provincial administrations on the whole were smaller self-governing copies of the imperial administration; they were not dependent on subsidies from the residence, but paid over their surplus to Baghdad after meeting their own expenses. The imperial army alone was of any use for defending the frontier or for keeping down rivalries between or in the provinces. The tolls that were levied on the growing provincial frontiers were burdensome for trade and traffic it is true, but do not at first seem to have been a serious hindrance to the economy. In itself the disintegration of the empire into separate states—towards the end of the first half of the tenth century an accomplished fact—need not necessarily have ended in decline and impoverishment; it was above all lack of stability, and the economic short-sightedness of the foreign military officer caste, which consistently undermined the prosperity of Iraq, Southern Persia and the Jazīra. The great vizirs of the early tenth century, in the first place Abu 'l-Ḥasan ibn al-Furāt (executed in 924) and 'Alī ibn 'Īsà (d. 946), raised the standing of their office to an extraordinary degree: equivalent to that of a prime minister or even of a civil regent. But ultimately they were crushed between the army and the court, without whose help it was impossible to solve the financial difficulties brought about to a large extent by these two institutions. The true head of the empire after 908 was the general of the guard Mu'nis as *amīr al-umarā'*, 'Senior general'; less than thirty years later the caliph expressly invested another general with full executive powers: Muḥammad ibn Rā'iq (936), who of course was no more able than his predecessors to make money out of the air. Some stabilization took place when a dynasty of Dailamite adventurers, the Būyids, who had the support of a private army in North-West and Central Iran, occupied Baghdad in 945 and fixed the dichotomy of public power, military and administrative under the Sultan, spiritual and legal under the Caliph. It made it easier for the Būyids to act effectively in that they were Shī'ites, but conversely the Sunnite caliphate found co-operation with them more difficult.

The weakening of the central power and the widening domination of foreign soldiers and slave troops led in Eastern Islam to curious developments in the towns. They can be explained as a rise in forms of organization which had occurred earlier, possibly as developments of Sasanid traditions. There is nothing of the kind to be seen in Egypt before the thirteenth century, let alone in North Africa and Spain. Early on—a precise date is not yet possible—there appear associations of unmarried young men, particularly in the towns of Iraq and Khorāsān. They led an existence pledged to the social virtues (nobility, generosity, courage) and somewhat alienated from their religious and social origins. These clubs of *fityān* (sing. *fatà*, young man, 'Junker'), from the ninth century called *futuwwa* ('youth') seem to have had a not very large membership in each separate place, but they maintained connections over wide distances between the towns.

A similar grouping which existed in numerous towns was the *'ayyārūn*, (approximately 'vagrants') recruited from the lowest reaches of society. In restless times they exacted more or less voluntary contributions from the rich. Occasionally, as during the siege of Baghdad under Amīn, they were armed by the government; but generally they were boycotted, as comes to light in the spiteful unreliability of the historical reports. More than once the authorities neutralised the *'ayyārūn* by creating vacancies for them in the *shurṭa* (police). In a manner not as yet made clear in detail, the *fityān* and the *'ayyārūn* amalgamated in the ninth century, and put themselves under the command of socially higher strata in common opposition to the government with its reliance on a foreign soldiery. Their main object was to secure influence over the urban administration, and in this they were frequently successful, especially in the eleventh and twelth centuries in the Syrian towns, where their variant of town militia was termed *aḥdāth*, and its head (*ra'īs*) in fact shared power with the governor from time to time. Although the *futuwwa* clubs had no prescribed religious allegiance they began after the late tenth century to join with the increasingly influential *ṣūfī*, the 'wool wearers', as these 'mystics' were called. The *futuwwa* provided a model of organization, mysticism (*taṣawwuf*) gave a spiritual bond, opposition to the abuses imposed by the rulers and discontent with the strict conventionality of official Islam and with the social relations which it seemed to condone, supplied a programme which could be fought for both intellectually and on the streets.

Social questions, animated by the religious ideology inseparable from them, had since the late ninth century weighed upon the rulers in the most painful manner. As long as economic prosperity endured in the capital the increasing differentiation of rich and poor was not pressingly dangerous; *'ayyārūn* on one side, withdrawal from the world and begging on the other, were adequate safety valves, though doubtless a growing disillusion with the state and with official Islam added their contribution to the weakening of the caliphate. The great social revolts of the ninth century were focused outside the centre of government: in Egypt, in the marshy regions of Southern Mesopotamia and the South-Eastern Persian province of Sijistān, treated as a Cinderella by nature and government alike.

In Southern Mesopotamia near Baṣra attempts were made to desalinate and denitrify the land for the cultivation of sugar cane, and saltpetre was obtained as a by-product from this work, undertaken by large armies of African slaves. The weakening of the government was sensed here too, and an overseer who, perhaps justifiably, claimed to be an 'Alid, roused the Zanj, the Africans, on the lower course of the Tigris, to rebel. With extreme discipline the black troops, though quite inexperienced, managed to organize and maintain a state. They did not get lost in utopian experiments, they even retained slavery and resisted the attempt to transfer their headquarters to towns like Wāsiṭ and Baṣra which they stormed several times. The government was very weak and above all the army was unreliable. Even the shock of a massacre in Baṣra (871) and a punitive expedition near Baghdad (879) were ineffective in moving the caliph's army to counter attack. Thanks to the charisma of its 'Alid leader and to its Khārijite ideology the Zanj regime was able to withstand both intense pressure from without and the disintegrative ethic of the Khārijite teaching on sin.

After fourteen years of bitter struggle the troops of the imperial regent al-Muwaffaq, brother of the caliph al-Mu'tamid, overthrew the slave state (883). Yet nothing seems to have altered much in the economic structure of the region. The surviving Zanj were integrated into the caliph's army, and thus were spared having to return to the hated drainage work. One wonders whether Muwaffaq would have succeeded in mastering the Zanj if at the decisive moment the leader of the Sijistānī *'ayyārūn* had not refused the alliance proposed to him by the Zanj.

Ya'qūb ibn Laith, the coppersmith (*aṣ-Ṣaffār*), represented the humbler urban population in the fight against the Khārijites who were still influential in the rural areas of his homeland; as his successes grew the Bedouin and the landless proletariat (*ṣa'ālīk*) flocked to him. His power stretched westwards to Fārs, north to Khorāsān, where he put an end to the rule of the Ṭāhirids in 873. Three years later he was defeated by the imperial army not far from Baghdad. Even so the government was ready to recognize Ya'qūb as the *de facto* ruler of Sijistān, under the supremacy of the caliph; he died before the conclusion of the negotiations (879). His brother 'Amr did not submit to the caliph but to a provincial dynasty, and the Ṣaffārids' maintained themselves, with changing fortunes, in Sijistān into the tenth century.

In contrast to the Ṣaffārids (867–903) the Ṭāhirids (821–873) were supported by the Islamic aristocracy and the bourgeoisie. They no longer resided in the old capital of Merv but in Nīshāpūr, more to the south and hence nearer to Iraq. By origin they were Khorāsānī *mawālī*. It is usual to begin the list of independent dynasties with the Ṭāhirids. It is true that the position of the Ṭāhirids was extremely self-reliant and they were even hereditary, but their strength was in fact drawn from the caliphal system of power which they upheld in Iraq and from which they received all kinds of support in Khorāsān. Resistance to Baghdad was quite out of keeping with their beliefs and their political convictions. The religiously based paternalism of the first Ṭāhirid is forcefully expressed in his famous letter to his son, the governor of Jazīra. It is a model of conscientiousness and sense of duty and so appealed to the caliph Ma'mūn that he had copies of it sent to all provincial officials.

It is characteristic of the mental climate in Eastern Iran and

Transoxiana that Ṭāhirids and Ṣaffārids, like the Sāmānids of Bukhārā (875–999), all traced their descent back to the Sasanids, regarding themselves as national Iranian rulers, though of the Muslim faith. One is reminded of the legend of the marriage of Ḥusain with a daughter of the last Sasanid, which was intended to give Iranian sanction to Shīʿite legitimacy; the legend is indeed also preserved in another version which reflects Persian pride even more strongly; in this the princess refused to marry the son (this time Ḥasan) of the Caliph ʿAlī, since she could only take a reigning prince as husband.

The 'moderate' Shīʿa, the party whose essential difference with the Sunna was over the teaching of the matchlessness of the Prophet's house and its right to the throne, doubtless originated in an Arab milieu but had gradually gained in influence in Iran and Iraq. In the hostility between ʿAlids and ʿAbbāsids the Persian opposition to the caliphate had largely taken sides with the ʿAlid camp. Persian national feeling was not however tied down confessionally. It had rather developed a sort of supra-confessional point of crystallization in the advocacy of modern Persian as a literary language. In poetry Rūdagī (d. 940/941) had already achieved distinction; in the sixties of the tenth century came the turn of prose, in translations (including the Koran) and revisions of Arab works. The attempt by the Sāmānids to raise Persian to the status of a language of government was not pursued by the Ghaznavids. Zarathustrianism, which as the real national religion had the most to gain, had only a short renaissance. Although its teaching was codified in writing in the tenth century (with two ends in view: one to consolidate the tradition, and the other to prove their 'possession of the Book' to the Muslims) and its apologia was skilfully adapted, the decline of the community could not be prevented. Whereas the Zarathustrians were still a force to be reckoned with at the beginning of the tenth century—in Fārs for instance, which was the cultural focus of Central and Southern Persia—a hundred years later they no longer played any significant role. The main motive for clinging to Zarathustrianism was lost when it became apparent that 'Iranianism' could be pursued unharmed within Islam and given a more universal validity, and even more important that islamization did not signify any foreign yoke. With a nostalgic and proud backward glance to the faith of their fathers, romantic as it was, the transition to Islam was smooth enough.

The Sāmānids were positively demonstrative in their loyalty to the caliphate, and were satisfied with the title of a ***maulà amīr al-muʾminīn***. With a few shortlived deviations they kept to the Sunnite path and assumed the Sasanid-caliphal mission of protecting the civilized Iranian territory (with the help of Turkish troops) against the Turks of Central Asia. From their seat at Bukhārā they ruled Khorāsān (together with modern Afghanistan) and Sijistān, and encouraged the efforts of their leading officials to strengthen the fragile unity of the political body by an increase of cultural consciousness. Under them the Persian historical tradition assumed the form it was to keep in later times. It was known to the Arabs from translations or adaptations of the *Khwatāy-nāmak* by Ibn al-Muqaffa' (executed in 757 or 758) and Tha'ālibī (*c.* 1020); it received the standard metric epic form by which it is known to the Persians from Daqīqī (d. between 976 and 980) who began it, and the great Firdausī (from Ṭūs in Khorāsān, 934–1020) who completed it: the 'Book of the Kings', *Shāh-nāma* (the Pahlavī word *khwatāy*, 'king', 'lord', in its modern Persian form *khudā* refers only to God). It is written in sixty thousand rhymed couplets of eleven syllables (for the rhyming half-verse) and like the Homeric epics is both the first and the greatest of Persian epics and of Persian national literature in general, the focus and material source of Persia's historical self-consciousness. The poet and his circle had to face the paradox, still alive today, that the destruction of the glorious Sasanid national state by Arab barbarians provided the conditions for rebirth and a universally significant cultural achievement. According to tradition the poet completed his masterpiece in 1010 under the orthodox first member of the Ghaznavid dynasty, a prince of Turkish blood. He was poorly rewarded; this though, should be attributed rather to its nationalistic, basically un-Islamic, undertones than to the reputedly Shī'ite inclinations of Firdausī.

The rise of the modern Persian literary language by no means caused a decline in Arabic. As the language of the Holy Book, of Arab-Muslim science, of government and international communication within the *dār al-islām*, it remained indispensable, quite apart from the fact that Persian was behind in the formulation of philosophic and scientific concepts and freely used Arab words and phrases, and Arabic surpassed it for a long time in flexibility of expression.

The 'moderate' Shī'a was at no time really organized; like the Sunnite *jamā'a* it represented a Community viable on account of its intensive sense of solidarity, and indeed it only gradually distinguished itself from the *jamā'a*. The respect of the Sunnites for the house of the Prophet and the co-operation of individual Shī'ites in upholding the *jamā'a* remained the rule despite all their animosity and exclusivity, and to a large extent disguised their differences in tenth century Baghdad. When in 873/874 the twelfth of the Shī'ite

Imāms, Muḥammad ibn al-Ḥasan al-'Askarī al-Mahdī, disappeared from the cellar of his house in Samarra at the age of hardly ten (according to legend even younger) the line of 'visible' intercessors came to an end. Until 939 four deputies (*wakīl*) took on the leadership of the movement, in so far as it is valid to use these terms. In this year in the Shī'ite view begins the 'great absence' (or concealment, *ghaiba*). The Imām, who is in fact the ruler of the world, works from his concealment; until his return (*raj'a*) it is, even more than in Sunnite Islam, the Learned in the Faith (*mujtahidūn*), who represent him before the faithful.

They see to the harmonization of life and teaching and guarantee, without themselves being organized, the order of the Community, working to some extent from the traditional centres of theology and jurisprudence of the Shī'a (such as Ḥilla in Iraq or Qumm in Iran). This accounts both for the greater flexibility of the 'Twelver-Shī'a' (*Ithnā'ashariyya*) and for their organizational weakness as compared with the Sunna in non-Shī'ite areas. It had become invulnerable to political vicissitudes and the chances of political moods, though it was unable to protect itself against persecution by those who thought differently; this absolutism of religious existence, which the Sunna never tackled with any speed or boldness, was not called in question again until the nationalization of the 'Twelver' Shī'a in the Ṣafavid period. Symptomatic of the attraction of strictly speaking unislamic, at any rate unkoranic themes is the accelerated expansion of the 'Twelver' Shī'a even during the 'little *ghaība*'; we have only to remember the rise of the Būyids in Iran and of the Ḥamdānids in Arab Syria and Mesopotamia. The convergence of Mahdī and Hidden Imām and the mystery of the Community which had been led out of its alienation clearly corresponded to a widespread feeling and fitted in with the relatively extensive rationalizing, indeed hellenizing overlay of the concepts of Islamic teaching.

Related in its themes though entirely different in intention and forms of thought is the movement, much divided in itself and yet a unity, which offered itself to the Muslim world as an alternative religious entity between the ninth and the eleventh centuries. Born of the *umma*, and superficially at least closely deriving from Scripture, the *Ismā'īliyya*, as the totality of this teaching can most simply be termed, is a complete religio-philosophic, political and social system which sought to perfect, burst open and replace Islamic orthodoxy from within. The main ideas are the same as those of the Shī'a, for the Ismā'īliyya is a branch or logical development of the ideology which led to the 'Twelvers'. Ismā'īl, the eldest (?) son of the sixth imām Ja 'far aṣ-Ṣādiq (d. 765),a figure also respected by the Sunna, died before his father, who had named him as his successor. The majority of his followers transferred their loyalty to another son of Ja'far; but a minority held to Ismā'īl and declared that he had not died and would one day return as Mahdī; others again recognized Ismā'īl's son Muḥammad as the last imām, the 'Lord of the Time' (*qā'im az-zamān*).

All these 'Sevener' groups were termed Ismā'īlī by their contemporaries. Exactly why the radicals, the 'exaggerators' (*ghulāt*) attached themselves to this chain of imāms is not clear. They shared with Islam as a whole the belief in the unity of God (*tauḥīd*), the divine mission of Muhammad, the Koran as the revelation of God and to a great extent the conviction of the binding force of the prescribed cult; in common with the Shī'a they believed in the need for the world to be divinely guided through an imām, in the hypostasy of the act or word of creation, the Logos, in the doctrine of the inner (*bāṭin*) meaning of the Koran, approachable through allegory, and in the function of the imām 'to fill the world with righteousness, as now it is filled with unrighteousness'.

The Sevener groups saw history as a cyclic phenomenon: they held a theory of emanation deriving from Plotinus, combined with the idea of the correspondence of macrocosm and microcosm—seven phases of emanation: seven 'speakers' in the history of redemption, among them Adam, Muhammad and Muḥammad ibn Ismā'īl, accompanied by seven 'silent ones', including Seth, 'Alī and the various founders of the 'Sevener' sects. It is clear that there was a tendency to deify the imām but it was expressly postulated only now and again. Gnostic modes of thought occur, with astrology and alphabetical mysticism in their train.

The ultimate aim of the moderate Shī'a was revolution but it had increasingly accommodated itself to the world in the meantime; on the other hand the Seveners of all persuasions were uncompromisingly bent on a new universal ordering of Islamic society. Secret societies arose throughout the *dār al-islām* from North Africa to India, from South Arabia to Khorāsān. They were strictly hierarchic, a member's rank corresponding to his grade of initiation. The manner of initiation into the seven- or nine-stage organization may well have been luridly elaborated in the reports of the non-Ismā'īlī sources which are all we possess, but the centrally conducted propaganda, often in the name of the unknown or unnamed Imām, is a fact. So is the tolerant, relativist attitude to other religions as all equally valid 'precursors', a tolerance deriving from the conviction that the truth of the secret teaching is universal. The Ismā'īliyya never tried to become a mass movement nor to convert all the lower orders to its doctrine. The system allowed the inclusion of hellenistic philosophy and science, thus appealed to the taste of the time, without compromising the basic hypotheses and thus one might say with a good conscience: the only Encyclopaedia of Knowledge which has survived from the period is from an Ismā'īlī conventicle, the 'Pure Brethren' of Baṣra (probably started in the 970s, for it was certainly known outside in 983/984).

With their strong stand against social abuses, the Ismā'īlī, shrouded in mystery though they were, were entirely up to date in their appeal, and manifold variants arose, borne along by a feeling of youthful strength and with no inhibitions about traditional Islam, which they proposed to supplant. They became the most serious, not to say the only, real threat to orthodox Islam both Sunnite and Shī'ite: as totalitarian and theocratic as they, but still unweakened by the vicissitudes of history and alluring in the authoritative force of their teaching.

However possible it may be to trace the origin of this or that single theme to another source, it cannot be sufficiently stressed that the movement was entirely independent in its spirit and manner of expression, and was felt to be so by its contemporaries. Where else would they have heard such language as that addressed to a leader of the Qarmaṭians, the 'emissary of the Messiah, who is Jesus, who is the Word, who is the Mahdī, who is Aḥmad ibn Muḥammad ibn al-Ḥanafiyya, who is Gabriel': 'Thou art the emissary, thou art the proof, thou art the she-camel (of the Prophet Ṣāliḥ, which, according to Koran 7 : 74–80, was hamstrung by the unbelievers), thou art the beast (Koran 27 : 83, which God will bring forth out of the earth at the end of time), thou art the Holy Ghost, thou art Johannes, son of Zacharias.'? It is difficult now to recapture the stirring enthusiasm aroused by this symbolism, this typological listing of the epochs, this play with time and the end of time, but it is all too clearly visible in its effect in the history of those centuries.

The first political manifestation of the movement is connected with the name of Ḥamdān Qarmaṭ (probably Aramaic: 'esoteric teacher') who set up a *dār al-hijra*, an 'abode of emigration' near Kūfa in 890. This being reminiscent of Medina, called the *dār al-hijra* of the Prophet, is as much as to say 'Residence of the Mahdī, founding place of his religion'. The Nabataean peasants, of whom he himself was one, joined him, and Arabs as well. Common ownership of cattle, furniture and jewels was introduced, revenues and earnings were handed over to the Community, the needy provided for out of communal funds; they were also said to hold women in common, but the reliability of the sources is not sufficient to put this beyond question. The government forced Qarmaṭ to move to Syria, where he soon died, but the movement there flourished aggressively until the caliphate suppressed it in 903 after bloodthirsty fighting. It did the same in South Mesopotamia in 906. The Qarmaṭian centre of Salamiyya in North Syria managed to survive. Meanwhile however the Qarmaṭians had begun in 894 to attach themselves in al-Aḥsā' (Baḥrain) to the 'propagandist' Abū Sa'īd al-Jannābī. Only five years later he succeeded in bringing the whole country under his control and founding a state. Similar attempts in Khorāsān and in the Yemen led rather to communities than to states; another Qarmaṭian state arose on Indian soil in Multān. Neither Hamdān nor Abū Sa'īd or even Dhikrawaih, the leader of the Syrian uprising of 900 and like Abu Sa'īd of Iranian origin, acted on their own authority; they were appointed by 'Fāṭimids', by the *ṣāḥib al-khāl* (He with the birth mark). The common enemy was the 'Abbāsids and with them the representatives of the orthodox order. A generation later an opponent summarized their programme: 'They said: 'Truth has appeared, the Mahdī has arisen, the rule of the 'Abbāsids, the jurists, the readers of the Koran and the teachers of tradition is at an end. There is nothing more to wait for; we have not come to set up a government, but to abolish a law.' (From the translation by W. Madelung.)

The Baḥrain Qarmaṭians had exceptional striking-power. The caliph's army was inadequate to ensure the security of South Mesopotamia or the route to Syria, even of the Pilgrimage. Like so many heretics the Qarmaṭians looked on the unconverted Muslims as unbelievers, whose property and life were outside the law. The massacres of the Mecca pilgrims which they perpetrated more than once and the abduction of the Black Stone from the Ka'ba (930) were intended to demonstrate that God no longer upheld the orthodox, that the days of conventional Islam, from which the Lord had withdrawn its charisma, were numbered and the era of the Mahdī was close at hand. To all appearances the Baḥrain Qarmaṭians gradually freed themselves of dependence on the Fāṭimids. The story that the return of the Black Stone (951), and for a high ransom, was in obedience to Fāṭimid instructions probably originates in Fāṭimid propaganda; but the Sunnite world was convinced that the 'double plot' directed against it had a single leadership. They were none the less perfectly aware that the Qarmaṭians, particularly in their social structure, represented a relatively conventional and respectable version of the 'Sevener' heresy.

Shortly before 930 the Mahdist excitement reached its climax. There are stories of Kūfans who hurriedly migrated to Baḥrain in order to set foot in the country of the Mahdī before his appearance.

In 931 the Qarmaṭian prince Abū Ṭāhir handed over his government to a young Persian who had shown himself by secret signs to be the Mahdī. Abū Ṭāhir also announced that the true religion, the religion of Adam, had now appeared; all faith until now had been false; the teachings of Moses, Jesus and Muhammad had been lies, and they nothing but deceivers. It is of course more than unlikely that Abū Ṭāhir expressed himself thus. We can be sure that the extremely tenacious and polemically effective formula of the 'Three Deceivers' was invented by opponents of the Mahdī. The unislamic character of this whole episode cannot be denied; it was soon brought to an end by the cruelty of the Mahdī's regime.

The shock of disappointment brought Qarmaṭians and 'Abbāsids together in the following years, without any concessions being expressly made on religious matters.

Qarmaṭian Baḥrain kept its independence and its organization until far into the eleventh century. Two sympathetic observers have left reports in which they describe the state: it was ruled by an oligarchy, consisting of the council of the *'iqdāniyya* with the ruler presiding; about 20,000 arms bearers held about 30,000 negro slaves. There were no taxes; the state clearly accepted responsibility for the economic existence of its members. The Qarmaṭians had no mosque, did not pray and kept no fasts, but they allowed the 'orthodox' who lived in their midst to follow their own customs. Internal trade was conducted with an internal currency. How the state procured the necessary foreign currency we do not know. Isolation and political insignificance brought stability: the Qarmaṭian order seems to have continued in al-Aḥsā' until the eighteenth century.

Egypt under the Fāṭimids and Ṭūlūnids

MORE important for the general history of Islam were the Fāṭimids, whose fate demonstrates in the most dramatic manner how independent were the Seveners from any territorial or national affiliations. Descendants of the Prophet through Fāṭima and Ḥusain, according to their disputed claim, they moved their organizational centre to Salamiyya in Syria in about 860, whence, as has already been recounted, they set up a strong-point in the Yemen. The 'propagandist', *dā'ī*, Abū 'Abdallāh from Ṣan'ā' in the Yemen established himself in 894 among the Kutāma Berbers (in Lesser Kabylia, west of Constantine) encroaching on a region which the Sunna and the Khārijites had heretofore shared between them. Discontent with the Aghlabids resident in Qairawān and the chronic tensions between the urban rulers and the Berbers of the mountain and steppe zones allowed Abū 'Abdallāh to consolidate his position as the champion of the Mahdī 'Ubaidallāh, and finally in 909 to inflict a decisive defeat on the last Aghlabid. This destroyed the last remnants of 'Abbāsid influence in North Africa. The collapse of the Syrian revolt had meanwhile forced 'Ubaidallāh to flee by dangerous detours through Egypt to South-West Morocco, where he was held prisoner for a time in Sijilmāsa, on the instructions of the Aghlabids. Abū 'Abdallāh had him set free and the Mahdī entered Ifrīqiya (Tunisia) as conqueror. After a short time he had his champion murdered, probably turning against him because of his oppressive financial measures, and took over the reins of government himself.

However, the Fāṭimids were not minded to remain petty North-African kings. The caprices of politics had landed them in this region, utterly provincial from the point of view of Islam as a whole. What they aimed at was the expulsion of the 'Abbāsids and the rule of a Fāṭimid caliph, as the true and only *amīr al-mu'minīn*; 'Ubaidallāh had assumed this title along with that of Mahdī on January 15, 910; hence right from the beginning their policies were entirely directed eastwards. They occupied Alexandria a first time in 914. But the Berbers did not intend to be degraded into acting as the instruments of imperialism; Khārijism offered the necessary ideological pretext for a revolution which between 944 and 947 shook the Fāṭimid government to its roots and was only defeated at the walls of their new maritime capital of Mahdiyya (Tunisia).

After the defeat of this last Khārijite-supported Berber uprising it yet took more than twenty years before they could contemplate the conquest of Egypt. After careful diplomatic preparation the Sicilian born freedman Jauhar entered Fusṭāṭ (now Old Cairo) in 969. He founded a settlement in the immediate neighbourhood which he named the 'Victorious ('Martian' city) of Mu'izz' (Cairo) after his Caliph: al-Mu'izziyya al-Qāhira. It was not long before it became one of the largest cultural centres of Islam. At the mosque of al-Azhar, erected by Jauhar before the entry of the Fāṭimid caliph (973), a Fāṭimid theological school was founded to provide an immediate solid nucleus for Shī'ite learning. The Berber Zīrids were given Ifrīqiya whose prosperity they maintained as independent representatives of the Fāṭimids. Although the Fāṭimids took little enough interest in their first territorial possession they had governed the Aghlabid inheritance well, though this involved increasing the already considerable burden of taxation, and in particular they had maintained the strength of the fleet; Sardinia, Corsica, the Balearic islands were and remained under Fāṭimid influence, quite apart from Sicily which had been coming increasingly into the Muslin sphere since 827. As it did later in Egypt, the strength of the dynasty in Ifrīqiya depended in large part on the strength of the economy nourished by active trade relations with the Christian Mediterranean world, especially with Italy.

The translation of a state or rather of a ruling class and its mercenaries from one country to another is a spectacle which can only be understood if we keep clearly in view the exclusively ideological adherence of the 'elite', its inner detachment from earthly ties, which it only valued as a lever and support, and if we remember that minority rule had for long been an accepted form of political existence. Spain had been ruled by 200,000 Visigoths, the Vandals in Africa are assessed at about 80,000; some 12,000 Muslims conquered Spain; the Ayyūbids in 1200 held Egypt with 8,000 men or thereabouts. The minority situation of the Muslims in the Near and Middle East in the first centuries of the *hijra* does not need to be stressed again. The Fāṭimids indeed never attempted to make Egypt Shī'ite; the esoteric teaching agreed only too well with their political requirements; but they gave the non-Muslims more freedom than they had ever possessed since the Arab conquest. In this way they secured the active sympathy of the circles important to the economy and the administration.

When the Fāṭimids came into Egypt she had been enjoying a

certain independence for a century past, after a period of colonial exploitation. As so often in Egyptian history she had a foreigner to thank for this prosperity. Aḥmad ibn Ṭūlūn, the son of a Turkish military slave, had come there as the representative of a Turkish general to whom the governorship of the country had been granted in 868, but he, following the usual custom, had preferred not to quit the Caliphal city of Samarra, where lay the real source of his power. The confusions of the Turkish military uprisings, the smouldering quarrels between the Caliph Mu'tamid (870–892) and his brother, al-Muwaffaq (d. 891) who administered (and saved) the empire, the unreliability of the provincial governors, and last but not least the rebellion of the Zanj, made it possible for Ibn Ṭūlūn to set himself up as independent in all but name. He used the revenue from the taxes levied in Egypt, apart from a relatively small lump sum for the Caliph, to build up the country's economy, thus perpetuating a prosperity which had already distinguished the land in the previous decades. State monopoly of grain had in fact protected the country from famine since the Ptolemaic period; the Arabs had added the cultivation of rice and sugar. Even with a slight reduction in taxes Ibn Ṭūlūn managed to maintain a (slave) army composed mainly of Greeks, Sudanese, Berbers and Turks, and to build a new capital to the north-east of Fusṭāṭ, the land being shared in lots between officers and officials: it was called al-Qaṭā'i', 'lots' (or 'fiefs').

In spite of opposition from the central government Ibn Ṭūlūn not only succeeded in maintaining his position in Egypt but extended his power to Syria, the 'bastion' coveted by all strong rulers of Egypt. An attempt by the Caliph to escape from the tutelage of his brother by fleeing to Egypt (882) was unsuccessful; but this failure did not prevent the establishment of peaceful relations with Samarra. After Ibn Ṭūlūn's death (884) the Caliph's government confirmed the governorship of Egypt and Syria for the next thirty years in favour of his son Khumārawaih and the Ṭūlūnid family (886). In the following years the power of the Ṭūlūnids was felt in northern Mesopotamia; in 895 the Caliph al-Mu'taḍid married Khumārawaih's twelve year old daughter. The luxury of her dowry and equipment inspired the rumour that the Caliph hoped to ruin Khumārawaih by this marriage. The extravagance of the young ruler (who was murdered in 896) rapidly weakened Ṭūlūnid Egypt. In renewing the fief for his successor the Caliph was in a position to increase the tribute. The dynasty quickly declined, and only eight years later the Caliph was able to contemplate the reconquest of Egypt. In 905 Fusṭāṭ fell, and Qaṭā'i' was razed to the ground.

The only surviving monument of the Ṭūlūnid period is the mosque which Aḥmad ibn Ṭūlūn built between 876 and 879; a half-size imitation of the Chief Mosque in Samarra its design reflects the general dependence of the Ṭūlūnid court on the artistic and cultural example of the caliphal city. The combination of Hellenistic with the predominantly Persian elements of style characteristic of Samarra was thus introduced into Egypt. Samarra was also the organizational model: the same structure in the army which had brought the caliphate to the brink of impotence and had made Ibn Ṭūlūn's rise possible, was introduced into Egypt and was no doubt the main reason for the short duration of this epoch of Egypt's de facto (though not de jure) independence, the first that she had enjoyed for well over a thousand years.

After the thirty years of the 'Abbāsid restoration the cycle began again. In 937 the weakened caliphate granted to the Turkish governor Muḥammad ibn Ṭughj (935–946) the right to hold the Sogdian ruler's title of *Ikhshīd*, which his family had held in their homeland in Central Asia—a symbol of factual independence. Nine hundred years later the same significance was given to the North Iranian title of khedive that confirmed the independence of the Ottoman governor of Egypt, Muḥammad 'Alī, within the Ottoman Empire. The government of Egypt almost fell to the great financier Abū Bakr Muḥammad al-Mādharā'ī (872–957). He was the most important representative of a family of officials and bankers which had virtually controlled Egypt (and often Syria too) since the death of Aḥmad ibn Ṭūlūn. At that time both in Baghdad and in Fusṭāṭ the princes and their families were all actively engaged in commercial enterprise. This made a certain amount of corruption inevitable, but was not on the whole injurious to the development of the economy. The attack on Syria was repeated, even Damascus was occupied. The Abyssinian majordomo Kāfūr governed for Muḥammad's successor until he himself was given Egypt in fief shortly before his death. The power of the Ikhshīds was based solely on the impotence of the surrounding world; scarcely a year after the death of Kāfūr (968) the grandson of the founder lost his country to the Fāṭimids.

Almost unnoticed, and without any influence on affairs in the central lands, Islam had begun to spread into the Sudan and along the East African coast. This development however, at least until the end of the first millennium, was solely a matter of the immigration of Arabian colonists or merchants, and not because of any conversions among the Nubian Christians of the Sudan or of the pagan populations on the Indian Ocean. Since 652 Nubia had been in treaty with the Caliphate—to be interpreted as tributary relations—whereby the Arabs had to supply corn and oil in return for slaves. The first significant Muslim settlement on the East African coast seems to have been made by the followers of Zaid ibn 'Alī. When their claimant died after his defeat in 740 they sought refuge far from the reach of the caliph and founded a few small coastal stations. In the course of time they were joined by other refugees. Maqdishū (Mogadiscio), the first place of any importance, was not founded until the middle of the tenth century; next came the settlement of Kilwa further south, by Sunnites, at the turn of the millennium. These colonies without a home country maintained themselves primarily by the slave trade—in the homeland of the Zanj. There are grounds for thinking that Islam was now and again adopted by native rulers; Africa south of the Sahara contributed nothing either then or later to the development of Muslim teaching, nor had it any cultural influence on the original Islamic countries. Strictly speaking this applies equally to Islam in North Africa at that time, if one is prepared to except the eastward orientation of the Fāṭimids. North Africa was an Islamic colony, and conversion went ahead slowly. Although they held tenaciously to the teaching once they had accepted it, the Berbers did not identify themselves fully with Islam until Berbers themselves founded dynasties and came to power in the eleventh century. Several attempts were made to create a Berber faith by modifying the Islamic model.

The most remarkable was certainly that made by Ṣāliḥ about 744. His father had already distinguished himself in fighting against the Arabs, and he himself was one of the Khārijite leaders of the Bargawāṭa. The religion preached by him was built on a Berber Koran of eighty suras as against the 114 of the Muslims. He presented himself as *Ṣāliḥ al-mu'minīn*, the 'Upright among the Faithful' prophesied in the Muslim Koran (66 : 5), and felt himself to be the Mahdī who would return before the end of time. The Muslim feast days were changed, prayers and dietary rules modified; but on the whole the Muslim religious precepts were retained and the alterations were slight; presumably they were accommodated to local customs.

In the Rīf, the coastal strip of Northern Morocco, Ḥāmīm, like Ṣāliḥ, proclaimed a Berber Koran; he lost his life in 927 fighting against the Spanish Umayyads. He too altered the dietary rules and the times of prayer. One gains the impression that what Ḥāmīm preached was a pale reflection of the 'heresy' of the Bargawāṭa. The latter in spite of all persecution survived into the eleventh century, and in fragmentary communities for another century after that, while Ḥāmīm's message only flourished for a short spell. The significance of these border phenomena is certainly basically their 'national' character. Once the political and intellectual lead in Berber Islam was transferred to the natives it became possible for the particular character of the population to make its own imprint inside the orthodox community. This development is apparent in the Almohad movement of the twelfth century.

The Arab West

In the eyes of the West the significance of Muslim North Africa is primarily that it was a basis for the conquest of Spain, that highly civilized outpost of Muslim culture whose survival in the long run depended entirely on renewed injections of Berber 'barbarian' power. It can scarcely be said that Muslim Spain in the period of its political stability had any marked effect on the rest of Europe; what the Christian world owed to it was the classical inheritance in philosophy and science rethought by Islam and formulated in Arabic, and available in Latin from the twelfth century, when it filtered through in the centres which had again become Christian—particularly Toledo, where extensive translation work was done. The less tangible but unmistakable influences of form and mood in the songs of the troubadours also belong to this period of decline. It must be borne in mind that the political and military strength of the Spanish Umayyads was smaller than might be assumed from the courtly splendour and cultural brilliance of Córdoba. The Umayyads had the fortune to rule in a country whose geography provided extensive protection; their Frankish neighbours, particularly after the death of Charlemagne, showed signs of political dissolution, and their only potentially dangerous adversary was Ifrīqiya under the Aghlabids, and chiefly under the aggressive Fāṭimids.

The 'Abbāsids were relatively quickly reconciled to the loss of the remote province of Spain; after 763 there are no more rebellions fomented by the 'Abbāsids to report. The hereditary hostility to the 'Abbāsids still persisted but it no longer prevented the influx of eastern Islamic culture under 'Abd ar-Raḥmān II (822–852); it even had official sanction and soon gave a Syrian veneer to Islamic life in Spain; in fact until the end of the tenth century and later, Spain can be called a kind of colonial area from the cultural point of view. In the East, her considerable and individual artistic achievement was accepted: in architecture not at all, and in poetry, which was open to every popular and national influence and quite counter to the classical norm, only in the second half of the twelfth century; it was then at least theoretically recognized and systematized, though not creatively developed further.

More wary than the Visigoths had been before them, the Umayyads protected themselves against a repetition of invasion from the African coasts by building harbours and fleets, so that their rivalry with the Fāṭimids found its vent almost exclusively on North

African soil. The fluctuations of the balance of power are best followed in the development of the Umayyad sphere of influence in what is now Morocco, where it often crystallized in an entirely modern manner around financial support for impressive projects. Thus in 955 'Abd ar-Raḥmān III helped his devoted Berber Emir of Fez to rebuild the mosque of Qarawiyyīn. A sign of the times was the institution of diplomatic relations with Byzantium in 839/840; these were occasionally renewed during the tenth century, without in fact yielding any political results. On the other hand Byzantine artists or craftsmen exercised an extremely important influence on the development of Spanish Arabian architecture and architectural ornament.

The Christian states in the north were quite invincible in their geographical seclusion, and were even able to press southward as far as the Duero in the years between the battle of Covadonga which in 718 (or between 721 and 726) put an end to the Muslim expansion, and the late ninth century. But they were too weak to withstand serious counter-offensives or to shake the supremacy of the Muslims, who were culturally and economically far in the lead. The failure of Charlemagne's expedition in the Basque country—the annihilation at Roncevalles in 778 of a part of his army led by Count Roland was important not only in the history of literature—stabilized the north-east frontier for many years to come; early penetration into Catalonia had given the Christians a favourable frontier—they reconquered Barcelona in 803; in the south-east the equilibrium was maintained for many generations. The invasions of the Normans, whom strangely the Arabs called *majūs* (lit. fire-worshippers) were indeed dramatic, and the fall of Seville in 844 came as a great shock, but the Umayyad state was not in any real danger from them.

The political structure erected by the Umayyads was not however at all securely grounded. The conquerors were small in numbers and divided between Arabs and Berbers; not until the tenth century was the Arab minority able to overcome the tribal tensions which it had brought with it from its old homeland, though in Spain they no longer had any real foundation. The great majority of Syrians, who soon felt themselves at home in southern Spain, divided up in their new homeland according to the five military districts (*ajnād*) of their country of origin. The supporters of the Umayyad dynasty had found their way in large numbers to Spain in the fifties of the eighth century but after that there were no more statistically important reinforcements of Arabs. When 'Abd ar-Raḥmān I (755–788) gave the name of the famous Umayyad residence near Palmyra, Ruṣāfa, to the palace he built before the gates of Córdoba he was not only expressing his personal nostalgia for the Syrian homeland but suiting the mood of the leading circles of his entourage.

The inevitable intermixture with the natives consolidated the hold gained by Arabdom and particularly by the Arabic language among wide sections of the population; Arab, and particularly Syrian Arab origin became less and less demonstrable as a claim to nobility. The attraction of Arab culture as one superior to the Romance tradition—quite apart from its prestige as the way of life of the rulers—is manifest in the absence of any literary documents in Romance language. The desperate philippic of the priest Eulogius (written in 859) is eloquent testimony: he harshly reproves his Christian compatriots for their mania for Arabic and their neglect of Latin. Yet an outburst such as this should not disguise the fact that the Romance tongue held its own in everyday life, and even the Arab-Berber ruling class gradually came to use two colloquial languages.

Assimilation, furthered by widespread Islamization and the generally conciliatory policy towards non-Muslims—the Jewish communities in particular flourished as never before, until the Almohad persecutions of the twelfth century—did not of course necessarily signify political harmony. Rebellions were frequent. The Arabs could not agree, and the Berbers especially were a disturbing element. The burgeoning towns, particularly the capital of Córdoba, were refractory; the *fuqahā'* of the dominant (since *c.* 800) Mālikite law school, who accused the government of godlessness on the least provocation, provided moral support for the malcontents. The cruel suppression of the 'Suburb Affair', an obstinate revolt against al-Ḥakam I (818), occasioned the first wave of Andalusian immigration, or re-emigration into North Africa, which was to become of great cultural importance. Other 'Suburbanites' occupied Alexandria and after their expulsion from Egypt took possession of Crete, where a Spanish Islamic dynasty held power until the island was reconquered by the Byzantines in 961.

After this uprising there grew up new centres of unrest in the rural districts. From 879 to 928 the reconverted Christian 'Mozarab' (from *musta'rib,* 'Arabized' [Spaniard)) 'Umar ibn Ḥafṣūn—notice the Arab name with its Romance ending ūn/ōn—and his sons held the mountain valleys to the west of Málaga from their castle of Bobastro. In 929, after he had once more taken over the subversive regions, 'Abd ar-Raḥmān III, perhaps the most impressive of the 'orthodox' rulers of his time, took the unprecedented step of exchanging his title of *amīr* 'commander' for that of caliph and *amīr al-mu'minīn*; the Friday prayers were now offered in his name, no longer in that of the 'Abbāsid caliph. It is surprising how peacefully this revolutionary deed was received in Spain with its strict Mālikite tradition. To later generations the fragmentation of an authority which by its nature is indivisible remained a perpetual stumbling-block, but his contemporaries, or at any rate his Andalusian subjects, understood that 'Abd ar-Raḥmān was not desirous of destroying the older caliphate nor of dividing the *umma* by assuming the title of caliph, but was only giving the logical confirmation to the situation by presenting himself as the true shield of orthodoxy in the Islamic west. 'Abd ar-Raḥmān III drew his moral justification from his latent war on two fronts, against both Fāṭimid heretics and the Christians, who in the last resort remained invincible in spite of every Arab success, and he saw the material ratification of the independence which he had achieved for the Umayyad dynasty in the fame enjoyed by Spanish Arab culture in Europe, in the dazzling attraction of Córdoba with its magnificent mosque and the city of residence erected by 'Abd ar-Raḥmān, Versailles-like, at its gates. This assumption of the caliphate is paralleled in Christian northern Europe by Charlemagne's ascension of the imperial throne, though the consequences are not of course entirely comparable.

Charlemagne's supremacy was only too quickly followed by partition and decline; the Umayyad caliphal state also was of short duration. The highly cultivated al-Ḥakam II (961–976) was able to maintain his father's legacy, but after his death, a 'majordomo' dynasty took control of the state. The fabled 'chamberlain' (*ḥājib*) Ibn abī 'Āmir al-Manṣūr (978–1002) was constrained to purchase the support of religious circles with the destruction of a part of the splendid library of al-Ḥakam, whereby he symbolically surrendered any pretensions to a worldly culture. He could march across Christian territory as he pleased and he even occupied Santiago de Compostela, but basically he had to leave power relations as they were. After his death the caliphate rapidly fell a prey to internal discord in which the increasingly bitter struggles between 'Andalusians' (Arabs and natives), Berbers and 'Slavs', i.e. Europeans imported as slaves from various regions, created a situation fraught with frustration for every side.

Even in the brilliance of the tenth century the maintenance of an army would have been the only means of overcoming the particularism of the different parts of the kingdom, and this was perhaps the principal difficulty of the Córdovan government. The wealth of the country was certainly considerable—the export of textiles, leather work, pottery, jewellery and weapons, particularly to Egypt, had assumed, for the period, extremely large dimensions—and allowed for the recruitment or 'purchase' of Berber, Christian Spanish and 'Slav' troops. But the foreign influence in the army had a decidedly destructive effect, similar to that in the east; though the Umayyads managed to enlist the collaboration of the Christians and Jews in many ways, they would only accept economic and not military employment.

Scarcely seventy years after the death of 'Abd ar-Raḥmān III his house lost its last vestige of power; after the fall of the Umayyads no Spanish Muslim again assumed the title of caliph. Much as the double caliphate was repugnant to the sense of solidarity and the traditionalism of the faithful it is clear that this challenging state of affairs furthered the emancipation of the *umma* from political institutions, and positively worked in favour of that independence which was the only means of achieving a supranational religious Community with a lasting development along its own inner laws and with an absolute and timeless validity. The Community always aspired to this emancipation from the contingencies of political change, but at the same time it firmly opposed the constitutional theories deriving logically from this tendency.

In the panorama of Islamic culture in the ninth and tenth centuries the contribution of Spain is in many ways original, for instance in the invention of new forms of the arch and in the cultivation of strophic poetry, often with elaborate metres and sometimes vernacular refrains. Yet seen as a whole she remained isolated and almost colonial, as can be seen in the great authority enjoyed there by the Muslim scholars from the East. In the analysis of feeling and in nature lyrics too a new note can be heard which perhaps, being related to European sentiment, awoke an echo in the songs of the troubadours. In the eleventh century Spanish Islamic culture came of age and became really independent, finding itself in the great prose writers and politicians Ibn Shuhaid (992–1034) and Ibn Ḥazm (994–1064); Ibn Ḥazm was also a distinguished jurist and historian of comparative religion; his chief work was on the Islamic heresies. It seemed as though the political disintegration had liberated men's creative powers and that the multiplicity of small centres had given wider scope for the multiplicity of talents.

The weakness of the European states who were responsible for the defence of the Mediterranean coasts and the northward turn of political life in general, combined with the incapacity of Byzantium to compete with the Arabs for superiority at sea, enabled the Muslims to settle almost at will on the islands of the western Mediterranean for nearly three hundred years, and to plunder the coasts of Provence and Southern Italy, even the Adriatic coast as far as Ancona and beyond, and at times to control them from their strongholds. But the presence of the Muslims added little to the cultural development of these regions. Sicily was different. Its conquest was started seriously in 827 (after a number of raids, the earliest in 652) and the island was not really wrested from the Byzantines until 878 with the fall of Syracuse (or even not until 902 with the surrender of Taormina); but thereafter it is possible to speak of a specifically Islamic cultural transplantation, though paradoxically it achieved its climax when the Muslim hegemony of the island was broken in the eleventh century by the Normans, and three cultures became integrated. The Umayyads had also set up naval bases on Sardinia and Corsica; in 870 Malta fell, and to this day remains (but only in language) an offshoot of the Arab-speaking world. The Narbonensis, which was occupied in 717 and again, after a reverse, in 719, had to be surrendered in 759; but the Arabs played a controlling part in the local struggles of Italy and Provence. In 837 when they answered the call of the Neopolitans and came against Benevento they gained a firm footing on the mainland. In 846 their progress was halted outside the walls of Rome, but not before they had plundered Ostia and even the church of San Paolo fuori le Mura. The naval defeat of 849 left their strongholds intact; their most important one, Bari, remained the centre for their attacks and raids in the Adriatic and inland, until it was surrendered to Byzantium in 871.

The political selfishness and jealousy of the south Italian dynasties on the one hand, and the parlous economic situation of the coastal towns on the other ensured a continuous series of Christian allies for the Muslims. For example in 876/877 Naples, Salerno and Amalfi joined the Saracen raid, organized in Naples, on the Roman coast. In 915 Pope John X succeeded at last in driving the Arabs from their stronghold on the Garigliano, whence they had threatened the security of Rome's outskirts for almost thirty years. In 888 the Muslims had secured the fortress of Fraxinetum (La Garde-Freinet) in Provence, and from there in 972 they even took prisoner the Abbot of Cluny on the Great St Bernard. Not until 983 was the Count of Provence with his north Italian allies able to suppress the Arabs. In 1015/1016 Sardinia was reconquered, and in 1034 the Italian sea cities, particularly Pisa and Genoa, were strong enough to carry the war into North Africa and with the booty they took in Bona (Bône), to indemnify Cluny for the ransom the monastery had had to pay for its abbot.

More important than territorial gains however was the renewed security of the west from attacks from without—in its effect comparable with the cessation of the Viking and Hungarian raids—and above all the restoration of freedom of movement in the western waters of the Mediterranean. The Italian sea powers gained in influence and the Islamic powers, withdrawing into their own world, ceased to maintain trading posts in Christian South and West Europe. Western trade in Muslim lands made contact with world trade. Enclave-like trade settlements such as the Italian sea powers held as concessions in the Levant—they had long been the custom in Byzantium as *mitata* for foreign merchants—do not seem to have been contemplated even by the Fāṭimids, the strongest naval power among the Islamic countries. Hence maritime initiative in the Mediterranean soon fell completely into the hands of the Christian merchants and governments, even if they did not secure all the wealth of eastern trade. At the same time piracy developed as an economic necessity among the North African coastal states, Ifrīqiya in particular, and was tolerated or encouraged by the native rulers according to circumstance. This 'form of life' was strong enough to withstand the pressure of the countries who were its victims until well into the nineteenth century.

Thus at the middle of the tenth century there were three caliphates, two 'right thinking' and one heterodox, apart from the various small potentates who decked themselves out with the noble title of 'princes of the faithful', like the Midrārid prince of Sijilmāsa who was murdered by the Fāṭimids in 958. The Muslim unified state had outlived itself, but it still remained an ideal. The sacred rank of caliph only coincided in the Fāṭimids with the apex of a functioning hierarchy; in the general Sunnite view it belonged to the 'Abbāsid ruler in Baghdad alone and could neither be transferred nor multiplied. Hence the promotion of a non-'Abbāsid ruler to the title of caliph could signify nothing more than a regional claim to autocephaly, a demonstration to the infidel of the role he had assumed as leader and protector. The sense of unity of the *umma* was, as far as can be judged, endangered by sectarianism, but not by cultural differences. Then as later the Muslim lived as it were in a single Islamic culture, which manifested itself in at least two forms (an Arab and an Iranian). The average believer had however always been more conscious of the binding than of the separating elements, and paradoxically the veil of distance promoted the sense of Muslim unity.

Seen objectively, the feeling of unity rested on two foundations: the theological juridical teaching in its Arabic formulation, and the Arab or Persian religiously neutral formation of the 'scribes' and literati which could be understood equally as a style of life and as the sum of literary-historical knowledge. The philological sciences formed the link; philosophy and the natural sciences belonged rather in the a-religious sphere but were (philosophy especially) tackled predominantly from a religious point of view; in any case they enlarged the common field of questions and subjects which engaged advanced Islamic culture in every linguistic area.

It runs against the nationalistic theories of modern Arabdom, though not against the general experience of humanity, that the climax of the Arab-Islamic culture occurred in a period of political decline, in which small states were a matter of course and the various political centres ceaselessly threatened and fought each other. But this was a situation in which cultural interests were not only fostered by the usually short-lived dynasties, but were converted into lasting achievements by discerning patronage. The Italian Renaissance provides a parallel, and again the view of Justus Möser (1720–1794), passed on by Goethe, that 'it was precisely the mass of small states that proved to be so desirable for the extension of culture in each one'. Möser in fact presupposed the peaceful relation imposed on princes and classes by the German Empire. The Islamic national states of the high and late Middle Ages could not count on that at all, however. There was no readiness to recognize the variety of the Muslim states in their structure of government and administration. Political instability was occasioned not least by the influx of border peoples into the central Islamic countries. These Turks, Dailamites and Berbers confronted the *umma* with a problem of assimilation which was indeed often miraculously solved, but which brought no increase to the cultured strata; after the eleventh century it began more noticeably to lead to a lowering of level. More and more uneducated aliens stood in leading positions in opposition to a more or less disinherited class of educated natives. The fragmentation of the states and the cultural aloofness of the new rulers at first could only be favourable to intellectual freedom and to the monopoly position of the educated in the sphere of court and administration. Be it noted marginally that from the middle of the tenth century for three or four generations the intellectual initiative went over to a great extent to Shī'ite-inspired hellenizing or iranizing circles.

The Horizon of Islam: Theology, Philosophy, Literature

THE horizon of Islam extended little beyond the boundaries within which it held sway. The non-Islamic part of the world, apart from the disputed or courted border lands, was included in trade relations in such places as Ceylon, Malacca and Southern China, or it might be visited by mercantile and diplomatic missions, for example the territories of the Khazars and the Bulgars of the Volga and South Russia and the Varangians in central Russia, or like Tibet and Kashmir it was at least accessible to the imagination. But the educated classes, even those living on the margins of the *dār al-islām*, took no real interest. The sphere of Islamic culture being so extensive, and the regions to a great degree self-governing, it was natural that active sympathy was concentrated in each case on a fraction of this multifarious phenomenon, each according to its religious and political location. This localization was the same for geographers and historians alike. Few seriously ventured to the boundaries of the Islamic oecumene or beyond; only now and again an adventurous explorer like al-Muqaddasī (writing in 985 and also an outstanding master of Arabic style) broke through the self-imposed frontiers. But even he regarded it as unnecessary to concern himself with non-Islamic areas. The universal geographical and cultural interests of such a man as Idrīsī (his *Book of King Roger II* was completed in the year of his death, 1154) or of a professional traveller like Ibn Baṭṭūṭa (d. 1369) showed themselves at this period only behind a veil of sailors' yarns and anecdotes of curious personal experiences.

Even to a writer of universal history, like Ṭabarī (d. 923), who also won fame as a commentator of the Koran, North Africa and Spain were not living realities. Transoxiana, Iran as far as the Hindukush, Byzantine Asia Minor and the Caucasus, the Arabian heartlands and Egypt (and even these latter unevenly reported) marked out the area which in the Toynbeeian sense formed a whole, comprehensible in itself, which the historian can encompass and identify himself with. The period did not see itself as involved in the opposition of

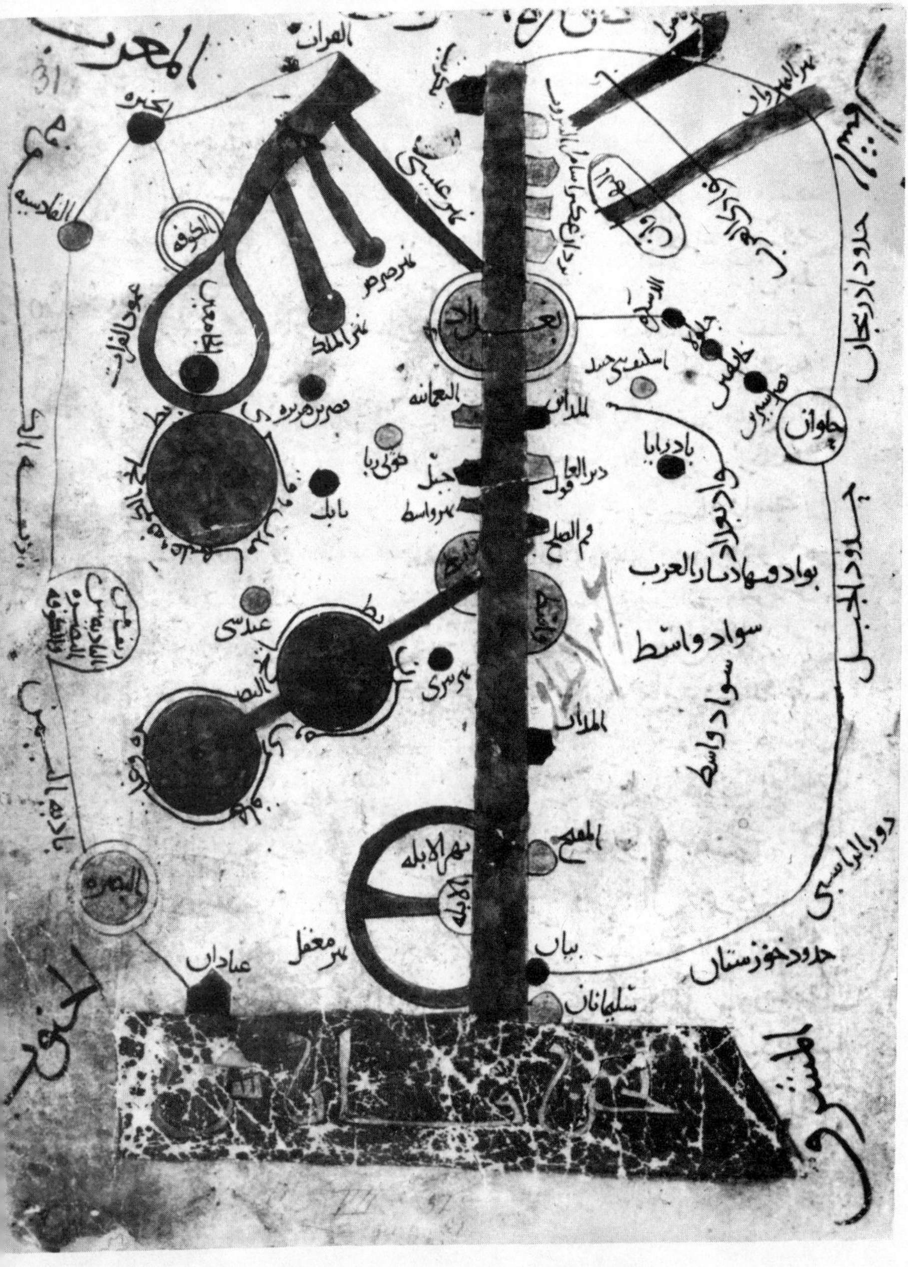

11 The course of the Euphrates in a map of Iraq. Miniature in the 'Book of Countries' by Iṣṭakhrī, 1173. *Gotha, Forschungsbibliothek*

12 Combat of a Muslim horseman with mounted crusaders. Silver inlaid water bottle, first half of the thirteenth century. *Courtesy of the Smithsonian Institution, Freer Gallery of Art, Washington D.C.*

east and west; the division into cultural spheres was delimited by confessional boundaries, not always to be cleanly separated from the national. Not until the eleventh century do we find the great Khwārezmian al-Bērūnī (973–1048) characterizing his Islamic world as poised between Indians and Greeks, though nearer to the Greeks and held together by the spirit of Arabic; of this latter he said that he would rather be abused in this language than praised in Persian.

When Bērūnī paid his homage to Arabic the Arabic renaissance had already fallen into a decline. In its wake the Ḥamdānids had set up their memorable rule in northern Mesopotamia, particularly round Aleppo, in the middle of the tenth century. But the renaissance had enriched the Arab inheritance with the work of Mutanabbī (d. 965) and prepared the way for the perhaps greater achievement of Abu 'l-'Alā' al-Ma'arrī (d. 1058): both poets of questionable orthodoxy who could only develop in the Shī'ite-tainted milieu of Northern Syria. The cultural expansion had been accompanied by a renewed ardour of faith against the returning strength of Byzantium, sustained mainly by Bedouins whose pugnacity has immortalized in Muslim memory the name of the prince of Aleppo, Saif ad-Daula (d. 967) as a hero of the faith. His efforts, like those of the Ḥamdānids, were vain; Byzantium won back Antioch and went on to regain the Armenian provinces and wide tracts of northern Mesopotamia; the military basis was too narrow, and the Būyids from Persia who had gained control of Baghdad looked on the Ḥamdānids as dangerous rivals; in 980 they put an end to their independence in Mesopotamia. After 991 the Ḥamdānids ruled in Aleppo as vassals of the Fāṭimids and only lost all independence in 1008. For half a century longer cultural centres survived whose brilliance still shines in the Arabs' mental image of their history.

The cultural excitement of those days can hardly be exaggerated. conventicles of thinkers of all tendencies rose up and strove for recognition; the monolithic orthodoxy which had in fact never existed except in the minds of obstinately pious believers, gave way to a luxuriant growth of the most varied ideas and smouldering crises of faith. Even so there is apparent an unmistakable tendency to standardize Islamic thought and Islamic life. The smaller law schools are obliterated or come near to dying out and the four surviving 'rites' (*madhāhib*) begin to recognize each other as orthodox, though violent quarrels continue for centuries more between the schools. The Mālikites, named after the Medinan Mālik ibn Anas who died in 795, are no longer to be ousted from North Africa and Spain; the Ḥanafites dominate in the culturally mixed centres, their founder Abū Ḥanīfa (d. 767) having appeared at the point of intersection of Arabism and Iranianism; the methodology of Shāfiʿī (d. 820) subject to much opposition, particularly from the Mālikites, was the first to make the *fiqh* universally into true jurisprudence and enforced a formal standard from which even the followers of Ibn Ḥanbal could not withdraw, although they stood against all newfangled theorizing and were up to a point the representatives of the original authentic orthodoxy. The Shāfiʿite postulate that the *sharīʿa* as a whole derives its authority in principle from the word of God and the example of the Prophet, and that therefore only the Medinan *sunna* ('tradition') is valid and binding, contributed as much to this standardization as the habituation of the Community to the mixed administration of the law, discharged partly by the executive, partly by the *sharīʿa* judges.

The *'ulamā'* of Baghdad also aimed at bringing unity to multiplicity. They recognized seven variants of the Koranic tradition as equally correct and valid; all further variations were to be rejected and suppressed, and the 'reader' Ibn Shannabūdh had to abjure his 'uncanonical' readings in 935. In a somewhat different spirit the theology of Abu 'l-Ḥasan al-Ashʿarī (873/874 to 935/936) pursued the same end in turning away from the Muʿtazilite movement whence it sprang. He used its methodology, applying rational as well as scriptural proof, and thus opened the way to an intellectualistic scholasticism inside orthodox teaching. Although he was opposed by the orthodox during his lifetime Ashʿarī was in fact very close to them in his treatment of the great controversies. In common with them he stood for the Uncreated Koran because of his reverence for the word of God and in view of God's omnipotence he denied to man the 'creation' of his behaviour (not its 'acquisition' by inner consent). He refused to accept the metaphorical interpretation of the anthropomorphisms in the revelation, yet he stressed the impossibility of understanding the reference to God's attributes such as eye, hand and throne as corresponding to the human experience of these things as objects.

The attempt to make a logical defence of orthodox teaching was also made by the second great 'father' of Sunnite theology, al-Māturīdī (d. 941) who worked in Samarkand. His school represents as it were the theological arm of the Ḥanafite rite. In contrast to Ashʿarī Māturīdī concedes that man has free will which gives a moral basis for reward and punishment, but also implies that God is bound by an absolute ethic. Here he remains bound to tradition (and to efficacious piety) in that he makes no attempt to adjust the fact of predestination with the will of man. In the sequel that moral concept which had inspired Abu Ḥanīfa, the Muʿtazilites in general and, basically, Muhammad as well, imperceptibly penetrated Ash'arism, so that it is possible to speak of a 'humanization' of orthodoxy in the following centuries.

The rise of mysticism (*taṣawwuf*) is to be understood as a reaction against the prevalence of dogmatic piety—which is surely indispensable as a scaffold of a universalist Community of faith—and against the pressure exercised by its bearers. Like every nuance of religious life in Islam mysticism too was anchored firmly in the word of God, that source from whose multiplicity it extracted the challenge to interiorize relations with the Creator. In an extraordinarily short process it developed it from asceticism through a refined analysis of conscience to the aspiration to a love-borne union with God, a development whose main phases can be connected primarily with the names of Ḥasan al-Baṣrī (d. 728), al-Muḥāsibī (d. 857) and Junaid (d. 909).

The second half of the ninth century was already acquainted with every facet of the love of God conceivable of formulation within the framework of a strict monotheism, and with every kind of exclusive surrender to the One, not all of which necessarily involved withdrawal from the world. Often the law received scant respect and the illuminati inclined to (at least intellectual) licentiousness. Ecstatics like the Persians Bāyazīd Bisṭāmī (d. 874) and al-Ḥallāj brought some embarrassment to the circles sympathizing with Sufism when they extended their consciousness of personality to full identification with the Godhead, or asserted this extension in their trance-born utterances. Bisṭāmī's seclusion protected him from administrative correction, but Ḥallāj, partly on his own doing, became involved in the Shī'ite disturbances over the tottering caliphate and was executed in 922 after a year's imprisonment, guilty in Sufic eyes for having divulged divine secrets to the profane, and in the eyes of his theological opponents as the advocate of an experience of God which appeared incompatible with the absolute separation of Creator and creation and hence incompatible with the irrevocable validity of the law derived from that separation.

One may justifiably speak here of a sharpening of feeling for the limits of what was laid down in the revelation and hence was compatible with the original true Islam; all the more since the great majority even of the ecstatically inclined Sufi teachers rightly knew themselves to be within these limits. But it is significant that the image of Ḥallāj occasioned 'temptation' (*fitna*), inner conflicts, for centuries, especially in the Persian and Turkish cultural sphere; it remained a phenomenon upon which minds parted company. His spiritualization was for many the summit of self-realization which could be reached by the faithful in suppressing the self and fusing it with the absolute transcendence. To ever-widening circles the individualistic religion of the mystic—individualistic even when it appeared as later in the form of brotherhoods or 'orders' accessible by initiation, gathered round a master—became the real Islam. An alienation was preparing between the religion of the *'ulamā'*, of religious law and in a certain sense of the state, and on the other hand the piety of the untaught, a free-moving faith, finding authority and fulfilment in experience and trusting in the guidance of adepts; the intuitive knowledge (*ma'rifa*) of the individual reaching out to union with God, in conflict with the systematic knowledge of divine

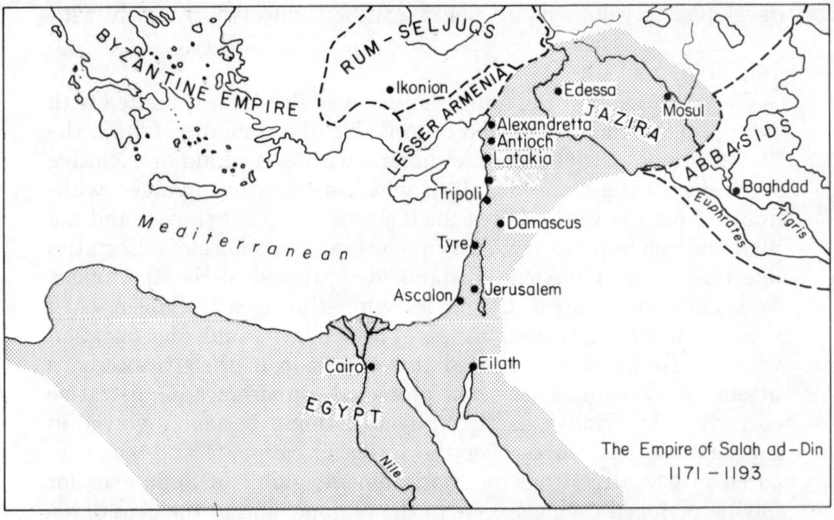

The Empire of Salah ad-Din 1171 – 1193

directives and their foundation in revelation and the example of the Prophet, pledged to the tradition of the learned, which curbs and protects the Community. The dividing line was drawn, not by a particular attitude to the Book and the Mediator, but by the primacy of the individual's experience of salvation as against the primacy of the collective salvation of the Community vouched for by the law. The spiritual heroes might of course find salvation without the law, but to safeguard it by teachable and inviolable tradition must remain the foundation of Muslim life and be recognized as the first task of those responsible for religion in the Community.

In examining Arab philosophy the question arises how far, taken as a whole, Hellenic thoughts and ideas were islamicized or Islamic ideas hellenized. Greek confidence in the power of human reason to tackle the mysteries of the universe—a certainty which included in it an appreciation of the irrational—could not be fitted into the structure of a revealed religion. What reason could provide, as in Judaism and Christianity, was a 'natural theology', the demonstration of the truths of the faith by human reason. But the decisive question was whether reason was to be measured against revelation or revelation against reason. The Neoplatonic form in which the Greek heritage reached the Muslims allowed the identification of God with the *prima causa* and the inclusion of supernatural understanding (and thus the function of the prophet) in the theory of perception. But what in Christianity had seemed 'a folly to the Greeks', the bodily resurrection and creation out of nothing (*creatio ex nihilo*), was also ultimately an insurmountable stumbling-block to the Islamic thinker. If the Muslim philosopher could not bring himself like Abelard 'to be no Aristotle, where this divided him from Christ' he lost the bond with the Community, if not his personal security. Yet rationalization even of Islamic theology was only possible with the help of classical philosophy, a contradiction which could be disguised but never entirely removed. Like Christianity, Islam is indebted to Greek thought for a deeper understanding of itself; the effect of Hellenism never spread beyond a few restricted circles; the Christian fathers were trained on Greek thought, while contact with the Greeks came at a later stage to Islam. It is not seldom asserted that the merit of Muslim philosophy is limited to its service in preserving the classical legacy and transmitting it to the West. This is not so. Its achievement must naturally be assessed in its Islamic context, as was done by the first great Arab philosopher al-Kindī (d. 873) when he studied the Greeks for the crumbs of truth which his own time could learn from them. He sees his task as one of perfecting their work and representing it in an Arab style and manner of thought. But for him the knowledge of the Prophet is superior to that of the philosopher; the truth contained in the Koran is of a higher kind than the judgments of philosophy. The Arab Kindī was followed by the more mature figure of the Arabized Turk Fārābī (d. 950), for whom philosophy possessed the greater scope. The Greeks are no more; but the surviving words of Plato and Aristotle allow a philosophical construction of the world within which natural theology working with Aristotelian logic is superior to the religion of revelation. The theology of the Koran corresponds in its effect to poetry, convincing the imagination with its rhetorical grounds of proof. The various religions are symbolic embodiments of the one universal truth; the One God bears many names. But every symbol does not stand equally near to the philosophically demonstrable truth. The ideal state to which Fārābī devoted the major part of his work and the vision of which reflects tacitly the political difficulties and dreams of his period, represents in the social sphere the same order which dominates both universe and individual. The universe is ruled by God, the state should be ruled by the philosopher as the most perfect man, representing pure reason: as king and spiritual leader, as imām, lawgiver and prophet. From the Muslim point of view only Muhammad could have played this role. Fārābī imputes the crisis of his time to the divorce of the philosopher from government. If the philosopher's influence cannot make itself felt the state is certain of downfall. Kindī was without doubt a pious Muslim, and Fārābī's thoughts were compatible with Shī'ite ideas; it is no mere chance that he ended his life at the court of Saif ad-Daula. The only great thinker who openly adopted the a-religiosity of the Greek tradition was the celebrated physician Muḥammad ibn Zakariyyā' ar-Rāzī (Rhazes: d. 925 or 934), a Persian by origin.

Rāzī must have been less isolated intellectually in his time than he is pictured by tradition; society would hardly have tolerated or indeed encouraged him as it did if he had really been entirely unique. He is linked to Kindī by his feeling for the educative and ennobling influence of philosophy and of scientific endeavour; his empiricism distinguishes him from the speculative thinkers of his period. The surety of his diagnosis, the cool precision of his descriptions of maladies has stamped Arab medicine for all time though few were able to maintain his high standard. In his tradition-ridden age Rāzī stood virtually alone in his truly classical self-confidence. Self-praise has always been a characteristic of the Arab style; pre-Islamic poets were already giving full rein to their enthusiasm for themselves. But it signified something quite new when Rāzī compared his authority to that of Aristotle and, in the knowledge that scientific truth was something he could only move towards, never master, envisaged investigatory thought as a process of overtaking and being overtaken; this for the first, and it would seem the last, time in classic Islamic thought. Since the Renaissance it has gradually become self-evident to us that intellectual life only perfects itself in the long run, and the achievement of the individual only gains its meaning in the unforeseeable context of future knowledge; this understanding in Rāzī is new and unprecedented in a mental climate where everything new is disreputable, where tradition signifies authority and the generation of the Prophet is considered as the irrecoverable best; where in short a certain cultural pessimism is almost inevitable. Rāzī's sense of power, reminiscent of Sophocles' 'man as the mightiest thing that walks this earth', has faded away; but it found its lasting expression in his consciously original autobiography.

The growing importance of the sects is illustrated by the fact that the only attempt to make an encyclopaedic survey of all knowledge was undertaken by educated Ismā'īlites. Their collection of fifty-three treatises has become famous (*Rasā'il Ikhwān aṣ-Ṣafā*); in it they attempted to embrace all the learning of their time and to present it from a consistent point of view.

In the conflict between sense of reality and faith in authority the former suffered (to us) unexpectedly from the inadequacy of the experimental methods and the lack of observable demarcations between subjective and objective reality, between what is empirically possible and impossible in a world wedded to the miraculous. This conflict also affected the adoption and improvement of classical science. Where theory ran no risk of becoming dangerous, investigation went ahead: optics, botany, pharmacology and empirical medicine are all deeply indebted to Islamic research. But the conceptual framework of late classical thought, and even Galen's anatomy and Hellenistic astrology, remained untouched though certain parts were known to have been superseded. A compromise had been reached up to a point with the (extraphilosophical) classical view of life and it was supplemented without attempting to make a new model of the natural world or to compare it with the knowledge guaranteed by religion.

A comparable conflict can be seen in literature, or rather in poetry which alone was important at this time. Here again it is a matter of seeking a balance between tradition and an originality which besides formal expression is concerned with self-observation and the observation of nature, and in general strives to extend the admissible repertoire, for example in describing buildings and sea battles or in historical biography. The fragmentation of the pre-Islamic ode into thematically independent sections led to specialization in refined love poetry and precious nature lyrics. As the mouthpiece of the great the poet enjoyed some social security, though it seems to us to have been bought rather dear with an excess of panegyric and polemical satire. It took almost two generations before true religious composition emerged—at first in sectarian circles—a delay which is understandable in view of the lack of encouragement afforded to poets in the Koran. But once launched it became an often impressive vehicle for the expression of ascetic and mystical feelings, while the style of court life provided a public for drinking and hunting songs. The refinement of amorous sentiment compared with the classical model of pre-Islamic verse can be seen in the work of such poets as 'Umar ibn abī Rabī'a (d. 719), Jamīl (d. 701) and al-'Abbās ibn al-Aḥnaf (d. 806), though their delicate verses in honour of love and woman stand beside the most coarse obscenities, the outcome of a society whose only female companions and love-objects are slaves and courtesans. By 900 theory was fast becoming a true science, but although poetry was closely bound to the music which also flourished at this time, theory concerned itself only with the words; it analysed figures of speech and imagery, developed the criteria of evaluation and even at times broke a lance for originality. But its acquaintance with Greek theory never succeeded in taking it beyond formal analysis and criticism.

A little ahead of literary theory, the history of literature developed in the ninth and tenth centuries; it was preponderantly the assembling of biographical anecdotes, confining criticism mostly to the consideration of single verses or sections of a poem. The individual biographies were arranged chronologically according to 'classes' (*ṭabaqāt*); for instance, the pre-Islamic poets, divided again into the 'great' and the less important, and the poets of the period of transition to Islam were grouped in separate classes. The most extensive work of this type, it is true, the *Book of Songs* (Kitāb al-Aghānī) by Abu 'l-Faraj al-Iṣfahāni (d. 967), starts with a hundred melodies, includes the verses set to them and attaches notes about the writers. As well as the biographical anthology there is the theme history in which the various motifs within the great categories (satire, elegy, panegyric) are treated and evaluated. Sometimes both types are combined in the criticism of a famous author like Mutanabbī or in the comparative analysis of characteristic verses of two poets felt to be stylistically opposed, for example Abu Tammām (d. 846), considered as the standard-bearer of the moderns, and the younger Buḥturī whose work is richer but formally more moderate (d. 897).

Only one new literary form grew up in the tenth century and came to fruition towards 1100 with al-Ḥarīrī; this was the *maqāma* (lit. 'Standpredigt'; a 'dressing down'), a short, narrative and dramatic sketch, sometimes witty, always gracious, which became a showpiece of verbal virtuosity and learning. Throughout the age the esoteric character of poetic speech remains striking. The preference for short metres often gives poetry a lightness rarely felt previously; the rhythm and rhyme of the Arabic penetrate the Persian poetry of the tenth century, which expresses in some ways a new beginning. Its particular achievement, the epic—first with historical, then romantic, and finally with mystical themes—did not in fact affect the Arab sphere though in compensation it flourished in the Turkish and Indian ambience. Persia for longer than the Arab world was able to keep herself free of the decadence of a concept of originality based upon pure form, which forced the poet to concentrate on the endless refinement of a very limited repertoire of motifs and on capping the ingenuity of his predecessors. But in the *'Arabiyya* at the time of the accession of the Būyids and the Fāṭimids there was no hint of degeneration. The literary innovator had as yet no bad conscience, nor was there in the Islamic world any of that apprehensiveness which in the problems of the eleventh-century crisis in politics, economics and primarily in religion put a stop to any expansion into a wider world view.

In art as well the Arab and Iranian cultural spheres fell apart. The arabesque; the high prestige of calligraphy as a medium and often as a work of art in itself; the ornamental and decorative element in general and the consequent tendency to abstraction even in motifs which were religiously unexceptionable, such as plants; the mosque or the mosque-school (*madrasa*) as the principal task of architecture; and in architecture above all stalactite arches (*muqarnas*) and domes as the technical solution to problems of space; all these elements are everywhere common to Islamic art, even though manner and function may vary from place to place and period to period. Yet the typical Persian layout of a mosque differs from the Arab. The Persian is dominated by the interior courtyard, the roofed portion is relatively small and the tendency to bold vaults and domes is unmistakably different from the 'Arab', whose quadrilateral ground plan is much less disguised by vaulting and decoration, which is as it were squat and solidly planted on the ground, even when an ambitious minaret draws the eye upwards, and the often fantastical optical allurements of the forest of pillars crouching under the flat roof distract the attention from the severe functionalism of the building. The ancient oriental-Persian architectural vision seems to stand beside that of the Hellenistic Mediterranean. But the elegance of late Greek forms is lost, or rather has been exchanged for the severity befitting the house of Allah.

The mosque with its courtyard, particularly in the early period, was a political as well as a religious place of assembly, and also the social meeting-ground and the teaching centre, where the sage sat leaning against a pillar and discoursed to the students on law or tradition; early on, certainly by the tenth century, cells for students were provided within the precincts of the mosque, in an annex to the sanctuary itself. Ritual ablution required a fountain with running water. The narrow nave of the average Christian church would be unsuitable for the long row of worshippers praying behind the imām; and the segregation of the women (and often of the ruler) determines a particular division of the interior. Beside the prayer niche (*miḥrāb*) rises the pulpit (*minbar*) with its steep steps, which is often moveable. From its height the preacher (*khaṭīb*) prays at the chief service on Fridays for the blessing of the Lord on the ruler, the conventional sign of his recognition by the Community; suppression of this prayer would be the equivalent of a revolution.

It is not true that there was ever a definitive prohibition on the representation of the human form. But undeniably after the ninth century a growing uneasiness gained the upper hand in increasingly wide circles, particularly in Arab-speaking Islam, and it even grew into a patent hostility to figural art. The reasons are many: the ancient oriental sensibility which we can find expressed in the Old Testament, ideas concerning the magical identity of images with their subjects, a specifically religious reluctance to make the Divine visible. This theologically based sensitivity is strong enough to paralyse figural sculpture, though not figural painting. Even in Samarra the private apartments were still decorated with wall paintings whose remains, incidentally, in contrast to those in the Umayyad castles, betray strong Irano–Asiatic influences. Ancient models, stylized into Islamic significance, certainly survive in Arab book illumination of the eleventh and twelfth centuries, but on the whole a certain orientalizing tendency heralds the final extinction of figural illustration at the end of the Middle Ages. In the Persian sphere however the miniature underwent an unprecedented revival at this period, its themes following, at a short interval of time, the development of the epic. Now and again it was even encouraged by theological approval, and book illustration in the lands under Persian influence remained one of the most sought-after and objectively impressive achievements of the Iranian brand of Islamic culture until well after the Middle Ages.

The *dār al-islām*, whose transformation from a political to a cultural unity was hastened by increasing fragmentation of states, conferred a double role on the non-Islamic communities of the People of the Book, in that it left them their own authenticity as institutions in public law, and at the same time brought them into (unpolitical) collaboration with the cultural whole. After Islam had gradually overshadowed all other religious communities in number, the state and society no longer needed to pay any heed to what were now minorities. The upsurge of a civilization based on Arabic, occasional waves of religious revivalism coupled with intolerance, the formation and perfection of an Islamic way of life and lastly political tensions with the unconverted world gradually sharpened the contradictions; in particular they isolated the infidel. But before the downfall there was, at least in the case of the Jews, a period of several centuries during which the economic and cultural expansion of Islam allowed sufficient scope for working in common and ultimately had the effect of arabizing the People of the Book.

The Arab conquest in Iraq first changed the Jews from a predominantly agricultural into a commercial people. When about 950 the silence of a period almost without documents is broken, we find Jewish communities engaged in long-distance trade on Islamic territory and beyond as far as India. Fāṭimid Egypt emerges as the centre of their economic power, but there are sizeable settlements almost everywhere in the lands dominated by the Muslims; in general, until

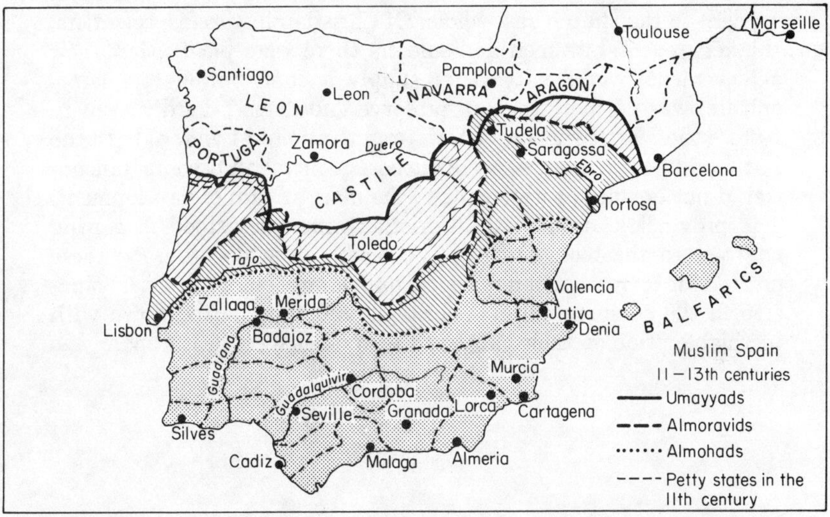

recent years their deep seated religious affinity and the lack of political backing from abroad has made the symbiosis between Jews and Muslims a much less painful affair than between Muslims and Christians. Though the material position of the Jewish communities was recurrently precarious it did not really take a definitive turn for the worse before the Almohads, and their inclusion in the Islamic cultural sphere brought them a golden age, especially in Spain and Egypt, but at times in Iraq and North Africa also. They became deprovincialized in every sense and even, strangely enough, made a more fruitful contact with classical thought through the detour of Arab philosophy than they had derived after the rapid percolation of Philonic influences in antiquity.

The case of the Christian enclaves is the direct opposite, with some reservations. It was certainly Christians who revealed antiquity and sciences to the Muslims in so far as these did not come from India, and the ninth and tenth centuries saw Christians and Muslims met together in the intellectual circles and even in the bureaucracy. The confidence and pride of the Christian churches seems as late as the eleventh century to have been largely intact. Yet their isolation from the real centres of Christian life soon began to make itself felt. Waves of the great movements which forced Church and state to intellectual discussion in Byzantium and in the West, which across the frontier kept putting the content and life of faith in question and making it a never-ending subject of controversy, only broke feebly among the oriental communities, neither did they raise any problems of concern to the church as a whole. Of Christian historians, scientists, thinkers, even statesmen and soldiers there were plenty; but their achievement, where it was not simply a contribution to Islamic culture, was no more than to preserve and defend, hardly even to restore these little enclaves which from the point of view of both the Latin and Greek churches were outposts which had become 'tangential' if not downright irrelevant to the main stream of development. The provincialization of the Christian minorities stood in glaring contrast to the blossoming of the Jews. From 900 to 1200 these created for themselves a new centre on Islamic soil by their participation in the common cultural heritage, and they looked down with justifiable pride on their backward fellow-believers in Europe.

The Downfall of the Caliphate

Fāṭimids, Būyids, Ghaznavids, Seljūqs

THE continuous decline in the power of the caliphate was shown to be irrevocable when al-Muqtadir (908–932) was killed during his struggle with the generalissimo Mu'nis. The petty princeling of central Iraq, which was all that remained of the glory of the 'Abbāsid ruler, was now driven to a perpetual search for a military protector. This role fell to various Turkish mercenary leaders, and then for three years (March 942 to January 945) to the last Arab majordomo, the Shī'ite-inclined Ḥamdānid Ḥasan. (He is better known under his honorary title of Nāṣir ad-Daula, *defensor imperii*, representative of a type of title which arose at this period and of which he was the first holder of any note.) A few months after his return to the centre of his power in his family estates in Northern Mesopotamia he was replaced by the Dailamite Būyids, whereby a dynasty of 'barbarians' based on Central and Southern Persia, only scantily arabized and of the Twelver Shī'ite confession, took over power in Iraq at the invitation of the Caliph. The Būyids were condottieri who had risen high in the service of the Sāmānids and later of Mardāvīj ibn Ziyār, a Gīlān prince who had built himself an influential position in Central Persia and apparently dreamt of the restitution of a Zarathustrian Iranian empire. However, he was assassinated in 935 in the typical dissensions of those days between ancestral Dailamite troops and mercenaries of mixed origin. The Būyids entrenched themselves in Persia south of the Sāmānid territory and succeeded in incorporating the often attacked but never conquered Baluchi of Kirmān into the *dār al-islām* for the first time.

The state lands were treated as a family possession; it was run in the first generation by the eldest brother, 'Imād ad-Daula, 'Pillar of the Empire' (d. 949) who resided in Shīrāz, and later by his nephew 'Aḍud ad-Daula, 'Arm of the Empire', who was without doubt the greatest personality of the dynasty and who between 977 and 982 held the whole territory of the house under his direct rule. Outside Iraq the Būyid regime followed the established pattern of provincial governors who had become independent; in Baghdad the Būyid military government took the administration out of the hands of the Caliph; they granted him estates and an income but withdrew his vizir. As the Sunnite 'prince of the Church' the Caliph was indispensable even to the Shī'ite *amīr al-umarā'*; an 'Alid caliph might have commanded obedience, a Sunnite caliph in exile could cause much trouble; there was no question of a Shī'ite majority. The legal continuity of the life of the Community and of the administration of justice remained the task of the caliphs and they, though much humbled on the whole enjoyed greater personal security under the Būyids than they had ever done during the previous century. Political considerations sometimes even turned the Būyids into champions of the Sunna. The fear of losing Syria to the Fāṭimids forced the Būyids into a policy of containment of the Ismā'īlis, which could only be welcome to the caliphate, while the attempts of the 'Seveners' to win over the Būyids did not begin to show any success until towards the end of their rule. The famous anti-Fāṭimid declaration issued by the caliph in 1011 was subscribed to both by 'orthodox' and by 'Twelver' theologians. The Būyid government drew its support in Baghdad primarily among the rich Shī'ite merchants and the 'Ṭālibids' (i.e. 'Alids) whom they organized though they were sometimes nonetheless embarrassed by their turbulence, and there is no denying that the Būyids gave assistance whenever possible to their fellow believers. 'Aḍud ad-Daula for instance sanctioned the funeral processions and self-castigation by which the anniversary of Ḥusain's death was celebrated and which even the women could join unveiled, though these processions always caused bloody riots between the sects and could not be held regularly.

The Ḥanbalites showed themselves in these events as the most energetic champions of the Sunna; it is thanks primarily to their tenacity that towards the end of the tenth century the first signs began to show of an orthodox restoration, coinciding it is true with the breakdown of concord and hence of striking power among the Būyids. By 1020 the Būyids were unable to protect Shī'ite preachers in Baṣra from disciplinary punishment by the Caliph. In 1015 the Ḥanbalites set fire to the mausoleum of Ḥusain in Karbalā'; in Baghdad and Samarra and even in Mecca, Medina and Jerusalem there were revolts which were less concerned with driving out the Būyids than with abolishing the public worship of the Shī'a. The rise of the Sunnite Ghaznavids, who set themselves up in 1027 as the protectors of the Caliph, strengthened his resolution by their gesture; a few years later the 'Abbāsid won back his right to have his own vizir. The hope of a genuine restitution of the caliphate seized the leading Sunnite circles. The Shāfi'ite chief judge Māwardī (d. 1058) published at that time a picture of the political institutions of Islam which is splendid in its own way. It reflects the atmosphere of this circle close to the court: its theses describe the prerogatives of the caliph in pretentious normative postulates which entirely ignore the reality of the last centuries and of the present, but present a blueprint supported by tradition for a political resurgence into caliphal leadership.

At the same time the intolerance of the Ḥanbalites towards the Mu'tazila and the scholastic theology of such as Ash'arī, indicates a narrowing down of the intellectual horizon, bound up with the intensification of Sunnite piety. Most significant of all however was that the Community was now able to maintain its own life without, even against, state power; the caliphate it is true functioned as an administrative and political support for orthodoxy; looked at more closely however it was the militant orthodoxy which allowed, and even forced, the caliphate to take on this function. At this time the four great Sunnite schools of law were increasingly inclined to recognize each other; the idea, which recurs again in the eighteenth century, arose to incorporate the moderate Shī'a as a fifth 'rite' in one comprehensive legal structure; finally the Twelvers under the Būyids had formulated their theological and juridical ideas systematically, and more than ever the '*ulamā*' now functioned as the medium whereby the parties formed their political policies. The failure of the 'idea of unity' was due primarily to the radicalism of the Sunnite reformers in Baghdad and their political allies abroad.

Great achievements were made under the Būyids and to a great extent thanks to them, both on Arabic and Persian-speaking soil. We should not be blinded into forgetting this by the lack of restraint in political and intellectual party strife or the splintering of the inherited territories arising from the dynastic conception which degenerated into fraternal feuds and particularism and finally resulted in the crumbling of the state. The Byzantine Michael Psellos was thinking of the epoch of the Būyids and Fāṭimids when he declared in 1060 that the Greeks, resting on their pride in the wisdom of their fathers, had been left far behind by the Arabs; true he bases his remarks more on their observations on classical philosophy and science, and on a general impression, than on a study of Arabic writings. Nonetheless the services of the Būyids for Islamic culture were considerable. The fulcrum of their power lay in Persia, however, so it is not surprising that they had a Sasanid genealogical tree compiled; their Persian orientation is even more clearly to be seen in the adoption of the Middle-Persian title of 'King of Kings', *shāhanshāh*, though at first it was only intended to indicate the position of the head of the family in relation to the other Būyid princes. The title roused great indignation in Arab Baghdad and was therefore not officially sanctioned by the Caliph until 1037 when it had been in use for more than half a century. (*Sulṭān*, however, which had already been used by the Caliph Manṣūr, does not become a regular part of the title until the Seljūqs.)

The decline of Zarathustrianism under the Būyids is to be ascribed in part to the fact that it was easier to emancipate oneself from the traditional religion under a 'Persian national' dynasty than under 'Arabic' foreign rule. The Būyid rulers were active in developing culture both in Baghdad and on Iranian soil. Hospitals were built in Baghdad and Shīrāz, an observatory was set up in Baghdad, and libraries founded in Shīrāz, Rayy and Iṣfahān. The Persian Avicenna like Firdausī before him was well received at the court of a Būyid prince; the historian Miskawaih, the geographer Iṣṭakhrī, the mathematician Nasawī who introduced Indian numbers into the Arab-speaking area, all leading lights of Arab learning, were protégés of the Būyids. Uneducated but devoted to learning as they were, they appointed as vizirs men of the highest literary refinement; and it was such men as the Ṣāḥib Ibn 'Abbād (d. 971), himself a highly esteemed writer, who made the Persis and Rayy (near present-day Teheran) the centre of patronage. The great littérateur Tauḥīdī, perhaps the only humanist 'existentialist' of his time, kept a record of the discussions which took place at the house of a minister of no particular note. Tauḥīdī's originality, combined with his sharp tongue, cost him his privileged position in the end, it is true. His accounts give an incomparable picture of the interdenominational educated class of the time, with its interest in Greek philosophy, ethnography and the biographical approach to politics and history.

The Būyids had transformed themselves remarkably rapidly from mercenary leaders, not to say brigand chieftains, to imperial administrators. But until the end they personified a military government, just as the Seljūqs did later. The official and merchant aristocracy of the recent past disappeared from political positions of importance, the great estates were transferred in large measure to the high ranks of the army. In return for military service there were non-hereditary lands or the tax revenue of certain districts. As an emergency measure this mode of compensation had already been tried in the late ninth century (a similar arrangement was also customary in Byzantium); the Būyids made it into a system. The conferred estates (*iqṭā'*) were now, unlike formerly, freed from the usual land tax. Whole districts were distributed, and their financial potential not only lost to the civil administration but actually unknown to it; the parallel with the Byzantine development of the *pronoia* is clear. Some remuneration, particularly of the lower ranks, was still paid directly from the state treasury, and often in kind: one must take care not to confuse the *iqṭā'* with the feudal fief; above all the *muqta'* in his estate did not represent the power of the state, and the 'fiefs' were revocable and exchangeable by order of the government and could neither be inherited nor sub-let. The burden of taxation weighing on the civilian was rather increased than reduced by the Būyids; taxation on industry was certainly intensified.

A relatively stable internal peace, new projects or the restoration of dilapidated irrigation works, bridges and streets, in short ordered administration achieved a certain prosperity and a stabilization of the currency which were favourable to long-distance trade. This was encouraged by the Būyids in every way. The security of the sea route to India was served by the annexation of the coasts of 'Umān and perpetual guerrilla warfare against the Qarmaṭians in Baḥrain. The greater freedom accorded to many of the towns is already a pointer to the basic weakness of Būyid power, but it was suppressed by bloody intervention wherever it appeared to constitute a threat. Yet the eleventh century saw a remarkable upsurge of the power of the towns, in Būyid territory as much as in Syria and Spain, which was due as much to the increase in economic activity as to the dissolution of the territorial state.

But the Būyids were not to be saved by the reorganization of the *iqṭā'*, the disciplining of the army, nor their care for public order. Their downfall was hastened if not brought about by family feuds—politically dangerous as instruments of regional separatism—and encroachment by the military caste. This consisted of Dailamite infantry, Turkish cavalry and smaller Kurd or Baluchi contingents of barbarians, and was itself torn by internal dissension. More difficult to understand, but probably even more important, was the fact that conditions of world trade were developing against the interests of the Būyids and the lands ruled by them.

The Būyid states were perpetually engaged in a kind of war on two fronts. The Fāṭimids threatened to establish themselves in Syria and the Turks of Central Asia—autonomous tribes, not to be confused with the Turkish mercenaries and military slaves—were gaining ground in the Irano-Arab world, much more easily once they had embraced Islam and belonged to the Community. The Būyids showed themselves less and less a match for the Turks as time went on, especially after they lost the bulwark of the Sāmānid empire when it fell, shortly before the turn of the millennium; but they managed at least to thwart the thrust of the Fāṭimids towards the north of

Mesopotamia, even though they could not expel them from Palestine and Syria.

Until the middle of the eleventh century Fāṭimid power seemed to be unbreakable and borne aloft on a wave of economic prosperity. A number of factors contributed: the disturbances in South Mesopotamia, increasing instability in the Persian Gulf which the Būyids endeavoured but failed to suppress, and the vulnerable frontiers along the Byzantine and Fāṭimid territories all worked against the Būyids; on the other hand the steep rise in Egypt's European trade which the Fāṭimids consciously encouraged by naval building, and the growth of their influence in the Red Sea made Egypt the centre and reloading point of international maritime trade. The consequences of this new orientation were already visible in 1000 when the Būyid silver currency lost value, tax-farming and office buying gained ground and the lack of ready money had to be made good with payments in kind.

Iranian military strength was also clearly insufficient for dealing with several tasks at the same time; they had to withstand the Turkish flood, curb the Arab frontier lands and keep off the Byzantines, who between 960 and 1020 were gaining strength and streaming back into the old frontier provinces—at this time Armenia again lost her sovereignty to Byzantium—and furthermore they had to recognize that their main base lay in a province whose population regarded them with suspicious passivity as the representatives of the foreign speaking and heretical Iranian power. In Iraqi eyes the Būyids, who found they had more and more to rely on foreign troops, had disqualified themselves as protectors of orthodoxy because of their faith; furthermore the Būyids were divided among themselves and hence unable to make any effective stand against the Turks, who identified themselves with orthodoxy. A change of front to the 'Seveners' such as the Fāṭimids aimed at would no longer have been of any help, since the beginnings of weakness were showing even in Egypt in the middle of the eleventh century, and there was no support among the population of the capital. Almost at the last minute a (Turkish) Būyid general al-Basāsīrī (d. January 15, 1060) came to oppose the Seljūqs with a Fāṭimid army and Fāṭimid subsidies. But the adventure foundered against the realities of Seljūq power and the Būyids' isolation. This last ambitious imperialist undertaking of the Fāṭimids is incidentally the only example of an Egyptian or Egyptian-supported conquest of Central Iraq and it is furthermore a significant indication of the prestige of the Fāṭimid state, whose first 80 years in Egypt belongs along with early 'Abbāsid Baghdad and the blossoming of Córdoba under 'Abd ar-Raḥmān III until the fall of the 'Āmirids, to the golden ages of Islamic culture, and constitutes the only one under heterodox leadership.

Indisputably the Fāṭimids were imperialists and saw their final goal in the expulsion of the Sunnite caliphate; the political situation restricted them however to the usual 'defence barrier' in Syria (which they sometimes extended beyond Aleppo into Mesopotamian towns like Ḥarrān and Raqqa), and to protecting the security of the trade with India through their influence in the Yemen (a stronghold in the Indus basin with Multān as its centre was lost to the Ghaznavids). This trend is inherent in the nature of the Egyptian economy; it outlived the dynasty and has even made itself felt today. Mecca and Medina, which were dependent on Egyptian grain deliveries, acquiesced without opposition in the profitable suzerainty of the Shī'ite ruler. The documents found in the *genizah*, the 'archives' of a Jewish synagogue in Cairo, mainly of the ninth to twelfth century and the most extensive collection of their kind from mediaeval Islam, give an impressive picture of the economic activity of the time; they throw a light too on the situation in the Jewish community, whose position under the Fāṭimids was more favourable than at any time in the first thousand years of Muslim history. Their treatment went far beyond mere tolerance and probably arose in part from the indifference of the inner circle of the Ismā'īlīs towards the externals of religions, an attitude which facilitated their foreign propaganda in non-Muslim circles and created a suitable psychological climate for the peace concluded in 1040 with Byzantium. But after the third caliph al-Ḥākim bi-amr Allāh (996–1021) had proceeded for a time against the Sunnites he turned suddenly against the Christians and Jews and destroyed numerous temples, including the Church of the Sepulchre in Jerusalem. This persecution, active between 1008 and 1015, may well have been induced by Sunnite counterpressure as much as by the changed religious sympathies of the Caliph. At all events a few years later the ruler felt himself to be the incarnation of the Divine Reason, or at least had himself worshipped as such. An outbreak of anger among the populace was coldly and cruelly put down. The Caliph also interfered strongly in the private lives of his subjects, for not very comprehensible religious reasons; soon after his accession he forbade women to go out of the house at any time on pain of death, and men to go out at night. Finally he disappeared in 1021 in a manner as yet unexplained, during a walk at night through the streets.

His successor eliminated the extremists who had deified al-Ḥākim; they found an echo in the Lebanon however, and the Druze who are still to be found there at the present day, their zeal undiminished, owe their foundation to this expulsion. They are named after their champion ad-Darazī (probably died 1019). This strange development has to some extent a parallel with the Nuṣairī who formed somewhat earlier in more or less the same region; both groups seized upon a number of motifs thrown off by Islam and wove them together with the help of Islamic symbols.

The religious ideology had, in the course of time, acquired its philosopical and juridical support and elaboration; it bestowed upon the Fāṭimids a rare homogeneity and the dynamism for their intra-Islamic conquests; but it was bound to incur irreconcilable hostility for the dynasty from the 'orthodox' and, what was really more dangerous, from partisans who because of personal differences became so to speak sectarians within the sect. By attaching themselves to a certain imam these latter found the means of giving organizational support to their dogmatic deviations. The death of the Caliph al-Mustanṣir, under whose long reign (1036–1094) the disintegration of Fāṭimid power had been exposed, had divided those loyal to him into Nizārī, the followers of his son Nizār whom he had designated his successor, and Musta'lī, the supporters of his second son, whom the army set upon the throne, whereupon Nizār and his son met a violent death in prison. Driven out of Egypt the Nizārī took over the leadership of the 'foreign' Ismā'īliyya, who congregated partly in Syria, but under the leadership of the famous Ḥasan-i Ṣabbāḥ (d. 1124) chiefly in the mountains of Western Persia.

These fanatical groups, especially the Persian, because of their terrorist practices and the aura of secrecy surrounding them, exercised from their inaccessible strongholds an influence out of all proportion to their size. On August 8, 1164, the Persian Nizāriyya from their seat of Alamūt, the 'Eagle's Nest', proclaimed the 'Great Resurrection', the paradise on earth which no longer recognizes any law. This (according to the plausible suggestion of Massignon) seems to be the source of a much cited legend about the 'Assassins': the leaders secured the loyalty of their followers by intoxicating them with hashish so that they experienced the joys of paradise as described in the Koran. Translated back into the every-day world they awaited with the greatest impatience the death which would take them once more to the bliss of which they had had a foretaste.

The Mongols alone were able to subdue the Nizārī, once they had destroyed their castles in 1256; but the sect survived, chiefly in India, divested of its apocalyptic political aims, and both here and in East Africa under the leadership of the famous Aga Khan it has accomplished the transition to modernism in a quite surprising manner without giving up any of its fundamental dogmas. The Musta'lī caliphs in Egypt seem only to have possessed to a small degree the gift of arousing religious enthusiasm. With the murder of Mustaʿlī's son in 1130 the Fāṭimid dynasty did not lose the throne, but the last four rulers of the house were no longer considered as imāms but simply as representatives of the promised 'Lord of Time', scion of the family of Mustaʿlī's grandson, who had been abducted as a child, and who would appear from concealment at the end of time.

This religious decline had been preceded by deterioration in the internal political situation. Alien governments now ruled everywhere in Islamic territory and the minority character of their following, together with the fluctuatingly negative apathy of the population, had the effect of making the rulers more and more the puppets of their soldiers. The Fāṭimids recruited Berbers, Negroes and Turks and with them smaller units of Arabs from the frontier lands; but instead of this diversity creating an equilibrium their rivalries corroded the authority of the caliph. Their original territories in North Africa had been entrusted to the Zīrids when the Fāṭimids had left for Egypt, and they in their essays at independence could rely on the hostility of the orthodox population to the Fāṭimids. They immediately spread to Sicily which the Fāṭimids had reserved for themselves. In 1047 they saw that the moment had come when they could free themselves from the Fāṭimids with impunity. In fact the Fāṭimids were not in a position to exact obedience by force of arms. In revenge they diverted to North Africa the Bedouin of the Banū Hilāl who had disturbed the peace on the Egyptian frontier for decades, and somewhat later the Banū Sulaim, who like the Banū Hilāl had emigrated from Syria because of their Qarmaṭian sympathies. These tribes settled by degrees in modern Tunisia and westwards as far as Morocco, and decisively furthered the arabization of these territories; at the same time they brought their nomadic way of life to these agriculturally highly developed lands and thus caused an economic catastrophe from which North Africa has not recovered to this day. The 'Arab' as the destroyer, responsible for the century-long decline of North Africa, is an image which still dominates the historical picture of Ibn Khaldūn (*c.* 1377) more than 300 years later, and the travel reports of the late Middle Ages.

The disloyalty of the Zīrids made it impossible to recruit Berbers any longer; the Cairenes rejoiced, but the government found itself even more helplessly caught in the nets of the pretorians. The fall of Damascus to the Seljūqs in 1076 put an end to the Greater Syria policy of the Fāṭimids; they had already lost Jerusalem in 1071, though they reconquered it in 1098, but this proved to be just in time to come up against the crusaders. What gave the state at the end of the eleventh century the strength for foreign defence and political resurgence at home were the Armenian mercenaries, at their head the vizir and high judge Badr al-Jamālī (1073–1094); this convert began as a military slave and rose to the rank of general in Syria. As a beginning he killed off the rebellious Turkish officials and officers and re-established public order. His son al-Afḍal was able to maintain it until he was murdered in 1121.

It is remarkable how little either the intellectual activity of the capital or foreign trade were affected by the disappearance of Fāṭimid power. Egyptian society, composed of 'bourgeoisie', craftsmen and petty merchants, henceforth excluded from the army and the executive, remained basically unaffected in spite of all the political uncertainty, and dominated the cultural life of the country until the end of the Middle Ages; their admittedly somewhat one-sided monument is the picaresque sections of the Thousand and One Nights.

The eleventh century was, if one may use the expression for a series of historical developments, a caesura in the evolution of the Islamic world. The Iranian actors retire, the turkization of the leadership in the newly emerging component states of the *dār al-islām* has become irrevocable; Turks lead the great new wave of Muslim expansion which turns primarily eastwards, opening up Afghanistan and the Indus valley to Islam. Although often only recently converted and subjected to Persian influences they appear as the cultural (not linguistic) representatives of Iran. The expansion of the Turks, largely caused by movements of peoples in the eastern parts of Central Asia and accompanied by the decline of the older states with a Turkish ruling class, like the Bulgars of the Volga and the Khazars, signifies an expansion of nomadism; it is both a symptom and a cause of the return to a barter economy, a cause too of the drying up of Arabian trade in the north-west; it makes a curious parallel with the contemporary founding of empires by the Berbers in the West.

The Turks like the Berbers are Sunnites; strict and aggressive orthodoxy is the source of their power. The Shī'a will shortly be excluded for centuries from the conduct of the greater states as the moulder of political destiny. Everywhere government is in the hands of armies which feel themselves to be more or less the possessors of the land; but the centre of power is not the territory but the dynast who rules, sometimes here, sometimes there, with an armed following and whose house embodies the homogeneity of the political structure. The earlier, already typical process is repeated: an empire supported by a vigorous, numerically small but war-minded people quickly rises to a climax of power and then disintegrates equally quickly into a number of small states governed by princes of the ruling house or its mercenary generals, which in their turn succumb to new empires. Not until the rise of the Ottomans, Ṣafavids and Great Moghuls in the fifteenth and sixteenth centuries is there an end to this catastrophic cycle which on the whole depresses the cultural level of the regions concerned. However, the instability of public affairs does not prejudice the expansion of Islam. The dynasties need the support of the *umma*; when their power is shattered the newly won territories remain within the Community. The scholars of religion and, though they of course are differently stratified sociologically, the mystical sheikhs, form the second support of which the executive has need. The rulers and the ruled find increasingly that their only common ground is their participation in religion and religious life. Hence the state cares above all for theologico-juridical education, and for the alumni of the 'religious' schools and their integration into the civil service, a concern which existed even at the end of the Sāmānid period, and grew increasingly important under the Ghaznavids and crucial under the Seljūqs, Ayyūbids and Mamlūks.

The Ghaznavids form the transition to the new period. Their short history in the territory of ancient Islam shows nearly all the characteristics of the new state forms. Alptegin, a general of the Sāmānid Turkish guard who was given the governorship of Khorāsān, fell into disfavour during a change of government and acquired for himself an independent state by conquering Ghazna in 962. After his death it survived as a kind of communal possession of the soldiers, though under Sāmānid sovereignty, and opened up Central and Eastern Afghanistan, which had so far remained pagan, to Islam. Subuktegin, the son-in-law of Alptegin, whom the army designated ruler in 977, consolidated the conquest, saved Khorāsān for the Sāmānids from a rebel and laid the foundations for further conquests, particularly eastwards. The volunteer fighters for the Faith in the frontier territories (*ghuzāt*) who previously had been mostly employed against the Turks, attached themselves in increasing numbers to the troops of the soldier state. This latter, however, in order to deal with the destructive effect of internal rivalries between the different parts of the army, was forced into a new war of expansion. Subuktegin's son Maḥmūd—note the Muslim name—exploited the possibilities inherent in the contemporary political system and by a series of large-scale campaigns created an enormous state composed of numerous and highly diverse national groups. It was held together by an army remunerated in cash derived from its considerable booty (not military fiefs) and thus directly dependent on the ruler and always immediately available; aggressively devoted to the

Sunnite form of Islam and to cultural iranization. In 999 the Sāmānids were 'liquidated', in 1009 Sijistān was wrested from the last Ṣaffārids and placed directly under Ghaznavid administration; in the following years the Baluchi in Mukrān were defeated; more important is the agreement with the Turkish Karakhānids, which left them Transoxiana while the lands south of the Amū Daryā (Oxus) including Khwārezm (Khiwa) fell to Maḥmūd. Here he set up a new dynasty.

A Turkish contingent of Oghuz under the leadership of the Seljūq family was settled on the southern bank of the Oxus to defend the country against possible inroads from the Karakhānids. At the same time more and more Būyid territories fell into Maḥmūd's hand; in 1029 Rayy was captured, and soon nothing was left to the Būyid princes but Fārs and Kirmān. Already in 1019 the Caliph had bestowed the title *Yamīn ad-Daula*, 'Right Hand of the Empire', on the Ghaznavid, and consideration was given to a plan to assume the Iraqi sultanate and thus provide the Caliph anew with a Sunnite protector; it never came to fruition.

Of great historical significance were the expeditions to India made between 1001 and the end of Maḥmūd's reign. They carried the Holy War as far as the south of Gujarat and into Kannauj, in the centre of India on the Ganges. In spite of a resistance which at times reached heroic proportions, the Indian princes being disunited among themselves were no match for the Ghaznavid cavalry and archers. Islamic imperialism celebrated one of its greatest triumphs; temple strongholds were stormed, their idols destroyed and their treasure plundered. The religious zeal of the troops shows unmistakable signs of their irreconcilable hatred of the heathen. Maḥmūd certainly laid the foundations for the greatness of Indian Islam, but he is also responsible for the virulent tensions which still exist today between Muslim and Hindu, although after the pacification of the conquered territories he treated those of other faiths correctly and even went so far as to admit Indians into his army. It was only the later rulers who indulged in those unrestrained acts of cruelty which are engraved in the memory of the conquered peoples. The blood-curdling reports in which contemporary and even later writers like Sa'dī (d. 1292) described the storming of the temple city of Sumnath (1026) are founded less on fact than on the general mood of the time.

But while Maḥmūd found it in him to acquiesce in the survival of non-Muslim religious communities he would not tolerate non-Sunnite communities within Islam. The 'Sevener' congregations in the Indus valley were destroyed and the Shī'ites on Iranian soil vigorously combated; when Rayy was conquered the great library of the Būyids was burnt down because of its Shīʿite character. Maḥmūd developed a zeal against sectarianism which other Muslim, particularly Sunnite, rulers only showed against threats of a political nature. He sought support for his autocracy in the principle of *cuius regio eius religio*, comparable to the Byzantine identification of national sentiment and faith, a tendency corresponding to the unqualified adherence of the vast majority to the religious community, rather than the dynasty, let alone the 'nation'.

The new empire offered unusual scope to the historian. Under Maḥmūd the greatest of all Muslim scholars, the Khwārezmian scientist, astronomer, chronologist and man of arts and letters Abū Raiḥān al-Bērūnī (973–1048) wrote his description of India, unrivalled in the whole field of Muslim scholarship. In common with other of his writings it is of unique importance apart from its factual content, because al-Bērūnī subjects his own position and the cultural situation in the Islamic world in general to a critical examination.

Maḥmūd, the most powerful personality among the Muslim rulers of his time, was able to maintain an equilibrium between the Iranian and the Afghano-Indian possessions of his dynasty. At his death the power of the Ghaznavids in Persia began to wane. The chief interest of Maḥmūd's son and successor Masʿūd was in India, and he failed to counter the ambitions of the Seljūqs until too late. Led by the brothers Ṭughril Beg and Chaghri Beg, the Ghuzz, (called 'Turkumān' [Turkoman] by the Arabs) occupied Central Persia and West Khorāsān within a few years and in 1040 at Dandāqān near Merv inflicted a decisive defeat on Masʿūd's army, which he had assembled too late and too hastily to meet them. They drove the Ghaznavids out of Khorāsān and soon became their successors on Persian soil. They made their capital at Iṣfahān and from there pressed unceasingly southwards. Finally in 1055 Ṭughril Beg was able to enter Baghdad, summoned by the Caliph. Shortly afterwards the Seljūqs added North Syria to the Iranian and Iraqi provinces of the traditional caliphate. Though under foreign leadership the eastern caliphal empire was now restored as a state for the first time for three hundred years; it was to endure for nearly sixty. The unity of this state was indeed endangered from the beginning by its extension over heterogeneous territories, and even more by the traditional Turkish form of organization which had already been fatal to the Karakhānids, because they assigned the administration of the empire to the princes under the supreme sovereignty of the head of the family, thus inviting separation and ultimate dissolution.

The Seljūqs were careful administrators and vigorous soldiers, but they would hardly have been so quickly successful had they not placed themselves firmly on the side of the Sunnite doctrine and thus obviated the need hereafter for the Ghaznavids with their Indian preoccupations. Where Subuktegin and his successors had taken Islam eastwards the Seljūqs spread the teaching to the west. In 1029, even before Maḥmūd's death, the Turkomans had turned against the Byzantine Armenians in Holy War. Under Alp Arslan (1063–1072), the second Seljūq ruler in Baghdad, the Turks broke through the Byzantine line of fortifications into eastern Asia Minor. The battle of Manāzkart (Malāzgard, Manzikert) in 1071 opened the way to the turkization of Asia Minor, the larger half of which was included in a *de facto* independent Seljūq state (theoretically a part of the larger Seljūq dominions) controlled first (1077) from Nicaea and after its loss (1097) from Konya (Ikonion). At about the turn of the century the crusader states of Antioch and Edessa isolated it from the central Seljūq territories. Despite the cultural flowering of the Rūm Seljūqs, which did not really reach its climax until later, in the last quarter of the twelfth century and into the period of the Latin Empire in Constantinople, the long-term result of the invasions of the Turkish nomads was the economic decay of Asia Minor, a decline in agriculture and above all in urban culture. The Greeks' loss of power also meant the beginning of inevitable economic and, apart from the capital, cultural decadence in those areas which still remained Christian but which slowly though continuously fell to Islam. The Rūm Seljūqs never seriously tried to annihilate Byzantium; their political ideal seems to have been dualistic: the *dār al-islām* was to be subject to them, but the Christendom of the *dār al-ḥarb* was to remain under the Emperor of Constantinople.

The united Seljūq state flourished for about forty years, and was, practically speaking, confined to Iraq and Persia. Administrative methods were improved, the regime took a lead in consolidating Sunnite Islam, learning was encouraged and for almost thirty years the outstanding personality of the Vizir Niẓām al-Mulk kept a firm hand on affairs, often against the opposition of the Caliph and even of the Seljūq Sultan, whose Atabeg (guardian and educator) he had originally been; but all this was not enough to eliminate the permanent sources of weakness. The economically strongest areas of Islam at the time, the city oases of Central Asia and Egypt, lay outside Seljūq power; the gulf between the ruling Turkish soldiery and the Persian or Arabic-speaking population remained unbridgeable. Indiscipline within the dynasty led to rebellions by the princes who held key positions as generals and governors, not only at every change of monarch but whenever the chances looked favourable. The Persian Niẓām al-Mulk attempted to replace the loose family federation with a centralized absolutism on the Sasanid model; but he came to grief in the central territories because of the political weakness of the civil administration and because of lack of money, and in the outlying Arabic-speaking areas because of the inadequate extent of Seljūq authority, which the local potentates of the most varied origin and legitimacy were constantly flouting. Mesopotamia and Syria were a flickering kaleidoscope of minor powers—city states, Bedouin and soldier princes—in the more or less stable geographical framework of a Seljūq 'Great Kingship', in perpetual feud with each other, with the central power and with the slowly sinking Fāṭimids.

In 1087 Niẓām al-Mulk saw himself forced to recognize the inner logic of the development of *iqṭā'* and to hand over 'military fiefs' tax free to the officers of the army, thereby abandoning himself to the hope that this liberation of the 'fiefholders' would make them treat the rural population more indulgently. He still insisted on a short-term tenancy and only officially granted the *muqṭa'* the right to a certain property value. But with the reliance on feudal contingents it was becoming not unusual for public rights to be usurped and landed property to be acquired which was not withdrawable as a fief. The development of a land-owning military aristocracy, a process favourable to local stability but also to the decomposition of the state, was completed paradoxically under the settled administration of the early Seljūqs. The connection of this development with shortage of money is clear in the similar though much slower process which went on in Egypt. It shows again in reverse in the success of the Mongol Karakhitai, who broke into Transoxiana from the east a generation after Niẓām al-Mulk's death (1092) and managed to maintain the strength of their army after they had finally eliminated the Seljūqs north of the Oxus by checking 'feudalization' with the help of money payments.

The state philosophy of the Seljūq empire was laid down in Niẓām al-Mulk's famous *Siyāsat-Nāma* (Book of Political Conduct) which he wrote shortly before his death. It agrees with the general Muslim concept that 'the empire together with the subjects belongs to the Sultan', hence regards the fief holders only as protectors. This concept was never disputed in theory but was never strong enough to effect this 'paternal despotism' in practice.

The Seljūqs are vividly remembered in the West because of their invasion of Asia Minor and their involvement in the first crusade.

From the Islamic point of view it was more significant that they took over the Sultanate in Baghdad and thus set the political stage for the successful 'reanimation' of Sunnite Islam. Certainly, even without Seljūq hegemony in Iraq the 'Sevener' heterodoxy would no longer have been capable of imperialist expansion; and certainly also it was the crusaders at the end of the eleventh century who drove a wedge between Fāṭimid Egypt and her outposts; even if they did not break it, they made the link more difficult between the Bāṭinite opposition and their Caliph. Even so we must recognize that the Seljūq regime had as its aim the consolidation of the Sunna and worked to this end primarily with intellectual weapons. That on January 1, 1060, the Caliph changed the honorific title of Ṭughril-Beg, Rukn ad-Daula ('Pillar of the Empire') to Rukn ad-Dīn ('Pillar of the Religion') has more than formal significance.

The disintegration of the religion of the law, encouraged not always consciously by the mystical movement that seized both the broad masses and the educated, the differences between the faith of the scholar and the simple believer, the religious malaise consequent on the persistent political and economic crises, the empty monotony of the anti-scholastic, anti-philosophical, in short anti-intellectual Ḥanbalite orthodoxy, all these factors, combined with the resolute strength of Ismā'īlī propaganda, had caused mystical circles to stress the *sharī'a* as an indispensable prerequisite of Sufic enlightenment as early as the late Būyid period, and encouraged the theologians to recognize mystical forms of piety. Yet the transformation came in fact from above. Niẓām al-Mulk stopped the persecution of the Ash'arite 'compromise theology' which approximated to the Mu'tazila in method and to Ḥanbalite orthodoxy in content, freed the capital from the political oppression of the Ḥanbalites and to the best of his ability furthered the study of the *fiqh* with emphasis on his own Shāfi'ite rite.

The Persian Ghazzālī from Ṭūs (1058–1111) was called to the Niẓāmiyya, and though he wrote his exhaustive refutation of the Bāṭiniyya and his encyclopaedic 'Restitution of the Religious Sciences' only after the death of the vizir (who fell victim to the dagger of an assassin in 1092) these works are written in his spirit. The basis of Sunnite Islam was now becoming a synthesis of religious law and a mystical type of intensified experience of God, described and analysed most sensitively by Ghazzālī, having lived it himself through ten years of withdrawal and teaching. It is he too, undeterred by sectarian dispute, who has provided the generous roof that still stands today and shelters both a theological rationalization of the truths of belief and the piety needed by the simple folk. The closing of the ranks in the Muslim Community could only be accomplished by legitimizing popular cult forms, particularly in the matter of Prophet—and saint—worship, and by relinquishing secular learned aspirations.

But the synthesis of Ghazzālī only won through gradually; in 1150 his works were publicly burnt, a not infrequent practice in that century, also performed on the Bāṭinite encyclopaedia of the 'Pure Brothers'. The retreat of scientific thought also took some time to make its mark. Niẓām al-Mulk was patron of the great mathematician and astronomer 'Umar Khayyām (d. 1122), more famous in the West for his quatrains (not all of them authentic). Ghazzālī

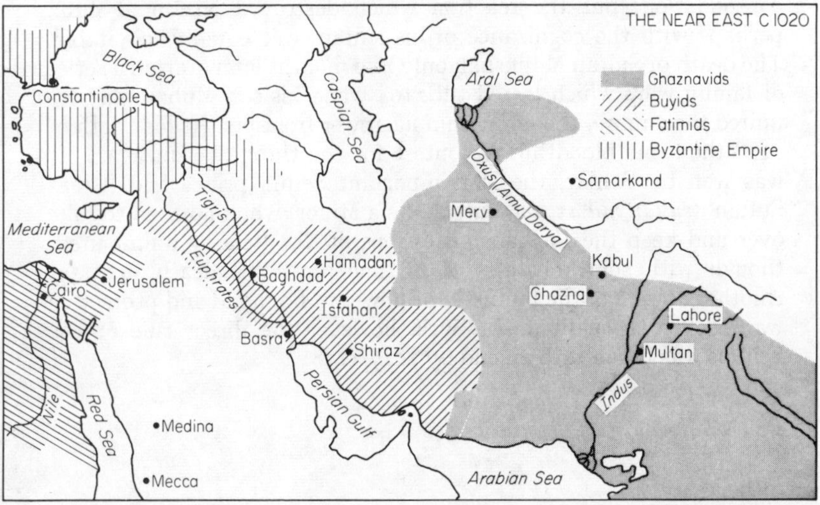

himself was a master of Greek philosophy, which he penetratingly combated in the doctrine of Avicenna. But the age was drawn increasingly towards security and nearness to God, to ecstasy and remorse, it longed to rejoice in human impotence and to enjoy the divine frenzy of the illuminati. At the same time it was intent on order and authority; it thought to meet the indiscipline of political life and the perpetual economic and military insecurity by turning back to the Community, for whose sake and by whose power alone life was to be endured.

In this atmosphere natural science especially was out of place; a perpetually more refined literary art and a grammatology to correspond could however persist. The little scenes in metrical prose (*maqāmāt*) in which Ḥarīrī of Baṣra (d. 1122) emulated a tenth-century model and combined erudite forms with popular motifs were the acme of subtle and elaborate writing. Love poetry was saved by the Sufis; the time of the great preachers and mystical poet-philosophers was drawing near. It should not be forgotten that Ghazzālī was also an outstanding writer. Only in Persia did worldly literature thrive, untouched by political oppression. The great historian of the second Ghaznavid, Baihaqī, died in the Seljūq period (1078); not long afterwards the romantic epic with an original theme took its place beside that based on historical legend.

The persecution of heretics inevitably accompanied religious consolidation; but the reaction which destroyed Niẓām al-Mulk, perhaps with the cognizance of his sultan, was equally inevitable. The death of Sultan Malikshāh only two months later started a series of family wars which lasted till 1104 when his son Muḥammad re-united the empire, though within narrower frontiers. At his death in 1118 the same bloodthirsty contest for the throne began again. It was won by Sanjar, the last important Seljūq prince and 'Great Sultan' (*sulṭān mu'aẓẓam*, outside Asia Minor) who managed to take over and keep the Persian possessions of the dynasty unimpaired, though with some changes of fortune, until his death in 1157. Another branch of the family kept power in Baghdad and protective watch over the caliphs. In Syria however the direct rule of the Seljūqs was brought to an end by 1117/1118.

The Latin States

THE crusades were basically a Latin Christian monologue. Their ideology, and even the political realities and practical motives which played a part in their realization are only to be understood to a very small degree as reactions to Muslim initiative; not until the establishment of the Franks in the Holy Land did there arise a situation like that of the cold war today, in which the mutually hostile momenta of the two sides increasingly affected and evoked each other. But until the end the destiny of the Latin states in the Levant was guided by developments which can be explained solely in terms of the changes of mental climate in the West, though naturally they were influenced by the practical experiences of the crusaders and the counter thrusts of the Muslim princes. Even when demographic or simply general economic considerations seem to us to predominate, it was almost exclusively internal western stimuli that fanned or withdrew interest in the crusades, and not those resulting from the situation in Islam, except in a remote and indirect manner.

Not every fight against the infidel is a crusade. The crusader takes the field in order to bring the Holy Sepulchre under Christian protection, spurred on by the church which guarantees him absolution and promises him heaven if he should die. Pilgrimage and *dilatatio regni Christi et ecclesiae* (the extension of the rule of Christ and of the Church) as the aim and specific spiritual privileges as the reward are the marks of the true crusade. As in the Muslim *jihād* the purpose of the fighting is not forcible conversion. The establishment of Christian rule naturally provides a fitting frame for a subsequent mission. The fundamental change which turned the defensive *bellum iustum* justified by St. Augustine into a religious war of aggression occurs at the turn of the millennium.

Under the impact of the Saracen attacks in Italy and particularly of the destruction of the Church of the Holy Sepulchre by al-Ḥākim, Pope Sergius IV made his first call in 1011 for a 'Battle of the Lord', and even promised to go across the sea himself to Syria. Sergius' encyclical was a failure. The basic features of a crusade do not appear until the struggles of the Normans against the Greeks in Apulia and Calabria and against the Muslim in Sicily; the feudal sovereignty of the Papal see over the island had legitimized the Norman claim to possession two years before they sailed. The Norman kings however allowed their Muslim subjects to keep their ancestral faith. In Sicily as in Syria and in Spain, the third region in which contact with the

Muslim 'heathens' led to religious conflict, it was at first sufficient to restore to the Christians their rightful leading position. This policy applied equally to the non-Latin Christians and to the infidel. It is in fact highly likely that the papacy under Urban II (1088–1099), when preaching the crusade, though of course it envisaged the liberation of the Holy Land as a primary goal, also had in mind to win back oriental Christianity as a long-term aim, which is one more weighty reason for the mistrust with which Byzantium regarded the movement.

In 1063 in Sicily it came to the intervention of St George at the battle of Cerami, so characteristic of the battles of the crusades; in 1064 for the first time large French cavalry contingents joined the Christian Spaniards campaigning against Barbastro 'so that the Christian truths be fulfilled and the infamous delusions of the Saracen be destroyed'. After the victory the Spaniards treated the vanquished far too leniently to please the French; in the incessant disputes among the small Spanish states of both religions political and military alliances were far from always coinciding with the alignment of the faiths. Even the Cid (from the Arabic *qā'id*, leader) Rodrigo Díaz, the Spanish national hero, won much of his fame in the service of Muslim princes and in battle against the Christians. The Catholic princes, particularly after the middle of the eleventh century when the *reconquista* had brought them large gains of territory, were in no way inclined to reap civil war and discord from a radical religious policy. It was only the anti-Christian rigour of the Almoravids towards the end of the eleventh century that stiffened the anti-Islamic position of the Christian rulers.

The crusaders were undoubtedly a possible source of relief from the perpetual threats to the Byzantine empire from the Seljūqs, but the ideology of the church militant, the prospect of armed clerics and not least the spectre of a Europe united under the rule of Christ filled the Greeks with dismay. Anna Comnena, daughter of the Emperor Alexios who had turned to Pope Urban II with a plea for help, saw the crusaders as misguided pilgrims, and their leaders as hypocrites whose true objective was Constantinople. Among the Christian communities of the East only the Armenians and the Maronites of the Lebanon felt an identity of interests in the proximity of the crusader army. The Monophysites of Syria, who were allied to the Muslims in language and culture, mostly remained passive, the Greek Christians were full of mistrust. The West had not assessed the position of the Christians under Muslim rule correctly. Since the advent of the Seljūqs it seems that the pilgrims had been increasingly exposed to what at first had been occasional disagreements, and then the raid of 1064, to be laid at the door not of the government but of the Bedouin, and lastly the difficulties of the Greeks in Asia Minor had given an exaggerated idea of the oppression of the Christians in the Muslim countries. It was in fact precisely in the Fāṭimid territory that a highly acceptable *modus vivendi* had been reached. The Muslims did not see the analogy to their concept of the *jihād* in the idea of the crusade. In Syria and Egypt the *jihād* had ceased for some time to be a living concept; the Rūm-Seljūqs on the other hand did see themselves as fighters for the Faith; India, Central Asia and the south of Morocco were the real lands of the *jihād*. The Franks in Syria were looked upon as helpers of the Byzantines; their arrival awakened no particular surprise. Even when they intruded themselves as autonomous powers in the confusion of small states under Seljūq and Fāṭimid sovereignty there were many princes who considered them first of all as possible and useful allies. The reality of the crusader armies also gave the Muslim princes some justification in overlooking the ideological motives of the newcomers.

The Muslims might indeed be forgiven for mistaking the character of the crusade. From the blood bath of Jerusalem and the cold efficiency with which it took possession after the conquest of the holy city, the crusade hardly facilitated its interpretation as an eschatological undertaking, in its true sense the last war, bringing in the empire of universal peace, the final establishment of the faithful, the eternal awakening into the dream of God, desire become reality, making the one all-embracing dwelling for truth—and in this closely resembling the *jihād*. It would have been easier to recognize the interpenetration of the earthly and heavenly spheres in the collective monologue at the siege of Antioch (1097–1098) when the discovery of the Holy Lance and the intervention of the dragon-killing saint showed clearly how the irrational elements were working in the service of victory. The Augustinian concept of a just and holy war was concretized in the fight against the aggressive Donatists, extended later to the concept of the fight against the heathen and served again, when the spirit of the crusade was beginning to sink, as the justification for combating heretics or even the political opponents of the curia. The *jihād* on the other hand had retained on the whole its original extrovert character; only in the defensive struggle against the Sevener Shīʿa was it brought into intra-islamic conflicts by the orthodox, though the Khārijites, for whom it was the sixth 'pillar' of the Faith, had always so used it. It would be wrong to go so far as to say that the Fāṭimids viewed the Latin troops on their arrival as instruments of an anti-Seljūq *jihād*. But they were undisguisedly pleased to see Antioch fall when a relief army under the Seljūq emir of Mosul was defeated, and they lost no time in exploiting the situation to take over Jerusalem. When the crusaders then turned against Jerusalem they naturally changed their attitude; the newly founded kingdom of Jerusalem had immediately to defend itself against an Egyptian counter-offensive.

At first Jerusalem claimed a certain primacy over the other three Latin states: the duchy of Edessa, an advance post against the Seljūqs of both Asia Minor and Iraq, the princedom of Antioch, which like Edessa was in the first instance more important than Jerusalem, and the duchy of Tripoli, which was a vassal state until the 1170s. The number of Frankish settlers and of Frankish troops, though strengthened by armed pilgrims, native soldiers, known as *Turcopolae*, and a growing number of mercenaries, was always small, too small to ensure the peace of the country. The regular administration and orderly justice practised by the crusader states seem to have won sympathy even from their Muslim subjects, as appears in the much quoted passage from the travels of the Spanish Muslim Ibn Jubair (he visited Syria in 1184/1185). But religious ties proved stronger than political allegiance however readily accepted, and even the native Christians saw no terror in returning to Muslim rule. The similarity in structure and interests (fighting, hunting, horses) of the leading military aristocracy both Christian and Muslim created friendships over and above the relations arising from symbiosis and occasional alliances. But the difference in customs, the sensible cultural superiority of the Muslims except in certain matters of military technique, and the unsettled political situation combined to make the religious difference dominant.

The fragmentation of Muslim power not only opposed the Fāṭimids to the Seljūqs but within Seljūq territory set the Great Sultan against the members of his house, the various princes against their Atabegs and the smaller district governors against each other and often against the other local powers, the Bedouin leagues or the larger towns. The endless see-saw of constant petty warfare with its mistrust and hatreds gave the crusaders the chance to occupy the coastal territories and keep them open for replacements of men and supplies. The seven crusades between 1096 and 1270 which have been singled out and separately numbered by the history books are of special importance mainly in the light of intra-European and European–Byzantine relations. The self-assertion of the Latin states can only be understood against the background of an incessant thin stream of immigration throughout the twelfth century, and the lively traffic with Italy and France which guaranteed the supply of arms, almost entirely the monopoly of Italian shipping. The arrival of pilgrims and the call of a fleet, the Pisan or the Genoan it might be, created the opportunity for the short and sharp campaigns which achieved such important conquests as Beirut and Sidon (1110).

The fragmentation of Islamic Syria and Mesopotamia was not only the result of the unruliness of the Turkish soldiery; it reflects the conflicts of interest of the large Syrian cities and the Jazīra, and also the self-sufficiency and self-consciousness of the inhabitants of such cities as Damascus and Aleppo. Even though they had Turkish masters, who could be very trying, they were more 'themselves' than standardized components of a large state. This accounts for the support which these often mutually destructive dynasties generally found among the Arab-speaking population in spite of their foreign origins. Seen from the overall Muslim point of view the crusaders were no real threat, particularly as they neglected to consolidate their possessions geographically and strategically. For this purpose the Franks would have had to reach the Jordan valley and dominate the road from Damascus through Ḥomṣ to Aleppo, or at least be able to block it at will. They made no serious attempt to do this. Aleppo and Damascus were attacked several times, but always without success, and communications between the Muslim centres were never interrupted. The duchy of Edessa was exposed on all sides, not least because of the ever precarious relations with Byzantium, and Antioch which protected Edessa to the east was not much better situated. On the Muslim side the possession of strong towns or fortresses guaranteed the power of the ruler over the countryside of the plains, which was incapable of protecting itself against razzias large or small. The survival of the Latin princedoms also depended on the maintenance of walled (harbour) towns, and fortresses inland.

The adventure of the crusader states, so full of consequences, at least for the West, lasted for almost two hundred years with an astonishingly small population. The duchy of Edessa and somewhat later the kingdom of Jerusalem could muster about seven hundred horsemen. No campaign is known in which more than fifteen thousand soldiers participated; as a rule the armies consisted of hardly a fifth of this number, and the Muslim armies also remained at about this size, although of course the reserves at their disposal far outnumbered those of the crusaders.

The fight against the Franks can hardly be termed a war of religion, though of course the continuous friction with the Christians led to a renewal of religious feeling and its translation into political terms resulted ultimately in a hardening of Sunnite orthodoxy, without which the various states would never have managed to combine into a unity independent of the Seljūqs. The presence of the

Franks acted as a catalyst; the Zengids and later the Ayyūbids exploited this circumstance and thereby won a clear advantage over their rivals and at least the passive support of the population. Thanks to the piety of the Zengids their Muslim opponents lost the sympathy of their subjects, especially when they sought to protect themselves by an alliance with the Christians. But during the rise and floruit of the Latins it was impossible to avoid such treaties, for the Latins held in their power such strategic places as the Ḥaurān (in present-day Jordan) and the Biqā', which areas provided Damascus with corn. The decline of the Būrids (1120–1154) in Damascus was clearly the result of their enforced and inevitable alliance with the Christians.

It has often been maintained and frequently disputed that the existence of the crusader states aggravated the hostility of Muslims and Christians. Certainly after the restitution of a unified Muslim state in Egypt, Syria and Northern Mesopotamia the Christians were treated more after the letter of the *sharī'a*, and soon were excluded entirely from public life. It may be true that the way the Christian churches associated with the anti-Muslim Mongols finally hardened the Muslim majority into its antipathy and contempt for the religious enclaves of the 'People of the Book' (*ahl al-kitāb*); but there were signs of this development before the Mongol period. The unusual liberality of the Fāṭimid period was turned to neutrality by the new Sunnite orthodoxy of the Ayyūbids and their successors, and ultimately disappeared completely.

Latin expansion suffered a temporary setback after the failure of the grandiose siege of Tyre in 1112. The town was not conquered until 1124; the important Egyptian port of Ascalon stood out until 1153. Only a few years before this the Muslims had achieved their first concerted resistance, significantly issuing not from Syria which was most closely affected, but from Seljūq Mosul. The harassed emir of Tripoli had already turned to the Great Sultan in Baghdad for help in 1108 and again after the fall of the city in 1109; it is curious that this Shī'ite notable did not rather look upon the Fāṭimid caliph as the protector of Islam's interests. With the consent of his brother the Great Sultan in Baghdad, Maudūd organized a Holy War and sought immediately an alliance with the previous Seljūq emir Ṭughtakin Būrī, who had made himself independent in Damascus. His murder in 1113 interrupted this development, but the Mesopotamian emirs cherished the spirit of the *reconquista* as his legacy. The next fifteen years were devoted to the struggle for Aleppo, for the time being tributary to the crusaders, and claimed both by the Mesopotamians and Damascus. The removal of Armenian lords from the area round Edessa, the crystallization of a 'Little Armenia' in Cilicia and the first land attack on Egypt in 1118—also the last campaign of King Baldwin I, the brother of Godfrey of Bouillon and the real founder of Latin power in southern Syria and Palestine —fall into this transitional period, which ended with the transference of the emirate of Mosul to 'Imād ad-Dīn Zengī in 1127.

His father Aq Sunqur had ruled Aleppo from 1084 to 1094 as the deputy of Malikshāh; he himself had been prominent in the *jihād* since his youth and had made a name in the provincial government of Maudūd and his Bursūqid successors in Mosul, and later in the service of the Seljūq central government as governor of Iraq and of Baghdad; Syria did not belong to 'Imād ad-Dīn's sphere of administration. Arab historians, looking back from the conquest of Edessa, have seen 'Imād ad-Dīn as the great fighter for the Faith. This he was, but only in the sense that he achieved the unification of Muslim Syria and Mesopotamia, without which all attempts against the Franks were fruitless, by every means within his reach and unburdened by any scruples. Apart from the campaign against Edessa in 1144 'Imād ad-Dīn had only twice seriously taken arms against the Latins, and this merely in a somewhat episodic manner. His first and decisive success was the dethronement of the Muslim dynasts of Aleppo (1128). In Jerusalem in the thirties a more detached policy had been adopted towards the northern princedoms. The second generation was at the helm; they did not feel immediately threatened by their encirclement, were orientalized in externals and were somewhat estranged from their western fellow-believers when these came to the rescue after the shock of the loss of Edessa in 1147. This second crusade, in which two kings participated, was started with the aim of winning back Edessa, whose fall not only exposed Antioch but because of the now unhindered communications with Mesopotamia, gave Aleppo the freedom of movement to threaten Damascus, the bastion to whose independence Jerusalem owed her prosperity. But the crusaders capitulated to the lure of a march on Damascus and when it misfired the unbeaten army decided to return home. This second genuine upsurge of enthusiasm in Christian Europe ended in disillusion and mutual recrimination. 'Imād ad-Dīn had been murdered before the arrival of the crusading army and his possessions divided between two of his sons (1146) who lived in Aleppo and Mosul. Nūr ad-Dīn, the younger brother, finding little hindrance because of Jerusalem's passivity, occupied Damascus in 1154; the kingdom was now confronted on north and east by a unified Muslim power. It is characteristic of the loose structure of the state at that time that Nūr ad-Dīn had to let almost a decade go by before his realm was sufficiently organised to allow him to make a decisive advance against the Franks.

Consolidation in his case was not only a matter of suppressing the Christian enclaves and subduing the recalcitrant officers; it was primarily the elimination of Shīʿite influence; in part by force, in part by the impact of new centres of teaching (*madrasa*) on the Seljūq model—Nūr ad-Dīn himself lies buried in one of the colleges which he founded in Damascus. Sufism helped to strengthen popular piety in the same way as it had done in Seljūq Asia Minor; it spread widely, often under the direction of Persian devotees. The radical Shīʿa of the Assassins survived even under the pressure of Ṣalāḥ ad-Dīn, and Rashīd ad-Dīn Sinān, the 'Old Man of the Mountain', remained until his death in 1193 a power to be reckoned with in Syria, deriving his strength from a double game against the Sunnites and the Latins. Not until 1273 did Baibars, the subduer of the Mongols, break their fortresses and destroy their independence.

To modern eyes it may seem hard to understand how the Jazīra, Syria and Palestine were able to enjoy a not inconsiderable prosperity in a time of never-ceasing petty warfare, when the governments of large and small areas alike were forever changing hands and the open land was all too often laid waste, when the Christian and Muslim rulers were constantly at variance and the Muslim towns were rent by civil wars; Baghdad indeed declined economically. Ibn Jubair speaks of the arrogance of her citizens, which stood in sorry contrast to the desolation of large parts of the inner city. Mosul on the other hand was an industrial centre which kept in contact with the upsurge in European trade through Aleppo and Damascus. The coastal cities, in which the Italian merchants enjoyed considerable privileges in return for transport services, became the depots for an important wealth of trade, in which Egypt also participated. In the larger cities there generally grew up small 'quarters' of foreign merchants, comparable to the *mitata* in Constantinople; counterparts, perhaps, of the Syrian colonies which had carried trade to Italy and what is now France at the end of Graeco Roman antiquity.

The Fāṭimid state was no longer able to use its wealth effectively in face of internal dissolution. Ismāʿīlism had no roots in the country, the renaissance stimulated by the Armenian vizirs collapsed when al-Afḍal was murdered (1121); in this the Assassins surely had a hand, or the Caliph al-Āmir (1101–1130) who was their minion. Nine years later the Caliph himself fell victim to an assault by the Nizārī. Palace intrigues, street fighting, confiscations of Christian property, rise and assassination of dignitaries in rapid succession, attacks on Franks performed without enthusiasm and fruitless alliances with

Nūr ad-Dīn, and after 1155 the rule of child caliphs in addition; the Fāṭimid government owed its respite solely to the fact that the Latin states were there between Nūr ad-Dīn and Egypt, and the union of the Sunnite forces was not yet completed.

In 1163 King Amalric (d. 1174) of Jerusalem intervened in the internal politics of Egypt, in order to use the riches of that land to strengthen his own kingdom. His plans foundered, but on the advice of his Kurdish Emir Shīrkūh, Nūr ad-Dīn was persuaded to send troops to Egypt in the following year on the invitation of an Egyptian emir who had fled to him. Like Amalric, Nūr ad-Dīn felt unable to dispense with the resources of Egypt for his final victory; the Egyptian fleet would allow him to cut off the sea links of the Franks and bring most of the European trade under his control. His expedition was successful, but the Syrians were slow to leave the country and the Egyptian emir called Amalric back. The performance of entry and departure was repeated once more. In 1168 Amalric made himself king of Egypt by occupying Cairo. The Fāṭimids now took it upon themselves to call in Nūr ad-Dīn. As Shīrkūh approached, Amalric avoided a battle and the Syrians entered Cairo on January 8, 1169. The fame of his nephew Ṣalāḥ ad-Dīn, known to the West as Saladin, has overshadowed that of Shīrkūh—who died two months after the conquest; the foundation of the Ayyūbid empire (named after Saladin's father) was however to a large extent his work although it was Saladin two years later who formally put an end to the Fāṭimid dynasty; and it was at his behest that for the first time for two hundred years the Friday prayer was offered up again in the name of the 'Abbāsid caliph in Baghdad. Having taken power in Egypt Saladin became dangerous to his overlords. Diplomatic skill and favourable circumstances, not least the early death of Nūr ad-Dīn in 1174, prevented a resort to arms.

The dependence of the ruler on his high officers was something that not even a Saladin could avoid. Just because the social and to some extent the political stratification of society was little affected by the person of the ruler the unity of the state had always to be re-won by fighting. In spite of his skill as a statesman and the resources of Egypt Saladin needed a strenuous ten years before he had a firm grasp of the territories that had been administered by Nūr ad-Dīn. The recognition by the Caliph (1175) of his sultanate over Egypt (with Nubia and Cyrenaica), the Yemen, Palestine and Syria only confirmed established facts, but it strengthened his moral position and formally legitimized the mission to which Saladin felt himself called: the annihilation of the Latin states and the reconquest of Jerusalem by the champion of the true Faith.

Saladin was wise enough to wait until Damascus, Aleppo and Mosul were united under his control, so that the mutually hostile Latin princes could be deprived of their power with a few heavy blows. Numerically inferior to the Muslims, with weak and inconsistent leadership, inextricably bound up in dynastic feuds and fully conscious of the weakness of their position, the crusaders rallied once more under King Guy de Lusignan for a final great military effort. A strategic error, due at least in part to the suspicious tension between king and knightly orders on the one side and the smaller princes on the other, led on July 4, 1187 to their crushing defeat at Ḥaṭṭīn, above the Lake of Genezareth, causing the Latins the loss of their last army of any strength and laying the way open before Saladin for widespread territorial gains and the occupation of Jerusalem on October 2, 1187. Tyre was saved for the crusaders only by the exhaustion of the Muslim army and the unwillingness of its generals to flout custom and extend the campaign into the winter. The duchy of Tripoli escaped virtually unscathed from the catastrophe, a strange example of the limited dimensions of even the most grandiose politico-military operations at that time. The fall of Jerusalem set Europe in agitation. From 1189 until 1192 English, French and German troops were quartered in the Holy Land. The re-conquest of Acre after almost two years of siege and the fortification of the coastal strip from Tyre to Jaffa was the thin reward of this last great military effort of the West.

A few months after the conclusion of an armistice between Saladin and Richard Cœur de Lion whose chivalric fantasies bear a good proportion of the blame for the lack of success of the third crusade, Saladin died, at only 55 years of age, in March 1193. Again it took some time for his brother to gain control, under the title al-Malik al-ʿĀdil, of the empire which Saladin had shared between his three sons. The 'world status' of the Ayyūbid state within the *dār al-islām* remained unaffected by these family quarrels however. In 1173 Saladin had sent his brother Tūrānshāh to the Yemen, and his successors were able to assert themselves in the greater part of the country until 1228; the 'protectorate' over the holy cities of Mecca and Medina was also preserved for the Egyptians. At this time an Ayyūbid emir pressed forward as far as Tripoli (in Libya), evidently with the intention of creating a more extended coastal base for the planned enlargement of the Egyptian fleet, with easier access to building material and a seafaring population. Although the religious fronts were hardening there were already signs of that exhaustion in the West which was occasioning a cooling of interest in the crusades. With an eye to the European trade and the offensive potential of the western powers, the Ayyūbids several times consented to treaties favourable to the Latins; the most famous is the ten-year peace between al-Malik al-Kāmil (1218–1238) and the (excommunicated) Frederick II, which restored Jerusalem and Nazareth to the Christians (1229); an agreement between two sophisticated politicians which caused a scandal among both religions.

The military activities of the crusaders were now concentrated on Egypt. Damietta was besieged and taken three times in one generation (1217, 1221, 1249–50), and twice a crusader endured crushing defeat while attempting to advance from Damietta to Cairo. The fall of Constantinople in 1204 and a certain disillusionment among the Europeans about the Latins in Syria reduced the influx of armed pilgrims more and more throughout the thirteenth century. Neither the personal idealism of St Louis nor the missionary preaching of St Francis of Assisi in Egypt (1219) could do anything to improve the increasingly precarious position of the crusaders. Once Jerusalem was lost, Acre, Tripoli and the Templar castles stood out like erratic boulders in the flood of the Mongol period. A horde of Khwārezmian mercenaries, driven along by the Mongol storm, was engaged by the Ayyūbid sultan and seized the city from the Christians for the last time in 1244.

Divisions in the Islamic World

The Almoravids in the West

THE rise and fall of the Seljūq empire more or less brought an end to the political interactions between the Muslim states centred on the Mediterranean and those oriented towards Central Asia and India. The Ghaznavids only kept independent from the Seljūqs in India; their possessions on the western side of the Hindukush fell to the Ghūrids, natives of the Afghan mountains, who in 1150 razed the 'western capital' of Ghaznīn (Ghazna) to the ground. Attacks by the Ghuzz and a last flare-up of Seljūq power under Sanjar only postponed the complete take-over of Afghanistan by this Sunnite dynasty. The Ghūrids came from the region round Herāt; by 1178 they were strong enough to attack India and occupy Peshawar; in 1182 they reached the coast of Sindh and in 1186 they took Lahore, the eastern capital of the Ghaznavids. In 1192 the defeat of the Hindu prince Pritthvī opened the way to Delhi, and it was taken in the following year by Aibak, the Turkish slave of the Ghūrid Mu'izz ad-Dīn. Ghūrid rule soon spread in the south as far as Gujarat, in the east as far as Bengal. The autonomy of these 'slave rulers' a few years later begins a new epoch in the history of Muslim India; though it falls chronologically into our period its historical implications lie outside it.

Repeating the history of the Ghaznavids, the Ghūrids lost their position in Iran and Afghanistan as soon as they were established in India. The Khwārezmshāhs, spreading out from the far west of the central Asiatic plain at the turn of the century, overcame the Ghūrid state, hampered by its remoteness from the economic centres, in two great campaigns, pushing forward in the typical fashion of a new loosely articulated great power supported by Turkish soldiers. It shared with its predecessors the weakness of having to spread for reasons of survival beyond the area which it ruled directly. In the fluctuating semi-nomad states every enduring centre of power might become overnight the initiator of a population movement which in its first impetus would be irresistible; within the territory contained by the Aral Lake, the Oxus and Jaxartes system, the Pamir mountains and the mountains of south-west Persia the only way to maintain political hegemony was by neutralization, which is to say by elimination of every possible rival. The predominantly Nestorian Karakhitai had ruled Transoxiana from about 1140; by deflecting every new horde of Turks southwards they contributed to the disorganization, particularly of eastern Iran. Their victory over the Seljūq Sanjar probably gave rise to the saga of Prester John.

Khwārezm was spared, protected by its geographical position far from the main attack routes into Iran, and ruled since Maḥmūd by a competent military government installed by whichever dynasty was dominant at the time. Its strength came from the increasing weakness of the Seljūqs. The victory of the Khwārezmian Shāh Tukush over the last Persian Seljūq (1194) made Khwārezm the strongest power in Iran. His successor 'Alā' ad-Dīn Muḥammad (1199–1220) during his reign of barely twenty years saw both the apex of the prosperity of the empire and its downfall. He drove the Ghūrids out of Khorāsān and seized the key towns of Transoxiana, Bukhārā and Samarkand. In 1210 he defeated the Karakhitai to whom he had been till then paying tribute, conquered Ghazna in 1214 and achieved (nominal) recognition even in far off 'Umān. Failing to secure investiture from the Caliph, he made preparations in 1217 for a great campaign to overthrow Iraq. As a first step he had the 'Abbāsid deposed by a meeting of religious scholars, possibly he also approached the Shī'a, which was not without influence even in Baghdad. An unusually cold winter frustrated his plan, and he was prevented from resuming it by the necessity of fighting the Mongols.

These troubles left Iraq and the Mesopotamian forelands untouched, and they only affected Seljūq Asia Minor in so far as new Turkish immigrants were for ever being driven westwards and helping to accelerate the de-hellenization of the country. The battle of Dorylaeum (1097) pushed the Seljūqs back eastwards; we have already alluded to the fact that Ikonion replaced Nicaea as the capital of a state organized by Iranian officials; it became a culture-conscious great power when the political units surrounding it broke up. It joined in the trade with Russia and Egypt, revived the towns which had been destroyed by the nomad Turkomans during the frontier wars and asserted itself politically *vis-à-vis* both Byzantium and the Syro-Mesopotamian princedoms. Unlike the Arabic-speaking countries where the Turkish immigrant rulers never managed to assimilate, they became naturalized in Asia Minor and enriched both the architecture and the literature of Islam by adopting its Persian form of expression as their own. The nomads and the hordes of Turkomans who were incessantly streaming out of Central Asia into this relatively secure Seljūq state were excluded from this advanced culture, turned to heterodox teachings and at times took arms against the government of the sedentary residents. Although they were put to rout, the discontented nomads were a constant burden on the empire of Ikonion. By 1243 its emaciated body was an easy prey for the Mongols, who let it continue as a kind of protectorate, but filled it with garrisons and provided the ruler with a 'High Commissioner' (*parwāna*).

The destiny of the Mediterranean lands unfolded in complete isolation from this chain of events. While the crusades had barely roused the faintest echo from Iraq and further eastwards and Saladin had found it impossible in 1189 to mobilize a North African relief fleet against the Latins, the Muslim West itself remained completely on its own politically, even within the Mediterranean zone. This isolation went hand in hand with cultural separation. The influence of the intellectual and artistic blossoming of Andalusia—coincidental with its political decline—hardly reached beyond North Africa, except perhaps for the monistic mysticism of Ibn 'Arabī (1165–1240) and the popularity of Andalusian strophic verse in the late twelfth century, a period generally open to the folk element in painting as in piety.

The break of the Zīrids with the Fāṭimids and the consequent immigration of Arab Bedouins introduced a development whose offshoots are still to be seen today. The economic decline of the Zīrid empire entailed political decline as well and led to the abandonment of Qairawān as a centre of power and culture; Tunis under a petty dynast, and Mahdiyya (Tunisia) under the last Zīrids were no longer able to maintain the Muslim supremacy in the Mediterranean, threatened by the rise of the Christian West. A direct consequence of the Zīrid catastrophe was that the North African Muslims made no vigorous efforts to save Sicily from Norman invasion. The Zīrids had earlier been concerned with the construction of a fleet but they had little good fortune at sea. When the Sicilian Muslims asked for help against Roger I in 1052, the relief fleet was wrecked off Pantelleria, thereby giving the Normans a free hand and furthermore reducing the Zīrid defence against the Bedouins at home. The landing in Sicily in 1068 promised better success, but it had to be interrupted when the Zīrids' black guards fell out with the Sicilian population they were called upon to defend. In place of naval warfare organized piracy began.

As a countermeasure the Italian maritime cities stormed and plundered Mahdiyya in 1087, though this had no serious effect on the situation. The Normans themselves had already concluded an agreement with the Zīrids in 1075 which according to circumstances took on the aspect of a trade treaty, an alliance or a constricting mandate. New petty states along the South Tunisian coast gave plenty of reasons for disputes and intervention. The crumbling of city culture in the Tunisian hinterland, the main area of support for Zīrid rule, had for some time been leading to the shift of the centre of Berber Muslim power westwards onto the Ḥammādids in their fortress of Qal'at Banī Ḥammād. When this position too became untenable because of the spread of the Arab nomads the Ḥammādids moved their capital even further westwards, finding a solid base in Bougie (Bijāya) with its hinterland of wooded mountains favourable to shipbuilding. And there the last Zīrid retreated when Roger II appeared before Mahdiyya with a fleet that to the Muslim prince seemed irresistible. The most important coastal towns of Tunisia (except for Tunis itself) paid tribute to Roger, who adopted the title of a king of Ifrīqiya. Native historians later celebrated the mildness and justice of his rule. It lasted for only eleven years, then the Almohads put an end to it.

The Arab immigrants were instrumental in undermining the power of the Berber dynasties of eastern North Africa and weakening the Arab city culture which flourished under their protection; they themselves however did no more than found a few petty princedoms and were content to lead one might say an unhistorical existence. It was the invitation or pressure of the opportunist Berber princes which made them gradually advance as far as central Morocco; they doubtless brought about the first (partial) Arabization of western North Africa, but they played little part in the great political syntheses of the following period. The most powerful epoch of the Maghreb was the work of Berbers who from two different, though both 'national' concepts of Islam, drew the strength to break through their demographic and cultural boundaries.

In 1035 some chieftains of the Lamtūna—the great league of tribes of camel nomads belonging to the Ṣanhāja, who camped in the western Sahara—went on a pilgrimage to Qairawān. They were shocked by the discrepancy between Muslim teaching and their native customs and applied for a missionary to be sent to them. It was difficult to find a scholar who was ready to go and share the life of the Lamtūna—an indication of the cultural gap. The rigorous Mālikite 'Alī ibn Yāsīn at last accepted the task, but he met with sharp opposition when he demanded the abandonment of unlimited polygamy, and required almsgiving and strict performance of prayer. The crisis was solved when Ibn Yāsīn and his close confidant Yaḥyà ibn 'Umar went off to the south with a small band of chieftains and founded a *ribāṭ*, a stronghold of potential fighters for the Faith, on an island in the Lower Senegal—the name of the river is derived from that of the Ṣanhāja—on the frontiers of the *dār al-islām*. The idea caught on, and it was not long before a considerable number of sympathizers joined the *ribāṭ*. The religious law was preached and administered uncompromisingly. The *sharī'a* of the *murābiṭūn*, those living in the *ribāṭ*, formed a closed unit. Reference to the Koran and the Sunna was superfluous, even suspect, discipline was rigid, submission to the teacher unquestioning. To be admitted the candidate had to endure a hundred lashes in order to be absolved of sins committed. Lateness at prayers was punished with five lashes, murder with death, other serious crimes entailed excommunication. Berber Islam, now taken seriously, became aggressive. The fulfillment of life in the *ribāṭ* was the Holy War, first undertaken against the pagan Negroes, but soon against those Berbers who lacked the true Faith. War leadership was taken on by a general who remained subordinate to the 'spiritual' authority of Ibn Yāsīn.

The northward *jihād* began in 1056; in 1059 Ibn Yāsīn fell in battle against the Barghawāṭa. Yaḥyà ibn 'Umar had already preceded him in death; the cousin of his successor Abū Bakr, Yūsuf ibn Tāshfīn, took over the command in the fight for Morocco in 1061, while Abū Bakr remained in the Sahara; he was, as almost always in such cases in Islam, the first and the greatest representative of his dynasty, the Almoravids. Spiritual leadership fell after the death of Ibn Yāsīn to Sulaimān ibn Ḥaddū, of whom nothing further is known, except that he soon found his death in the fight against the heretics and his succession was transferred to the legal scholars as a whole. The *fuqahā'* of the Mālikite *madhhab* ('rite', law school) were given a legal status in the government, which summoned and paid them for advice. They had no executive power, but their verdicts on religious law (*fatwà*) defined the rights and duties of the faithful and in difficult and dubious situations they gave religious legitimation to the decisions of the prince. The influence of the *fuqahā'* grew with the consolidation of the empire. Although they were independent of the government it can be seen again and again from their attitude that it was not the dynasty or the state but the Muslim Community which was the highest unit, and by whose interests they were guided.

In 1062 Yūsuf founded Marrākesh, the 'southern capital' of Morocco until our own time. The petty princes were quickly set aside one by one and the Shī'ite nest in Tārūdānt exterminated. Wherever the Almoravids came 'illegal' taxes were abolished, wine poured away and musical instruments destroyed. Yet it would be wrong to think that islamization affected every sphere of life of the Lamtūna, now the thin upper stratum of a growing empire. Polygamy was restricted to the measure permitted by the *sharī'a*, but woman, who remained unveiled, retained her traditional influence. Almoravid princesses appear more than once in politics; and the dark coloured *lithām* which is still customary among their distant relations, the Tuareg, today, the cloth which veils the lower half of the men's faces, remained until the end of the dynasty as a sign of aristocracy, only allowed to the Lamtūna.

Yūsuf subjugated the whole of Morocco, though the Barghawāṭa stood out, but Fez fell to him definitively in 1069 and in 1082 he reached modern Algiers and built himself a united dominion which stretched eastwards as far as the Ṣanhāja, in Lesser Kabylia, to whom he was related. While Yūsuf shifted his centre of gravity northwards, Ibn 'Umar continued fighting against the Negroes, and in more than fifteen years of campaigning destroyed the 'golden' kingdom of Ghāna (not identical in extent with the new republic of this name); in 1086 Ibn 'Umar lost his life in the *jihād*. At the same time Kānem was islamized; it developed in the thirteenth century into an extensive empire embracing Bornu which carried on trade relations with Tunis, a lasting gain to the Muslim *umma*.

Meanwhile the Christian *reconquista* had been making progress not only in Sicily but in Spain, where its success was not without effect on the disunion of the Andalusian Muslims. The disintegration of the Umayyad caliphate brought about a flowering of cultural life in the same way as the disintegration of the 'Abbāsid empire had done in the East. The small princely courts encouraged the poets to the best of their ability; their presence signified prestige and also provided entertainment; moreover they were useful propagandists. The brilliance of a refined way of life, a disposition for enjoyment which lightheartedly exceeded all the bounds set by religious law, a finely wrought delicacy of behaviour which lent an appearance of frivolity to the outbreak of passions often all too brutal, a stylish extravagance that became less easy to justify with every year that passed when independence was only to be maintained by tribute and recruitment of mercenaries, this frenzy of sensibility drew its bitter charm from the awareness of the approaching end. The poet-king Mu'tamid of Seville (1069–1090) captured the spirit of his age in one line: 'Fling yourself into life as onto a quarry, it lasts no more than a day.'

As in the Italian Renaissance, education, sensitivity to the arts, self-analysis (conducted in a manner unexcelled in the *dār al-islām* in reference to the emotions of love by Ibn Ḥazm in his 'Neckband of the Dove'), a feeling for style and *recherché* courtesy all go together with relentless intrigue and perfidious cruelty. The ruler not only puts his enemy in chains—and when overthrown is himself thrown in chains—he will kill traitors with his own hand in violent anger; even Saladin struck down Reginald de Châtillon when he was taken prisoner at Ḥaṭṭīn, to redeem an oath. The kaleidoscope of small states is also reminiscent of the quattrocento, and the multiplicity of forms assumed by social life, and the fictitious nature of power, which crumbled at the first assault. But what distinguishes the period of the *reyes de taifas*, the kings of the petty states, from the Renaissance is the shallowness of the intellectual movement, which is not concerned with redefining the human image or the liberating mastery of philosophical, artistic and technological problems, but simply with the exhaustive refinement of tradition, though this tradition does become ever more unrecognizable in its 'Andalusian' guise, and clearly distinct from the oriental Arab legacy. Crystallization of the national popular spirit in the *zajal*, a strophic verse composed in a language approximating to the Arabic spoken in Spain, was first completely achieved in the Almoravid period, to which belonged the celebrated poets Ibn 'Abdūn and Ibn Zaidūn (both d. 1134), and the most famous of all 'strophic' poets, Ibn Quzmān (*c.* 1087–1160) who wrote both in the language of the court and in that of the people. The famous 'Elegy for Valencia' was written by the learned mathematician and philosopher al-Waqqāshī early in 1094 when the city was about to surrender to the Cid, and here already is a remarkable example of this genre, similar to, and perhaps prefiguring, the later Spanish *romance*. The influence of the form extended to the Hebrew of the Spanish Jews; the liking for (stylized) realism allows the Romance popular idiom to be introduced into the *kharja*, the final rhyming couplet of each verse. Formal similarities in the complicated strophic structure reveal an even stronger Spanish–Arab influence on troubadour poetry than just parallels of material, mood and apparatus.

It is impossible to exaggerate the colour and variety of Muslim Spain in the ninth and tenth centuries. The opposition between Berbers, 'Slavs' and 'original inhabitants' (*baladī*) which destroyed the caliphate of Córdoba was mirrored in the states which succeeded it and in the tensions between them which condemned them all to impotence. The most important Berber states were the petty kingdoms of Granada and Málaga (annexed by Granada in 1057). An *Apologia pro Vita Sua* written by the last Granadan Zīrid after his deposition by the Almoravids gives an unequalled insight into the problems facing these princes, hemmed in by an increasingly powerful Christendom, threatened by party rivalries as much as by the

13 The Giralda. Minaret of the Almohad mosque in Seville, now the bell tower of the cathedral, 1170–1180. *Foto Jeiter*

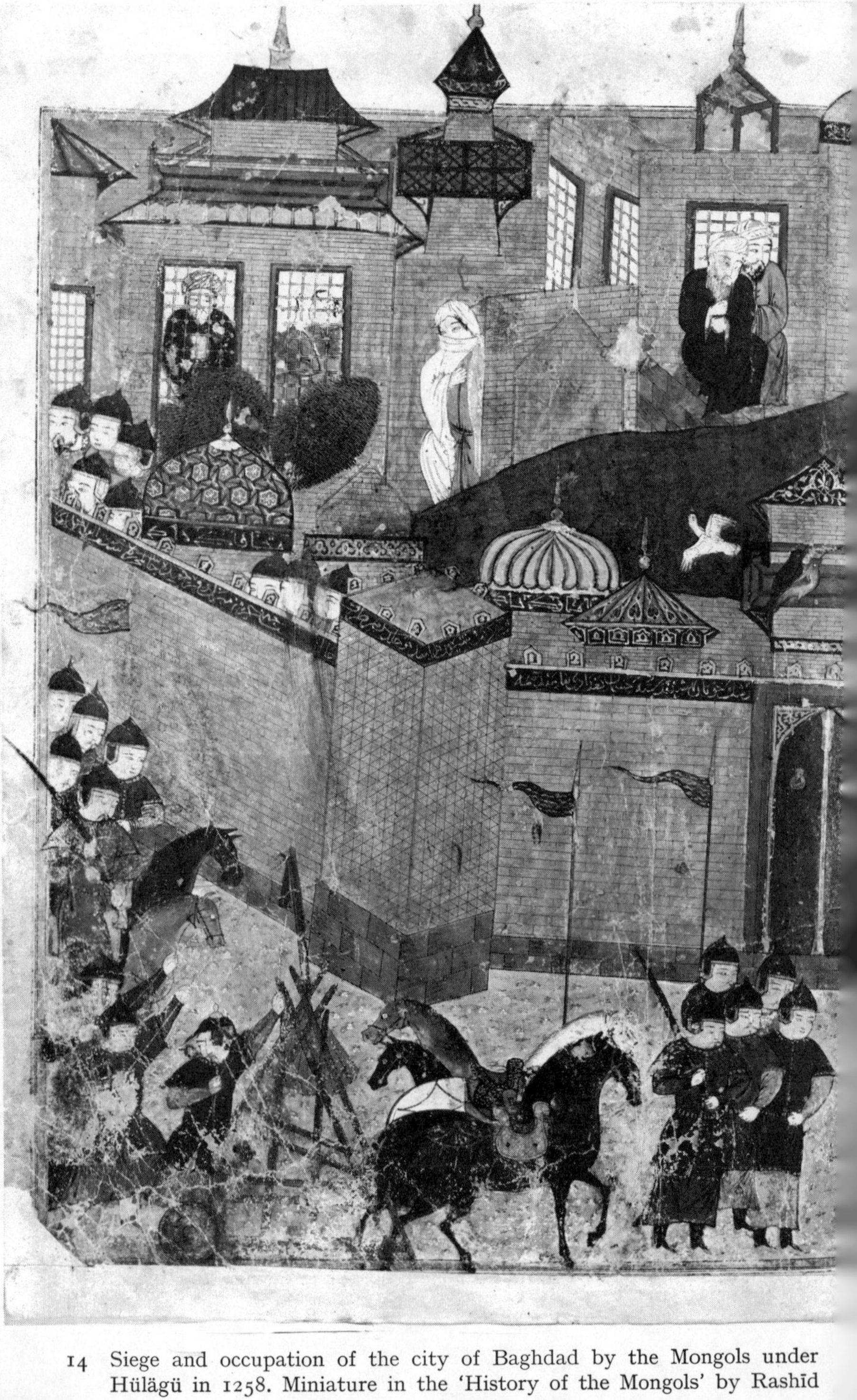

14 Siege and occupation of the city of Baghdad by the Mongols under Hülägü in 1258. Miniature in the 'History of the Mongols' by Rashīd

Photo Bibliothèque Nationale, Paris

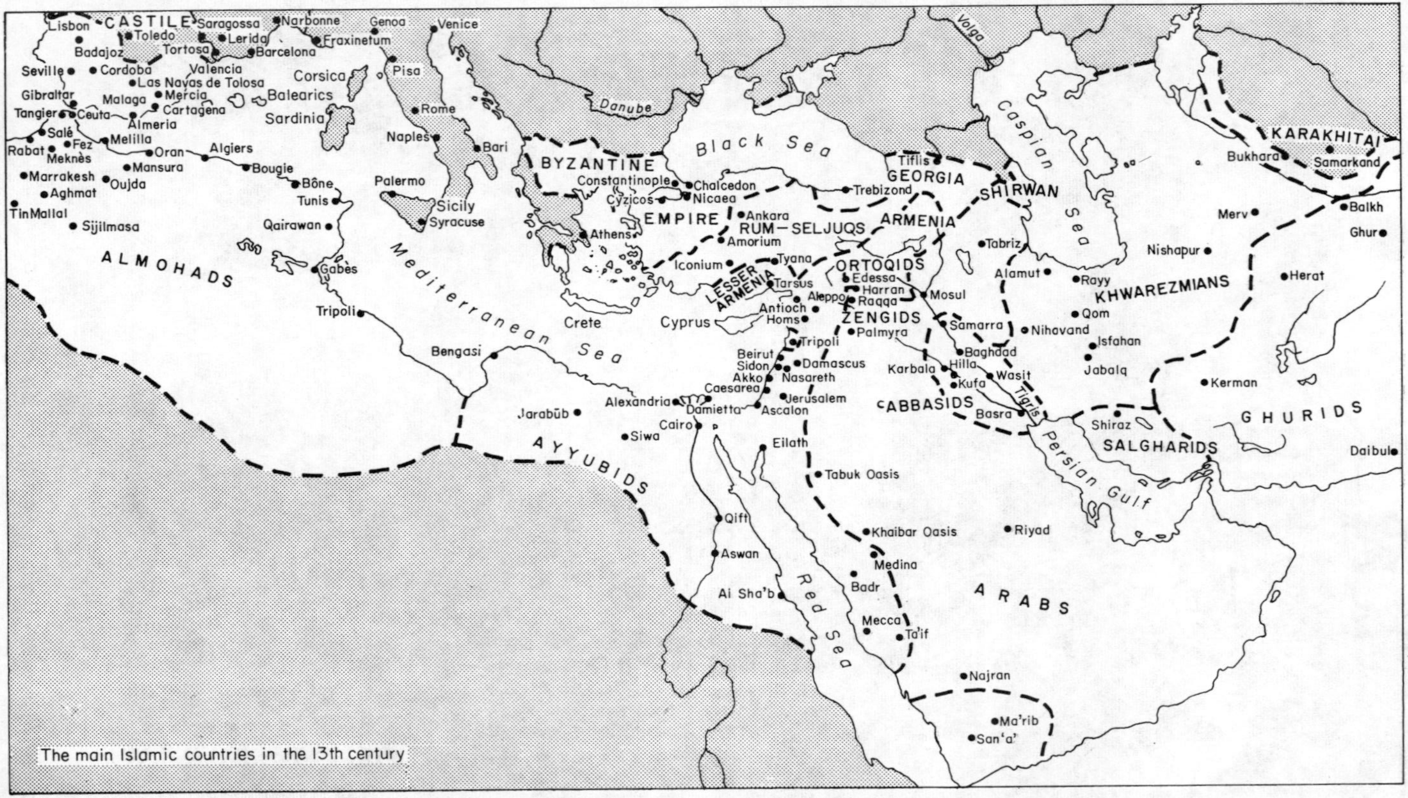

The main Islamic countries in the 13th century

fear-driven avidity of the Muslim potentates. The 'Slavs' had the upper hand in Almería and Denia, Valencia and the Balearics. There were 'native' rulers in the former capital and in nearby Seville, in Badajoz and Murcia, in (now Portuguese) Silves, to name only a few towns, and of course in Saragossa and Toledo.

Following the complete disintegration of the military authority in Córdoba Jahwar ibn Muḥammad seized power. He came of an influential family of officials and set up, as *primus inter pares*, a kind of oligarchic republic in the city. His son succeeded him and gradually turned the administration into a kingdom, but by 1070 Córdoba was incorporated in the rising fortunes of Seville, under the Banū 'Abbād. This dynasty too, founded by a judge, had built up its supremacy within a similar republican constitution until it achieved absolute power, giving Seville a position of dominance (though not an excessively strong one), in south-west Spain.

The multiplicity of centres of power and the small areas involved also allowed of a number of special developments, of which perhaps the dominance of the Jews in Granada under the Banū Naghrālla (*c.* 1030–1066) was the most curious. Samuel ibn Naghrālla, Talmudist, grammarian and poet, had been *nagīd* (principal, prince) of the important Jewish community in Granada in 1027, and as leading official recommended himself, apart from his personal qualities because he was neither Arab nor Berber, to the Zīrid whose throne was none too secure. Recognition of a non-Muslim as vizir was inadmissible by law—the famous Egyptian Jew Ibn Killis (d. 991) had not become vizir to the Fāṭimids until his conversion to Islam—this therefore caused a ferment of ill-feeling among the Muslims, and it ultimately cost Samuel's son Joseph and many of his co-religionists their lives in a pogrom. It is not impossible that Joseph provided the incentive for the building of the famous Alhambra. However that may be, his rise, like that a hundred years earlier of Ḥasdai ibn Shafrūṭ (d. 970), the Jewish doctor of 'Abd ar-Raḥmān III, to be minister of finance, was a symbol of the blossoming of a bilingual Hebrew–Arab culture in Muslim Spain; its importance is given eloquent testimony by such men as Salomon ibn Gabirol (Avicebron; *c.* 1022–1058), a poet and neo-Platonist of world stature, and after him from the same school the astronomer Abraham ibn Ḥiyya (d. 1136) and Abraham ibn Ezra from Toledo (d. 1167), the Aristotelian Jehuda hal-Levi (also from Toledo; d. 1140) and above all Maimonides (*c.* 1135–1204) of Córdoba.

Pushed down by the Almoravids, oppressed by the Almohads and Christians who became more and more intolerant throughout the thirteenth and particularly the fourteenth century, the Jewish scholars of the two centuries after the reconquest have earned the gratitude of the West for their collaboration on Latin translations of both Arabic and Jewish science and philosophy in Toledo. The emigration of young Maimonides with his father, who found him employment as court doctor to Saladin in Cairo, can be seen as a symptom of the regrouping of Jewish life, which clearly now was focused in Fāṭimid and Ayyūbid Egypt. The surviving correspondence of Maimonides when he was the head of the Cairene community shows the extraordinary respect enjoyed by the Arabic-speaking Jews among European Jewry: a reflection of the esteem which the rising West rarely admitted to feeling for the Arab–Muslim orient, already so accomplished and indeed slowly beginning to atrophy.

The conquest of Toledo by King Alfonso VI of Castille and León in 1085 may not have been entirely unexpected, but it confronted the other princes squarely with their own insecurity. Mu'tamid of Seville whose territory must be Alfonso's next objective, joined with the princes of Badajoz and Granada in calling on the Almoravids for help. An embassy of *qāḍīs* conveyed the request. Yūsuf ibn Tāshfīn agreed, but demanded that Algeciras be handed over to him as a landing-place and naval base. The emissaries did not feel themselves authorized to agree and returned to Spain to consult their ruler. Meanwhile Yūsuf made his *fuqahā'* submit their conclusion to him that the occupation of Algeciras even if carried out against the will of its present ruler would be in the interests of the fight for the Faith, and in keeping with the Law, and soon himself followed the army which was despatched to Andalusia without delay. In Seville he was received by Mu'tamid and the other princes. Alfonso took up a position near Sacralias (Zallāqa) north-west of Badajoz, and on October 23, 1086, he suffered a heavy but not a decisive defeat. Valencia and Saragossa were saved but the Berber regiments which Yūsuf left behind were unable to hold back the Christians who had rallied; disputes among the petty princes paralysed Muslim arms, as before the intervention. Invited for a second time by Mu'tamid who this time appeared in person, Yūsuf returned in 1090 to Spain, where he was soon convinced that the political weakness and moral disintegration of Andalusia was only to be controlled if the Almoravids took over direct rule.

The Spanish lawyers pressed him to the decisive step: one more example of the primacy of the *umma* over the political structures of the day. Yūsuf had the proclamation endorsed by the *qāḍīs* of Granada and Málaga, who declared that the princes were unfit to rule, and by the greatest scholars of the East, among them al-Ghazzālī, before he carried out his decision. Only Saragossa was able to stand out for a few years, but fell in 1110 to the Almoravids as well, though eight years later the Christians seized it from them. Not even the violent measures of the Almoravids, hated in Spain for their lack of culture and their severity, were able to hold up the *reconquista*, this time conducted from Aragón, for any length of time. The intolerance of the *fuqahā'*, who gained increasing influence in the executive under 'Alī ibn Yūsuf (1106–1143), made it easy for Alfonso to inspire thousands of Mozarabs to migrate into the depopulated Christian territories. The deportation of Christians to Morocco sanctioned by Averroës' grandfather, which followed on the defeat of Armisol (near Granada) in 1125, indicates the sense of crisis.

Religious Reform and Berber Nationalism

The Almohads

But only a few decades after the death of Yūsuf ibn Tāshfīn (1106) a new and even more powerful wave in the heartland now engulfed the one which had made the Ṣanhāja nomads into the lords of an empire the like of which had never as yet been seen in the Maghreb.

After the victory of Zallāqa, Yūsuf had found himself required to incorporate the Almoravid empire into the Sunnite state system, to name the Caliph of Baghdad in the preacher's address at official prayers (*khuṭba*) and to have the domains which he had conquered conferred upon him by the Caliph and held by him as *amīr al-muslimīn*, 'Prince of the Muslims'—carefully distinguished from the 'Abbāsid *amīr al-mu'minīn* 'Prince of the Faithful'. With this title the Almoravid power received, at least in the eyes of the jurists, a quasi-religious sanction. How far the exercise affected the population cannot be ascertained; it demonstrates the theoretical binding force of the construction whereby political power in the *dār al-islām* could only issue legitimately from the successor of the Prophet.

Incorporation into the Sunnite 'state system' did not however protect the Almoravids from opposition. The reigning oligarchy was unable to secure a sufficient basis from among the remaining Berbers and 'Alī ibn Tāshfīn was obliged to resort to Turkish and Christian mercenaries to give his government the necessary support. The Christians, Spaniards and Catalans led by the famous Reverter, who had first fallen into the hands of the Almoravids as a prisoner, were prized not only because of their orderly line tactics in battle, but were first and foremost required to collect the taxes, for which they hunted out the tribes remote from the centre (as had to be done to those still surviving in Morocco as late as the twentieth century) making their expeditions into a kind of round tour of the territory. Discontent with the employment of infidel mercenaries and with the 'illegal' taxes certainly helped to confirm opposition to the regime, but the ideological basis of the opposition was specifically religious.

From the beginning the Muslim had been charged with responsibility for preserving the Community against objectionable practices.

If he was unable to set things to rights himself then he should express his objection or at least protest in his heart. There is however no corresponding duty on the part of the ruler to let the purifier act or even to listen to him. He operates at his own risk. Hence this 'alteration of the admissible' becomes almost of necessity a collective slogan for those discontented with the regime.

The Almoravids had undertaken to improve morals, the aim of their great opponent Muḥammad ibn Tūmart was to re-establish a correct Islamic way of life. Ibn Tūmart, a Berber of the Hargha tribe of the Maṣmūda, hence a mountain peasant and no nomad, studied first in Andalusia and then in the Islamic east; he came to perceive that the Mālikite *fuqahā'*, the intellectual backbone of the Almoravids, distorted Islamic teaching on important points and robbed it of its richness, with their submission to the letter of the revelation and their authoritarian concentration on applied law (*furū'*). Ibn Tūmart contrary to the legend was not with Ghazzālī in the east, but he probably had relations with Ash'arite scholars and adopted from their theology both the scholastic method operating with rational argument (*kalām*) and the rejection of any anthropomorphism. Like the Ḥanbalites, the Mālikites in North Africa had also turned decisively against the allegorization of the self-statements of God in the Koran, which make God hear, see and sit on His throne, so as to avoid the inescapable arbitrariness inherent in the rationalistic interpretation.

This attitude corresponded in large measure with that of the populace, but it roused the ire of the educated whose mind the Caliph ar-Rāḍī spoke when he attacked the Ḥanbalites in 935 for thinking that 'their hideous repulsive faces were in the likeness of the Lord of the Worlds'. Ibn Tūmart embodied the same hostility to the 'humanization' of God (*tajsīm*); he tried to introduce into the Maghreb a kind of Ash'arism, modified on important points by the teaching of Ibn Ḥazm. About 1100 Ibn Tūmart returned from the east. He went slowly from town to town as a moral reformer preaching everywhere and collecting round him a growing band of followers. Wine drinking, musical instruments, luxury, the veiling of the Almoravid men and the freedom of their unveiled women were the ever-recurring themes of his summons to self-examination and reform. Clashes with the authorities were inevitable. Ibn Tūmart retired to his tribe, built a mosque in Tīnmāl (Tīn Mallal) in the High Atlas and set about systematically to work out his teaching and an organization to promote it. The elimination of *tajsīm* and its replacement by the profession of God's undivided unity (*tauḥīd*) went, as so often in Islam, hand in hand with the conviction that it was necessary to defeat his opponents politically as well; their humanization of the concept of God made them 'polytheists' (*mushrikūn*, literally 'associators', because they associate other divine beings with the unity of God, in this case the humanized divine qualities) and hence infidels as well. Power in the Community must lie in the hands of the bearers of the genuine tradition of the Prophet.

The impact of the new movement was the result of a number of converging stimuli. The discontent of the Maṣmūda at being excluded from power played as much a part as the nationalization of the form of religion advocated by Ibn Tūmart: for the first (and last) time the call to prayer was chanted in Berber and the Friday sermon preached in Berber; Ibn Tūmart wrote at least one of his religious works in his mother tongue before he published it in Arabic so that it could circulate more widely. The return to the true tradition as the foundation of an absolute theology and an equally intransigently expounded law (*fiqh*) provided the psychological support to the moral aggressiveness. At the same moment as in the East a beginning was made to accept the equal validity of the solutions of several school traditions in the service of the unity of Sunnite Islam, Ibn Tūmart insisted that two well-educated *mujtahidūn* could not but come to the same conclusion on the same question.

Like every Islamic government the Almoravids had to recognize that it was impossible to defray the expenses of the state economy with the taxes permitted by the *sharī'a* alone. As long as conquests provided rich booty the ruler could manage with 'poor tax', 'land tax' and 'poll tax' paid by the tolerated *ahl al-kitāb*, and with the revenue from customs dues. When conditions were stabilized however it was impossible to cover expenses without burdening the income of the towns, trade and industry. With wearying monotony the new dynasties abolished the 'illegal' duties, only to reintroduce them again after a short time. The Almoravids saw themselves forced to tax the turnover of almost all types of goods, even of locusts, soap and skewers. It was of course popular to abolish such taxes; it made little difference that they soon had to be reimposed.

His contemporaries saw Ibn Tūmart's movement as an uprising of the Maṣmūda; the empire that arose from it was known even in Europe as that of the Massamuti. Joachim of Fiore identified one of the seven heads of the apocalyptic beast as Melsemutus, i.e. Maṣmūdī, presumably meaning the Almohad prince 'Abd al-Mu'min. Those in the movement called themselves 'confessors of unity' (*al-muwaḥḥidūn*, Almohads) after the kernel of their theology. They experienced the movement as theological; centuries later their princes, who were well versed in the religious sciences, were termed *pontifices* by the Mahgrebi convert to Christianity Leo Africanus (*c.* 1495–1550).

In the course of his missionary and organizational activity Ibn Tūmart had developed from a moral reformer to an authoritative teacher (to the '*faqīh* of the Sūs') before he realized that he himself was the Mahdī promised to the Community at the end of time who would fill the world with righteousness. We do not easily enter into the mind of a man who can identify himself with an eschatological-apocalyptic figure; the conditions of our existence place personalities which undergo experiences of this kind in the ranks of the pathological or at least on the fringe of collective life. But in the Islamic world it is still possible in some circles for a man to feel that he is the final saviour of the Community, the promised Mahdī, and to be accepted as such. The Mahdī of the Sudan, the *Mad Mulla* of Ogaden (Somaliland; 1899–1905, d. 1920) and a Mahdī from Shī'ite Ḥilla in Iraq, still living in Mosul, are familiar and quite possible phenomena. Among the Berbers, who are a classic case of confirmed anthropolators—early fathers of the church, such as Tertullian and Lactantius had already referred to this peculiarity—holiness of the kind that could create significant social structures was quickly recognized, and a rapturous personality cult a frequent religio-political phenomenon. When Ibn Tūmart gave himself out among a small circle of followers to be the Mahdī it clearly caused no great astonishment. The physical signs attributed by tradition to the Mahdī were discovered and a genealogy which linked Ibn Tūmart with the Prophet, giving him the indispensable patronymic 'Abdallāh—the Mahdī like the Prophet Muḥammad must be called Muḥammad ibn 'Abdallāh—; and the force with which he drew men to him was to them as to him the best proof of all.

Ibn Tūmart declared himself to be the Mahdī in a text written by himself; it allows us to feel the atmosphere in which he worked. 'The following', he writes 'is the promise of God which he made known to the Mahdī, the true promise which he does not change. His obeyer is pure, more pure than any before or to come, as it has been seen in no one nor will be again; there is none like him among men, none that can set up against him or contradict him . . . to none can he remain unknown, none can neglect his command. If any comes against him as an enemy he is rushing headlong to destruction and has no hope of salvation. He cannot be approached save by what he approves; all things issue from his command. All happens according to his will, but this is also the will of his Lord (God). To recognize him is an essential religious duty, obedience and devotion to him is an essential religious duty, and to follow him and be guided by him.

. . . The bidding of the Mahdi is the bidding of God, only he who knows him not ascribes it to himself.'

It goes without saying that the Mahdī was named from the pulpit in the official Friday prayers, and that later the official documents of the Almohads added to the customary Islamic naming of God and honorifics of the Prophet a formula (*tarḍiya*) expressing the satisfaction of God with the infallible (or sinless) Mahdī. Ibn Tūmart endeavoured unmistakably to model his life and work to run parallel with the life and work of the Prophet. Tīnmāl appears as the end of a *hijra* like Medina, the Community founded there corresponds to the *umma,* his proclamation takes place under a carob tree, corresponding to Muhammad's receiving homage in Ḥudaibiya. Ibn Tūmart's companions received the same title of 'Helpers' (*anṣār*) as the converted Medinans. Seen from the outside this provides the foundation of a community organization which used Berber customs and political usages in an original way and managed to overcome the principal weakness of the Almoravid movement: the small number of followers who could be won for it, and to create a structure in which religious loyalty could be bound together under the Mahdī or his successors with the tribal loyalty of larger groups, and groups capable of enlargement.

The closest circle round the Mahdī (as later round the Almohad caliphs), men who were at the same time his cabinet, were 'the Ten', also called *ahl al-jamā'a* or 'the Community Council'; directly under them was the 'Council of the Fifty' which, significantly, is known equally in Arabic as *ahl khamsīn* and in Berber as *ait khamsīn.* The 'Ten' were appointed by virtue of their personal achievements, and the 'fifty' were chosen from among the 'People of Tīnmāl'—corresponding to the Companions of the Prophet (*ṣaḥāba*),—from other Maṣmūda tribes, unspecified Ṣanhāja, and from a group of 'Aliens', i.e. non-Maṣmūda. An incipient opposition was quelled in the *tamyīz* (literally: 'distinction, separation', but in fact a massacre). Even after the final victory it appeared to be necessary to eliminate the unco-operative tribes in a second 'sifting' (1149). To widen the basis of support, tribes of non-Almohad origin were fraternized and paired with Almohad ones; this too is an echo of one of the Prophet's measures: soon after his arrival in Medina he tried to fraternize *muhājirūn* and *anṣār* by pairing them individually. To the Almohad tribes 'of the first hour', all of them Maṣmūda, who developed into a kind of religious aristocracy were later added the tribe of the first Caliph, the arabized Zanātic Kūmiyya of West Algeria.

A seat in the 'Ten' was to all appearances heritable in certain clans;

the most eminent was that of Abū Ḥafṣ 'Umar (d. 1175/76), with his Berber name Faskāt ū-Mzāl—Ibn Tūmart had given him the name 'Umar in memory of the great companion of the Prophet and second Caliph—his grandson was to be the founder of the Ḥafṣid dynasty of Tunis (1236–1534). The further following of the regime was also ordered in a hierarchy; if the chroniclers are to be trusted there were about twenty ranks whose series of grades was given dramatic expression in the frequent parades. The descriptions give the impression that these distinctions were only upheld on paper. Special mention is due to the two classes of *mu'adhdhin* (literally prayer-caller) and *ṭālib* (literally student); these were in fact scholars of lesser status who read aloud the Koran and the writings of the Mahdī to the marching army and led the prayers of the community. They alone were allowed to serve without weapons.

As soon as circumstances permitted, Ibn Tūmart began the *jihād* against the Almoravids, from whom the helm of state must be seized. 'Abd al-Mu'min had gone abroad to study in the east but met Ibn Tūmart in Bougie in 1117 and attached himself to him unconditionally, distinguished himself as a leader and was officially recognized three years after the death of the Mahdī in 1133 as his successor. It is said that the 'Ten', of whom 'Abd al-Mu'min was one, kept the decease of Ibn Tūmart a secret until the Caliphate of 'Abd al-Mu'min had been accepted on all sides—he did not belong to any of the original Almohad tribes. One may wonder whether this dissimulation be not a legendary gloss on the facts, and whether in reality the 'Ten' did not attempt an oligarchy during this transitional period. The fight against the Almoravids seems at first to have been in the nature of a guerrilla war. At any rate the Almoravid regime continued to function though it suffered ever greater losses of territory. The plain to the north and west of Marrākesh was almost encircled; about ten years after Ibn Tūmart's death 'Abd al-Mu'min reached the Mediterranean in the region of Oran.

With the death of 'Alī ibn Yūsuf (1144) the usual internecine strife began over the Almoravid succession, and almost at the same time their Christian mercenary general Reverter fell in battle. The Zanāta went over to the rebels, the new Almoravid prince Tāshfīn ibn 'Alī was killed in an accident. After a long siege Fez was taken and with the conquest of Marrākesh in April in 1147 Almoravid rule came to an end. By 1151 'Abd al-Mu'min had swept away the small dynasts who had established themselves in eastern Algeria on the ruins of the Almoravid state and took into his service the Arab nomads whom he had defeated at Sétif. Nine years later he held the whole of Tunisia and Tripolitania. Shortly before this he had destroyed those groups of Barghawāṭa which had survived the war of extermination waged against them a century earlier by the Almoravids. It was probably after his entry into Marrākesh, which has to thank him for the truly regal mosque of the Kutubiyya, that 'Abd al-Mu'min was persuaded to adopt the title of an *amīr al-mu'minīn*, thus officially placing himself on an equality with the 'Abbāsid caliph and freeing himself from the latter's spiritual sovereignty. To control the administration and particularly the taxation of the immense Almohad territory, the largest ever to be ruled from Morocco, he set up a land-register (*taksīr*) from Sūs to Barqa (Cyrenaica), as a chronicler informs us with some little exaggeration. It is to say the least difficult to imagine this land-register and the tax collection based upon it. A glance at the world atlas of his contemporary, the great Sicilian Arab geographer Idrīsī, shows how vague and confused were the notions of the period about the geography of the lands tributary to the Almohads.

With the decline of Almoravid power Muslim Spain, having developed no inner sympathy with the Lamtūna, fell back into fragmentation. Unenlightened and unteachable, a plethora of petty princedoms, like Badajoz and Málaga, Valencia and Ronda, not to mention Rueda and Cáceres, demanded an independence they were in no position, either military or financial, to maintain. Meanwhile in 1147 Lisbon was lost to the Christians for good, the Castilians extended their campaigns as far as Córdoba, the counts of Barcelona occupied Tortosa and Lérida. The Almohads had already begun to gain a footing in the peninsula by 1145. In the following year Cádiz fell to them, but then it took them more than a decade before they had control of southern Spain with Granada, and had seized Almería back from the Christians. Seville became the Spanish capital of the Almohads, and the Giralda today bears witness to their power and the splendidly severe feeling of their style. 'Abd al-Mu'min was five years in Spain before he entered in 1162 the newly built fortress of *Ribāṭ al-Fatḥ*, the 'Victory Fortress' (today Rabat, the capital of Morocco) where he died the following year.

'Abd al-Mu'min was wise enough to allow his Berbers sufficient participation in the government to keep them contented; but for the administration he needed the educated Andalusians. The duality of the Almohad state structure, which needed to keep a balance between the caliphal executive and the theocratic continuity incorporated in the 'Ten', did not prevent him from establishing the succession in his family; this he did as early as 1154. Shortly afterwards he installed his sons in the most important governorships, but characteristically he gave them advisers from the leading groups of the

Almohad aristocracy. His son Abū Ya'qūb Yūsuf took over power without incident. He fell in the holy war before Santarém in 1184. The next three rulers also, of whom the most important was 'Abd al-Mu'min's grandson Ya'qūb al-Manṣūr, 'The Victorious' (1184–1199), mounted the throne without having to put down any rebellion, a dynastic stability almost without parallel in the *dār al-islām*.

This stability allowed the two great monarchs Yūsuf and Ya'qūb to lend their support to intellectual aspirations, although it cannot have escaped them that these had implications incompatible with the theocratic premisses of their rule. The isolation of court society from the subject population, so frequent in Muslim states, may have made it easier for Yūsuf to feel that his encouragement of Averroës (Ibn Rushd) was not dangerous politically. Averroës was the most outstanding of Arab Aristotelians and the last Arab thinker whose work spread beyond the boundaries of language and religion to have an influence on Christendom. He continued the dialogue with Greek philosophy and religion, begun by Ghazzālī with his classic critique of Avicenna, with an equally classic critique of Ghazzālī, and in a sense concluded it, since the discussion was not carried on further from the theological side. Averroës shows the Janus face of the religious scholar and the a-religious philosopher, not easily understood by western man today. In the end it is true he feels the need to demonstrate the harmony of rational conclusion and the content of revelation, helping himself thereto with the stoic teaching of the multiple layers of truth, but to our way of thinking there remains the same gap as there is with Fārābī and even with Kindī, though there it is rather more naïve.

Ibn Ṭufail, Yūsuf's physician (d. 1185), attempted to establish the harmony of reason and revealed religion in a different manner from Averroës. He took up again a motif introduced into literature by Avicenna, and described the development of an orphan on a desert island, who acquires through his reason the essential insight into God and the world. When the hero of the story later becomes acquainted through the vizir of the king of a neighbouring island with the principles of the revealed religion he understands its fundamental identity with the truths he has worked out by reason. This novel-like story of Ḥayy ibn Yaqẓān ('Living, son of Awake') had filtered via Hebrew and, later, Latin into English literature by 1708, and had a marked influence on Defoe's story of Robinson Crusoe (1719).

The speculation of these scholars approximated in its intellectual basis and its leaning, and even in its matter with the political thought of the rather older Ibn Bājja (Avempace; d. 1138), a universal scholar who is said to have been poisoned by the *fuqahā'* of Fez.

Opposition to Averroës also came from the *fuqahā'* (this time Spanish) who inevitably took exception to his Aristotelian theories of the eternity of the world *ab initio* and to his denial of divine knowledge of particulars. Since Ya'qūb needed the support of the *fuqahā'* in the fight against the Christians they forced him to condemn Averroës; the Caliph however exercised the greatest possible mildness and exiled him to Africa; his philosophical writings were burnt. Once Yūsuf was free to act again as he pleased at home, after the victory of Alarcos north-east of Córdoba (July 19, 1195)—the last great triumph of Muslim arms on Spanish soil—he summoned Averroës to his court in Marrākesh; but the Caliph and the philosopher both soon died, within a short time of each other.

Yūsuf too had two faces. From the very beginning the risorgimento movement of the Almoravids had aggravated the generally lax treatment of Christians and Jews. The Christian communities in North Africa were in any case no longer very strong, and they soon vanished completely; the Jews, who opposed full assimilation, were oppressed to the utmost. Yet it was reserved for the Almohads to exceed the bidding of the *sharī'a* in their zeal and to resort to coercion on African soil. Upon the conquest of Tunis the *ahl al-kitāb* were faced with the literal alternative of Islam or death; this had never been more than theoretical, and in any case was only permissible with regard to the heathen. A series of executions provided a forcible illustration of the new interpretation. The Caliph Ya'qūb submitted the Jews to particularly embarrassing regulations concerning dress, out of mistrust for the true feelings of those converted by force. His successors softened them, but without waiving the insistence on yellow garments and turbans—in the interests of easier supervision, and in order to humble them. As could hardly be expected otherwise these Jewish communities returned openly to their traditional beliefs after the fall of the Almohads. The native Christians finally disappeared from the stage under the Almohads. Only foreign mercenaries and merchants were allowed to practise the Christian religion.

In Spain such procedure was quite impossible. But even there the Jews were weakened economically by high taxes, and the 'arabized' Christians were driven into opposition by annoyances of every kind and in many cases driven to emigrate into the 'reconquered' territories. The regime soon made its peace with the Mālikite *fuqahā'* and no separate *madhhab* (law school) corresponding to the principles of the Mahdī grew up. Their fanaticism had a patent political aspect in the efforts to present a consolidated Muslim south to the *reconquista*. It achieved little more than a hardening of the religious fronts and growing impatience, among an increasing number of the population, to become Castilian subjects.

Unrest in Africa had prevented Yūsuf from utilizing the victory of Alarcos. It is characteristic of the situation that the same Alfonso VIII of Castille who was defeated at Alarcos inflicted a crushing defeat on Yūsuf's successor, seventeen years later almost to the day, at Las Navas de Tolosa, a little south of Alarcos. It would be an exaggeration to view this battle as the beginning of the liquidation of Almohad authority; but clearly henceforth Spanish affairs paled into insignificance before the problem of maintaining the heart of the empire in Africa. It was not very long before the decline in power was manifest in dynastic difficulties. The successor of an-Nāṣir who was defeated at Las Navas, al-Mustanṣir, fell victim to the Almohad sheikhs. His death in 1223 was the occasion of the first civil or war of succession since the beginning of the dynasty. The next two rulers failed in their attempts to find a balance of power and met a violent end, one in 1224, the other in 1227. Under them the Almohad sheikhs had ruthlessly seized power and endangered the military and administrative stability of the state, but now al-Ma'mūn, a man born and bred in Spain, endeavoured to save the empire with a thoroughgoing reorganization.

The last decades of the century had not only brought dangerous uprisings, especially that of the Almoravid side-line of the Banū Ghāniya, who landed in North Africa from their stronghold on the Balearics and were not put down until 1204; the ideology of the *muwaḥḥidūn* was increasingly losing its persuasive power. Political satiation combined with the seductions of Spanish urban culture loosened the cohesion among those who carried the structure of the state; the tribes and the subject regions were vociferous with particularist demands; the position of the Almohads was becoming precarious. Therefore Ma'mūn ceremonially renounced the doctrine of Ibn Tūmart in the Great Mosque of Marrākesh and denied him the dignity of Mahdī which is only due to Jesus. The execution of a number of rebellious Almohad sheikhs underlined the rejection by the Caliph of the teaching which alone was able to justify his position. But Marrākesh was occupied by Christian mercenaries, as it had been under the later Almoravids; they were the only troops on whom the Caliph could rely. It almost goes without saying that the hoped-for success was denied to Ma'mūn's act of desperation. The brazen bond that had held the empire together was burst. The Ḥafṣid governor of Ifrīqiya more or less withdrew from the imperial commonwealth; an Almohad prince rose up in Ceuta, another in Marrākesh and Sijilmāsa; in north-east Spain Saragossa fell to a Muslim dynast. The personal ability of Ma'mūn's son ar-Rashīd, who once more proclaimed the teaching of Ibn Tūmart, could no longer halt the collapse. In 1230 the Almohads gave up the four-cornered coins introduced by 'Abd al-Mu'min and the later mintings with an inscription running in a quadrilateral; the conventional round coins which were reintroduced no longer bore the symbol of the Mahdī; one more sign that the dynasty renounced the 'law by which it had come to power' and sought to make itself acceptable to orthodoxy by normalizing itself.

Overnight Spain was once more fragmented into small and smaller princedoms, and they were absorbed with amazing rapidity by the renewed advances of the Christians. In 1236 Ferdinand III of Castile took possession of Córdoba. Seville also fell, after a long siege, in 1248. Aragón had already concluded the conquest of the Balearics (1233). There remained only one refuge for Spanish Islam: the Naṣrids of the Banu 'l-Aḥmar of Arjona fortified themselves in Granada in 1238 and unperturbed by humiliations managed to pursue a policy crafty enough to hold this Muslim enclave until 1492. They even had to provide Ferdinand with a contingent of their troops for the conquest of Seville. While Spain was slipping from its grasp the Zanāta tribes were undermining the African foundations of the empire. The Banū 'Abd al-Wād (also called Banū Zayān) seized West Algeria with Tlemcen for themselves in 1235; only the political indiscipline of the Berbers, unrestrained by any uniting religious experience, allowed the Almohads to hold on in Marrākesh until 1269. They found themselves obliged to seek support among the Arabs and thus to be drawn into their tribal quarrels. The Banū Marīn ruling from Fez since 1248 ultimately gained control over Northern Morocco.

The triad of Ḥafṣids, Zayānids and Marīnids then repeated in the thirteenth century on the larger scale the triad of Aghlabids, Rustamids and Idrīsids which had shared out Muslim North Africa between them in the ninth century.

Withdrawal and Mysticism at the end of the Caliphate

THE Maghreb of the mediaeval period had reached the climax of its development under native leaders, and the states in the succeeding period of decline were also 'national' in the sense that they were ruled by Berber dynasties. In the Near East the development was different, and at the end of our period it was only under the Rūm Seljūqs that the nationality of the dynasty and the Muslim population coincided to any extent. The Ayyūbid state, which one might perhaps call a family feudal unit, held together by free Kurd and 'bought' Turkish soldiers, became increasingly Turkish. The steadfast faith of Sunnite orthodoxy was the cement that held government and governed together. And as long as religion was not at stake the subjects gave their princes the same apathetic obedience which the Fāṭimids had enjoyed. The dynasty remained 'Kurd' in the eyes of contemporaries, though from the point of view of education and culture they were arabized, and Ayyūbid Syria was indisputably the intellectual centre of the *dār al-islām* until Egypt under the Mamlūks relieved her of this role.

The 'Abbāsids were not only named in the prayer, they were even allowed to have a certain influence; sometimes their representatives were summoned to solve political disputes within the ruling house. The attempt to win back supremacy at sea in the Mediterranean from the Italians, with whom gradually the Southern French and the Catalans were beginning to compete, was given up as too costly. The army organization with its remuneration in kind and from the *iqṭā'*—the vassal, like the later occupant of the Ottoman *tīmār*, had usually to collect the yield pertaining to him for himself—made long campaigns unfeasible. After all Saladin's efforts the Latins were by 1200 again in possession, with minor interruptions, of the Palestinian and Syrian coast, and of Cyprus as a naval and arming base as well. The attempt of the Rūm Seljūqs to break out eastwards into the Arab plains laid a defence burden on the Ayyūbid princes which was almost intolerable. The Egyptian economy was still state-run in many sectors; occasional concessions to private enterprise led to disturbances. European trade swelled to ever greater proportions in spite of the military hostilities. There are reports of an incident in which no less than three thousand European merchants were arrested in Alexandria. The economic exhaustion which accompanied Saladin's wars showed in the breakdown of stability in the Egyptian currency and in the forced loans which neither Saladin nor his successors were in a position to repay. The shortage of money was by no means due to military expenses alone; of equal effect, under Saladin's government, was the strict restraint imposed by the *sharī'a* on tax levies.

Attacks by the Latins might strengthen the unity of the Ayyūbid family; but on the whole a peace based on minor concessions seems to have replaced the heroic expansion of Saladin's time. That the almost incessant feuds of the Ayyūbid princes did not have more effect on the general prosperity is a symptom partly of the relatively small number of troops involved, and partly of the indifference of the population. These disputes took on a harsher tone when after the death of al-Malik al-Kāmil (1238) his youngest son aṣ-Ṣāliḥ Ayyūb endeavoured to reunite the crumbling empire once more. Animosities within the family were increased, the Latins interfered, and the Khwārezmian mercenaries in particular brought an ugly form of war into the land.

After the conquest of their land by the Mongols Khwārezmian soldiers under the leadership of their king Jalāl ad-Dīn Mankobirti who had previously fled to India, set out, burning and ravaging through Iran, to carve out a new home. Their compaigns with no strongholds or bases behind them perhaps reproduce something of the atmosphere of the early migration period in Europe; ruthlessness was at any rate their only hope of securing a political basis. The Ayyūbid confederate princes of the Jazīra used this force to further their rivalry with al-Kāmil, and then Jalāl ad-Dīn moved into Rūm Seljūq territory, where he was decisively beaten in 1230. In the following year he fell a victim to private vengeance, and was celebrated by many of his contemporaries as the champion of Islam against the heathen, that is to say the Mongols; but the mercenaries remained; many years later they were annihilated in South Palestine after the victory of aṣ-Ṣāliḥ whose enemies they had helped to fight, at his instigation. Jalāl ad-Dīn, king of an army without a country, and the Khwārezmian army without king or country are symptoms of the havoc which the Mongol invasion inflicted even in its first phase on the old order of Muslim South-West Asia.

The times demanded ever more extensive militarization. Care of the army was the foremost concern of the rulers, each of whom sought to surround himself with his own troops. Regiments, called after the name of their first 'buyer' (*ṣalāḥiyya* after Saladin, '*ādiliyya*, *kāmiliyya*) would continue after his death as political entities, and their rivalries added their part to the tensions existing between the various princes. The administration of Egypt, characteristically, remained on the whole unchanged, though an emir was added to each ministry (*dīwān*) who was to implement administrative measures, by force if necessary. The civil service, predominantly Coptic Christians whose church had experienced a certain revival under the Ayyūbids, would not have been capable of this on their own authority. The later Ayyūbids seem to have been concerned to keep and even to extend their Kurdish populated possessions. Nonetheless the Turkization of the army was an irresistible process. This was in no small measure due to the military policy of aṣ-Ṣāliḥ, disapproved of by his father. Unfortunately for the dynasty, aṣ-Ṣāliḥ died in 1249, just when Louis IX, the saint, had occupied Damietta in the seventh crusade. His wife Shajar ad-Durr, born a slave, held the throne for their son Tūrānshāh, who reconquered Damietta. But he was slow to understand the situation in Egypt and was murdered a few months later, whereupon the Turkish Mamlūks, the 'bought' war slaves, recognized Shajar ad-Durr as ruler—one of the very rare occasions when a woman was admitted to the first place in the state in the Islamic Near East. At her side stood the Turkish general Aibak, first as *atabeg*, and soon as her husband. A struggle for power ensued between the spouses, in which first Aibak and then the Queen met a violent death, and a Mamlūk emir took the helm as the first of a long series of 'slave rulers'.

Contemporaries saw in the extinction of the Ayyūbids the transference of power from Kurds to Turks. In retrospect the assumption of power by the Mamlūks means primarily two things: first, the logical consummation of military governments essentially based on *iqṭāʿāt*, whereby the state had now to some extent become the communal possession of a military ruling caste; second, the establishment for centuries to come of a foreign dominion whose representatives staked all on not being absorbed into the Arab-speaking majority by assimilation or acculturation. They themselves tried to lead the life of a warrior aristocracy constantly refreshed from outside, intellectually isolated from the protected and exploited subject population. The effectiveness of the organization was proven by the victory over the Mongols in 1260. Why the resident population endured this system has only one explanation, apart from the long-standing separation from the government to which they had become accustomed, namely that religion alone counted in life, a religion which coincided with the culture even though the culture itself had also drawn in those of other faiths.

It was not only the decline of the Seljūqs in Iraq which moved the

'Abbāsid caliphs of the twelfth century to make an attempt to win back executive power; the spirit of the times was in favour of strengthening an intellectual centre round the person of the caliph, which was for many possessed of peculiar sanctity. The faithful in all walks of life were finding increasing solace in religious thought and works. The time had come when men drew inspiration and turned in piety to the figure of the Prophet, curiously parallel to the rise in the west of a piety focused on the person of Jesus.

The world was now filled with recognized and unrecognized saints, miracles became a part of every-day life, pilgrimages conducted the believer from one potent sepulchre to another, feeling, soon backed by a speculation not untainted with pedantry, relinquished to God the administration of earthly things, through the medium of a complicated hierarchy of saints who appeared as the real lords of the world; the duality of rule by princes and by saints reflects the overlapping worlds of the mortal state and the immortal Community. Adherence to the *umma Muḥammadiyya* gave a security of existence which the world was no longer able to offer. The greatness (in both senses) of the Muslim Community, authenticated in its history, led into the bliss of paradise by its founder and advocate, was apprehended in Muslimhood as the decisive fact of the individual's existence, a truth which, like the Muslim brotherhood as a whole, exonerated him from the necessity of metaphysical verification of its structure and operation. What decides is being, not doing. In collective piety hope, even confidence, in God's grace triumphs over the previously dominant fear of God's majesty and anger. Theologians, particularly the Ḥanbalites, remained closer to the moderate spirit of the earliest days of the religion in feeling and experience, but they battled in vain against the overwhelming desire for mystic self-effacement in the loving and beloved Godhead, and for the introduction of a lyricism into the practice of religious services which rings strangely in the light of tradition, using music and love poetry and even dancing and psychosomatic techniques as instruments of ecstatic withdrawal.

This penetration of song and music (*samā'*) into the Sufic-inspired service coincides in time with a new upsurge of Byzantine church music about 1100. It has perhaps not heretofore been made sufficiently clear that until some time in the seventeenth century Islamic, like Western culture, gave hearing precedence over sight in its ranking of the senses, preferred the spoken to the written word, at first out of theory, later because of its psychological efficacy. This was a disposition calculated to stimulate hyper-excitability at the expense of scholarly critical precision, an excitability which was in any case evoked by living conditions, among them the ever precarious food supply.

A wave of individualistic hunger for God engulfed the Community; but it was characteristic of the mentality of the *umma* and perhaps of the structure of the experience sought that this desire for individualistic fulfilment should seek to realize itself more and more within the framework of organized orders or brotherhoods (*ṭarīqa*) under the leadership of an adept. The contradiction between the absolute transcendency of God and the unification of the soul of man with the divine source harassed the theologians; the believers and those who led them on the path of mysticism were glad when their experience was clothed in theologically unexceptionable formulae.

Ibn 'Arabī, one of the most 'extreme' mystics who was not in very good odour with the orthodox, succeeded with his pantheistic monistic theosophy in restoring their good conscience (to borrow a phrase from Hellmut Ritter) to the unhappy Sufis who had misgivings about their feelings and practices. He saw creation as the self-revelation of God as the single real being, sensible to apprehension in things; and he explained creation, in metaphoric anthropomorphism, as a mirror in which God admires Himself, and man as the most perfect mirror. Thus Ibn 'Arabī guarded himself against accusations of 'incarnationism' and self-apotheosis, interpreted the mystical search as the search of God for Himself, and freed from suspicion of moral ambiguity the practice of a piety which came near to being a cult, with the beautiful young man as its centre. The 'Beloved' represents the beauty of God and God loves Himself in him and through him.

Not all the theologians were convinced; but the realistic metaphor gave to mystical poetry a repertoire of motifs and images rich in allusion both to this and the other world; it contributed to the achievement in this (and the subsequent) period by Sufic lyric and epic writing, particularly in Persian, of a harmony between perfection of formal expression and (in the lyric) a deep and multifariously significant content, such as has hardly ever been equalled within or, for that matter, outside the Muslim culture area.

Ibn 'Arabī was a Spanish Arab; but it was in Persia that mysticism and pantheistic illuminationism felt his influence most. Persians or Iranized Central Asians play a strikingly prominent role too in the development of the orders and in religious philosophical intellectual life altogether, in the twelfth and thirteenth centuries in Arab territory. 'Abd al-Qādir al-Jīlī (d. 1166) came from Gīlān, south of the Caspian sea, and from his circle developed after his death the great order of the Qādiriyya. He was a Ḥanbalite theologian in whose *madhhab* the total rejection of mystical practices was not unusual, but he nonetheless succeeded in reconciling the religion of the law with ecstatic individualism. The saint remains subordinate to the Prophet. Ecstasy must not compromise purity of behaviour, ascesis does not exonerate from the duties towards family and Community. What it depends on is the 'great *jihād*' against the arrogant will to exist, and the surmounting of the 'hidden polytheism' of self-worship. The saint possesses no magical power, but God's grace allows him to divert the usual course of nature in case of necessity. Popular belief however was all too ready to overlook this distinction and to fear and honour the blessed man himself as an autonomous source of the power of grace and the curse.

In the Qādiriyya, as in the innumerable subsequent orders—sisterhoods too were founded in Egypt and Syria in the thirteenth and fourteenth centuries, but did not survive—the state of trance was achieved both by invocation of God in endlessly repeated brief formulae (*dhikr Allāh*, which is comparable to the *mnéme theoú* adopted by the Byzantine Hesychasts at almost the same time) and by certain other practices; for instance a dance symbolizing the movements of the planets among the Maulawī (Turkish: Mevlevi) who grew out of the following of Jalāl ad-Dīn Rūmī, and a savagely excited behaviour sanctioning the more primitive levels of religious experience among the Rifā'iyya order, which like the Qādiriyya is to be traced back to an Iraqi saint of the twelfth century. The candidate attaches himself to a master and at a certain degree of spiritual progress is clothed in the garment of the order. The order gains legitimacy through the spiritual descent of the founder from 'Alī the fourth caliph through a 'chain' (*silsila*) of transmission, a specifically Shī'ite feature which at that time even penetrated 'orthodox' piety.

Altogether this epoch provided a wider field for popular piety. *Futuwwa* (chivalry) made contact with Sufism in a development that was to some extent reciprocal: the Sufi adopted ideas from the *fityān*. One of the most important points of contact was the organized holy war at the frontiers of the *dār al-islām*, and also at the 'inner' frontiers; in Damascus for instance (according to Ibn Jubair) a *futuwwa* organization combated the terror of the Assassins with a counter-terror. A group of this kind tended to become the political spearhead of the lower classes, and in periods when the public authority was weak it could become a real power factor, as for example in Baghdad, where the *'ayyārūn*, unmistakably a *futuwwa* group with anti-'Abbāsid and 'proletarian' aims, held power from 1135 to 1144

Like the Sufic orders the *fityān* traced their societies back to 'Alī, cultivated a 'spiritual genealogical tree' and evolved an elaborate ceremonial. For Sufism 'altruism' (*īthār*) towards the members, which had always been proclaimed by the *fityān* of all types, was a step on the path of mystical perfection; the *futuwwa* made the piety of communal behaviour the determinant ethical factor. Regard for a good name by no means loses importance for the *fityān*, but the morality by which they behave is individualized; it is for the insight of the individual to decide which place each thing occupies within the divine ordering of the world. As a postulate at least a religious motive is attached to doing and not doing. With so much innovation adhering to the ceremonial of the brotherhoods and the bridges connecting with the heroes of early Islam being so easily discernible as useful mythologies, it was inevitable that a considerable number of theologians, who may well have also been upset by the Shī'ite flavour, took up a careful, and often a positively hostile attitude towards the *futuwwa*.

Public opinion was favourable enough to the movement for the Caliph an-Nāṣir li-dīn Allāh (1180–1225) to dare to use the help of a reorganized *futuwwa* to strengthen the influence of the caliphate beyond Iraq into the lands of Islam. When the Iraqi Seljūqs died out (1194) he was enabled to unite in one hand the power which for 250 years had been divided between caliphate and sultanate, and work towards a truly autonomous 'church state'. He concerned himself with the Shī'ites of Iraq; the mosque of the 'Occultation of the Mahdī' (*ghaibat al-Mahdī*) in Samarra is his work. He also came to an understanding with the neo-Ismā'īlī of Alamūt in 1208. But long before this, in 1182–83, an-Nāṣir had been clothed by the Elder of the Baghdad *futuwwa* with the 'garment of the *futuwwa*'. At the same time he had abolished all the *futuwwa* societies and only allowed that one to remain 'which put on the trousers (*sarāwīl*, the characteristic sign of the societies) from him and recognized him as master'. This meant then that henceforth only that *futuwwa* should survive in whose chain of transmission (*silsila*) the caliph was included. This court *futuwwa* found some response outside Iraq and many princes enrolled; how far their filiation was politically significant and how far purely a snob game is difficult to say.

At about the same time as this reform the power of the caliph spread beyond Iraq and asserted itself at times in Khūzistān and south-west Persia. This weighed sufficiently on the shāh of Khwārezm for him to prepare an attack on Baghdad; even so the strengthening of the caliph was doubtless beneficial for the *futuwwa* centralized in his person. But the Mongol catastrophe swept away the court *futuwwa* before it had been able to prove itself properly, and left only the 'bourgeois' *futuwwa* which was less politically exposed and bound to no particular system of government. This survived in various local forms at different periods, and was particularly hardy in Turkish territory.

It would be mistaken to speak of a decline in Greek-inspired learning during the period of the expiry of the caliphate. Mathematics and astronomy, medicine and the propaedeutic branches of philosophy retained their attraction, and the discovery of the lesser circulation of the blood by Ibn an-Nafīs (d. 1287) entitles this period to some fame. Neither is the gradual exhaustion of scientific productivity to be laid at the door of the public authority; in so far as this intellectual contraction can be seen in the twelfth and thirteenth centuries it is due to nothing else than a change of interests among the Muslim intelligentsia. The conservation of the *umma* had become a primary preoccupation, and the troubles of the time, soon made more oppressive by the assault of the heathen Mongols, required all its strength to maintain the Community intact. Energies had to be concentrated and men had to forgo the luxury of extending those branches of knowledge that were indifferent to religion, and even possibly dangerous. The security of the Community lay in the certainty of the apostolic tradition. Everything new was rejected and feared more than ever before, and consequently any research that gave itself out as original or indeed any activity which distracted from the religious goal of life. In spite of intellectual agitation the period was anti-intellectual, even anti-rational. Gnosis or intuition (*ma'rifa*) stood high above the knowledge gained by thinking (*'ilm*); tradition (*naql*), not reason (*'aql*) deserved trust; faith blunted the critical will and the critical ability. Religious satisfaction was derived from the fallibility of the human mind; man's weakness was God's glory, humility before God his only honour. It is not fortuitous that an-Nāṣir made the sheikh 'Umar Suhrawardī (1145–1228) his court theologian and frequently used him as his ambassador. Clearly the sheikh, a strict Sunnite, but tolerant of the moderate Shī'a, must have been welcome to Nāṣir because he developed a theory of state which, in rising order, co-ordinated *futuwwa*, Sufism and the Caliphate; yet the caliph can hardly have failed to notice how much the mentality of his adviser reflected the spirit of the time when he expressed such opinions as that philosophy was a conspiracy of the Infidel to destroy Islam, or declared that the miracles of the saints were immeasurably superior to the activities of the philosophers. The same caliph it was who gave his consent for Suhrawardī to 'wash off' the *Kitāb ash-shifā'*, Avicenna's philosophical encyclopaedia, and did not prevent another zealot from similarly destroying other philosophical writings.

The lack of counsel and direction in this period gave orthodoxy the upper hand. The aim was God, but a God who took it amiss if man sought independently to master the totality of his creation. Originality disguised itself as commentary, and progress, in so far as it was conscious, led to a bad conscience. The more impenetrable to reason the world appeared, the nearer to God it felt. The only study that flourished, which was directly serviceable to religion, was tradition, biographies of the 'transmitters', interpretations of the Koran; and with it the neutral registration of facts, to which was soon added the systemization of information important to the technique of administration. History-writing and its twin, the life-histories of important personalities, have great achievements to their credit. In 1234 died Ibn al-Athīr, whose 'Complete Book', a world history (understood as the history of the *dār al-islām*), is an unusually sensitive and mature work, particularly remarkable in the delicate understanding of the events taking place on the borders of the Islamic world in their significance for Muslim society. The collection of obituaries *Wafayāt al-aʿyān* by Ibn Khallikān (d. 1282) represents the high point of a certain kind of scholarship, which knows nothing of 'development' or entelechy, matched perhaps by the biographical 'Handbook of the Educated', *Irshād al-arīb*, by Yāqūt (d. 1229). The West has nothing remotely comparable to offer at this period. This is the more remarkable since the rare western autobiographies of the time, those by Wibert de Nogent (1053–1124), Suger de St Denis (1081–1151) or Abélard (1049–1142) are in no way inferior to the autobiographies of Nāṣir-i Khusrau (d. 1088) or even of Ghazzālī.

This is not the place to examine the intellectual exchange which the crusades stimulated between Christendom and Islam. The gift from the Arab world to the Christian of a wealth of cultural goods, from objects of daily living through details of heraldry and armament to a general broadening of experience was not, of course, reciprocated; it would seem that the Muslims contented themselves with a few technological and strategical borrowings from the Latins. The crusades in spite of their failure were of value only to the West; for this reason they must be excluded here.

The victory of the Mongols over the Khwārezmians in the year 1220 horrified the eastern Muslim world. It was shocked at the ease with which the victory was won and at the cruelty of the battles against these heathen intruders who had come into conflict with the Khwārezmians over the control of the Central Asian trade routes, but this did not awaken it to the need for a common defence. It was not to know that the Mongols under Genghis Khan were seeking to realize the ideology of the world state: 'One god in Heaven, one ruler on earth'; yet it sensed that it would not be a match for the disciplined brutality of the enemy. The celebrated physician 'Abd al-Laṭīf of Baghdad (d. 1231–1232)—Central Persia and Afghanistan had just fallen into the hands of the Mongols—was indeed utterly appalled by the barbarism of the heathen, but he saw only too well why the Khwārezmians were inferior to them. 'The Khwārezmian shāh Muḥammad ibn Tukush was a thief and a violent man, and his soldiers were a rabble . . . ; most of them were Turks, either infidel or ignorant Muslim. . . . He was wont to kill a part of a tribe and take the rest into his service, with their hearts full of hatred against him. Neither towards his own people nor towards his enemies did he show any deliberate policy . . . Then these Tartars came against him who are the sons of *one* father, with *one* word, *one* heart and *one* leader whom they obey.' (From the German of de Somogyi.) In the circumstances observed by 'Abd al-Laṭīf and in systematic terrorism lay ultimately the secret of the Mongol successes.

After the conquest of Iran, Genghis Khan turned eastwards; but he died in 1227 before his empire was consolidated enough to allow a further advance into Islamic territory. His sons directed their force westwards and gave the caliphate a final breathing-space. Then in 1256 Genghis Khan's grandson Hülägü continued the advance. The Sunnite public thanked him for the destruction of Alamūt with which he began. The Persian Shī'ites were blamed for turning Hülägü against Iraq. Al-Musta'ṣim, caliph since 1242, missed the right moment to capitulate; perhaps the Shī'ite-minded dignitaries at his court deliberately gave him the wrong advice. After overthrowing a feebly conducted defence the Mongol army pressed into Baghdad on January 17, 1258. The city was spared, the Caliph taken prisoner and forced to hand over his treasures, but a few days later he was executed. It is said that he was wrapped in a carpet and shaken to death; for had a drop of his blood touched the earth, the world would have begun to shake.

Psychologically Sunnite Islam has never recovered from the disappearance of the true caliphate; in political theory too the decline of the authority from which all legitimate authority derived left a gap impossible to fill. But the *umma* had already reached its full maturity, and achieved an independence founded on itself. For centuries the Community had always been able to extricate itself from the vicissitudes of history; political catastrophes had ceased for many a long year to signify religious menace. The greatness of the Islamic *'ulamā'*, perhaps also of the Islamic sense of community, lay in the tendency, never avowed in the ideology, to persist complete in itself and regardless of the contingencies of state. It was this religious and cultural immunity in Islam which was to its followers the ultimate proof of its divine mission. And, in the period of political confusion and exhaustion, the period without a caliphate, has the faith not spread out in a third wave to every quarter of the globe?

Chronological table

106	The Kingdom of the Nabataeans is incorporated into the Roman Empire.
273	The city state of Palmyra is destroyed by Aurelian.
From 502	The Ghassānids in Byzantine service as the 'Romaic Arabs'.
525	Death of the south Arabian Jewish king Dhū Nuwās; south Arabia becomes an Abyssinian satrapy.
c. 570	The dam breaks for the third time in Ma'rib; final disintegration of ancient south Arabian civilization.
c. 570	Birth of Muhammad.
597	The Yemen under Sasanid domination.
602	End of the Lakhmid dynasty, who had served the Persians as a frontier guard in Ḥīra.
c. 610	Muhammad receives his call.
c. 611	The Arabs inflict a defeat on the Persians at Dhū Qār.
c. 615	Emigration of a section of the Muslim Community to Abyssinia.
622	Muhammad's *hijra* with his followers from Mecca to Medina; beginning of the Muslim era.
624	Muhammad wins a victory over the Meccans at Badr.
625	Defeat of Muhammad by the Meccans at Mount Uḥud.
627	Inconclusive 'Battle of the ditch' outside Medina.
628	Muhammad marches to al-Ḥudaibiya and concludes a treaty with the Meccans.
629	Expedition into Byzantine territory and defeat at Mu'ta.
630	Conquest of Mecca.
632	Death of Muhammad (June 8th).
632–634	Caliph Abū Bakr; quells uprisings in Arabia, invasion of Mesopotamia and Palestine.
634	Victory over the Byzantines at al-Ajnādain (July).
634–644	Caliph 'Umar; greatest period of conquests by the Muslim Arabs.
635	Damascus surrenders to the Muslim (September).
636	Defeat of the Byzantines at the Yarmūk; decisive battle with the Persians at Qādisiyya.
639	Marshal 'Amr ibn al-'Āṣ crosses the Egyptian frontier.
642	Byzantines evacuate Alexandria; victory of Nihāvand gives Persia to the Muslim.

644–656	Caliph 'Uthmān.
649	Beginning of naval war against Byzantium and conquest of Cyprus.
651	Yazdgard, the last Sasanid, is murdered in Merv.
653	Compilation of the revelations of the Prophet and official edition of the Koran.
656–661	'Alī, the last of the four Rightly Guided Caliphs.
656	'Alī is victorious over his political enemies in the Battle of the Camel near Baṣra (9 December).
657	Battle of Ṣiffīn; struggle for power with the Syrians under Mu'āwiya.
658	Massacre of Khārijites (Secessionists) by 'Alī's army.
661	'Alī murdered (January 24th); his son Ḥasan renounces the caliphate; beginning of the rule of the Arab Umayyad dynasty (until 750).
661–680	Mu'āwiya I; beginning of the second great period of expansion.
662	Ziyād ibn Abīhi governor in Iraq.
667	The Arabs occupy Chalcedon, threaten Byzantium and invade Sicily.
670	Beginning of operations against the Berber and the conquest of north Africa by 'Uqba ibn Nāfi'.
680–683	Yazīd I; uprisings and counter-government in Mecca.
680	Ḥusain ibn 'Alī killed at Karbalā' (October 10th); he becomes central figure of the Shī'a through his martyrdom.
684–685	Mu'āwiya II.
684–685	Marwān I; aggravation of tribal feuds leads to the battle of Marj Rāhiṭ (684) between Qaisites and Kalbites; growing weakness of Arabs.
685–705	'Abd al-Malik; period of internal reforms: Arab coinage; Arabic as official language.
685–687	Religious and socially motivated uprising of al-Mukhtār in Iraq.
691	Construction of the Mosque of 'Umar (Dome of the Rock) in Jerusalem.
692	Occupation of Mecca by al-Ḥajjāj ibn Yūsuf; end of the 'pious' counter caliphate of 'Abdallāh ibn az-Zubair.
695–714	al-Ḥajjāj ibn Yūsuf governor in Iraq.
698	Final expulsion of the Byzantines from Carthage.
705–715	Walīd I; conquest and islamization of the central Asiatic centres of Bukhārā and Samarkand in the campaigns of Qutaiba ibn Muslim.

705 The church of St John in Damascus is rebuilt and fitted out as a mosque.
711 Ṭāriq invades southern Spain; beginning of conquest of Spain; first expedition to Sindh.
715–717 Sulaimān; unsuccessful siege of Byzantium.
717–720 'Umar II; tax reform; converts freed of poll tax, but included in responsibility for land tax.
720–724 Yazīd II.
724–737 The Khazars (*c.* 650–975) prevent the Arabs from overrunning the plains of south Russia.
724–743 Hishām, the last Umayyad statesman.
728 Death of Ḥasan al-Baṣrī, the most important religious figure (ascetic and incipient mystic) in early Islam.
733 The northward expedition of the Arabs is halted by Charles Martel near Poitiers.
740 Rebellion of the Fāṭimid Zaid ibn 'Alī in Kūfa.
743–744 Walīd II; dissension and fighting in the Umayyad dynasty; construction of the desert castle of Mshattā in Transjordania.
744 Yazīd III; Ṣāliḥ proclaims a religion in north Africa which he claims is based on a Koran revealed in Berber language.
744–745 Ibrāhīm.
745–750 Marwān II; nominal re-establishment of the unity of the caliphate and reform of the army.
746 Abū Muslim co-ordinates the Shī'ite opposition and agitates for the 'Abbāsids in Khorasan.
747 The Shī'ites raise the black banner of the 'Abbāsids in Khorāsān.
750 Marwān is decisively defeated at the battle on the Great Zāb.
750–1258 'Abbāsid dynasty; repression of the Arabs, eastward and north-eastward orientation of caliphal policy.
750–754 Abu 'l-'Abbās as-Saffāḥ; extermination of the Umayyads and their chief officials.
751 Battle on the Ṭalas, at which the last Chinese army to be sent to central Asia is crushingly defeated.
754–775 al-Manṣūr; dissociation from the radical Shī'a; uprisings of 'Alid pretenders.
755–788 'Abd ar-Raḥmān I emir of Córdoba, founder of the Spanish Umayyad dynasty.
757 Death of the Iranian writer and translator into Arabic, Ibn al-Muqaffa'.

762 Newly founded Baghdad becomes the imperial capital.
767 Death of Abū Ḥanīfa, the founder of one of the four orthodox law schools.
775–785 al-Mahdī; the Barmakids as vizirs (until 803); struggle against new Mazdakite and Manichaean movements.
778 Failure of Charlemagne's expedition in the Basque country and decimation of parts of his army under Roland at Roncevalles.
785–786 al-Hādī.
785 Construction is started on the Umayyad mosque in Córdoba.
786–809 Hārūn ar-Rashīd; caliphate at its zenith and floraison of Arabic literature.
793 Death of Mālik ibn Anas, the founder of an important and widespread law school.
806 Conquest of Tyana and advance as far as Ankara.
808 Foundation of Fez by the Shī'ite Idrīsids (788–985).
809–813 Al-Amīn; end of the political influence of the Arabs.
c. 810 Systemization of the legal sources by ash-Shāfi'ī (767–820).
813–833 al-Ma'mūn; cultural and scientific floraison: tendency to independence in the provinces.
816–838 The Mazdakite-communist sect of Bābak gains ground in Azerbaijān and west Persia.
821–873 Eastern Iran virtually independent under the Ṭāhirid governors.
827 al-Ma'mūn decrees the '*miḥna*'; he proclaims the theological teaching of the 'Mu'tazila', which founded speculative dogma in Islam, to be binding; the government takes sides for the 'createdness' of the Koran.
829–830 Uprising of oppressed Copts.
831 Fall of Palermo.
833–842 al-Mu'taṣim; removal of the seat of government to Samarra; the caliph becomes the puppet of his Turkish guards.
842–847 al-Wāthiq.
844 The Normans attack Spain and occupy Seville.
847–861 al-Mutawakkil; return to Sunnite orthodoxy, dismissal of the Mu'tazilite chief judge.
852–886 Muḥammad I in Spain.
855 Death of Aḥmad ibn Ḥanbal, founder of a traditionist and strictly orthodox law school.
857 Death of al-Muḥāsibī, an important representative of early Islamic piety and theology.

861–862 al-Muntaṣir; beginning of a decade of government by Turkish soldiers.
862–866 al-Musta'īn.
866–869 al-Mu'tazz; the Ṭūlūnids governors in Egypt (868–905).
869–870 al-Muhtadī; uprising of Negro slaves in southern Iraq under an 'Alid leader (883 overthrown).
870 Conquest of Malta.
870–892 al-Mu'tamid; the great collections of classical traditions by Bukhārī (d. 870) and Muslim (d. 875).
873 The 12th imam disappears: according to Shī'ite belief he works as 'the Lord of Time' from his concealment until his return.
873 Death of the first great Arab philosopher al-Kindī; death of Ḥunain ibn Isḥāq under whom translation from the Greek reached its height.
873 Deposition of the Ṭāhirids in Khorāsān by Ya'qūb aṣ-Ṣaffār, whose dynasty (the Ṣaffārids) continues until 903.
875–999 The Sāmānids in Bukhārā; cultural floraison and wakening of Persian national consciousness.
877 Aḥmad ibn Ṭūlūn occupies Syria; Beginning of construction of the mosque of Ibn Ṭūlūn in his garrison town of al-Qaṭā'i' [in Old Cairo].
878 Fall of Syracuse: Byzantium loses Sicily.
879–928 'Umar ibn Ḥafṣūn and his sons keep the Spanish Umayyad state at bay, causing unrest in rural and mountain areas west of Málaga.
888 Arabs installed in the fortress of Fraxinetum (La Garde-Freinet, Provence) until 983.
890 Rise of Qarmaṭians in Iraq, a secret sect with community of goods.
890–1008 The Arab dynasty of Ḥamdānids in north Iraq and north Syria as outposts against Byzantium.
892–902 al-Mu'taḍid; religious and political unrest.
897 Foundation of the Zaidite state in the Yemen.
902–908 al-Muktafī; fighting against the Qarmaṭians.
908–932 al-Muqtadir; caliphate increasingly loses power; Anti-caliph 'Abdallāh ibn al-Mu'tazz.
909 End of the Aghlabids (since 800) and collapse of 'Abbāsid influence in north Africa.
910 Adoption of the title of caliph by the Fāṭimid 'Ubaidallāh.
912–961 'Abd ar-Raḥmān III; height of Spanish Umayyad empire.
922 Execution of the mystic al-Ḥallāj.

923 Death of the historiographer and Koran commentator aṭ-Ṭabarī.

929 Adoption of the title of caliph by the Emir of Córdoba, 'Abd ar-Raḥmān III, as protector of orthodoxy in the West.

930 The Qarmaṭians remove the black stone of the Ka'ba from Mecca.

932–934 al-Qāhir.

934–940 ar-Rāḍī; the theologian al-Ash'arī (d. 935) introduces Mu'tazilite methodology into orthodoxy and opens the way for scholastic intellectualism.

937 The Turkish governor in Egypt Muḥammad ibn Ṭughj (935–946) is given the Sogdian ruler's title of 'Ikhshīd'.

940–944 al-Muttaqī; the Ḥamdānid Nāṣir ad-Daula (942–945) the last Arab majordomo of the caliphs.

941 Death of al-Māturīdī, the second great theologian of the Sunnites, who defended orthodox teaching by means of logic.

944–946 al-Mustakfī; the Shī'ite Būyids (945–1055) assume military and administrative control in the caliphal empire.

944–947 Revolution of the Berber against the Fāṭimids.

945–967 The Hamdānid Saif ad-Daula, celebrated hero of the Faith in the struggle against Byzantium.

946–974 al-Muṭī'; the philosopher al-Fārābī (d. 950), author of an 'Ideal state'.

961–976 Ḥakam II of Córdoba; after him internal collapse of the caliphate.

962 The Turkish general Alptegin founds an independent state upon the conquest of Ghazna.

965 Death of the court poet of the Hamdānids Mutanabbī, one of the last great Arab poets.

969 The freedman Jauhar conquers Egypt for the Fāṭimids; foundation of Cairo.

c. 970 The 'Missives of the Pure Brethren', an Ismā'īlī encyclopaedia of knowledge.

973 A theological college is founded at the Azhar mosque in Cairo and becomes the centre of Shī'ite intellectual life.

974–991 aṭ-Ṭā'i'.

977–997 Consolidation of the Ghaznavid possessions under Subuktegin.

991–1030 al-Qādir; general survey of Islamic political institutions by al-Māwardī (d. 1058).

996–1021 The Fāṭimid Ḥākim decides he is the incarnation of the divine intellect; persecution of Jews and Christians.
996–1030 Maḥmūd of Ghazna; conquest of north-west India.
999 Deposition of the Sāmānids by the Ilkhan of Turkestan and the Ghaznavids.
c. 1010 Firdausī (934–1020) finishes the Persian national epic 'Shāh-Nāma'.
c. 1030 Book on India by the naturalist and sociologist Bērūnī (973–1048).
1031 Fall of the Umayyads in Spain; disintegration into petty states.
1031–1075 al-Qā'im; the poet Abu 'l-'Alā' al-Ma'arrī (d. 1058).
1036–1094 al-Mustanṣir; political and religious break-up of Fāṭimid power.
1037 Death of the Persian philosopher and physician Ibn Sīnā (Avicenna).
1040 The Seljūqs under Ṭughril Beg defeat the Ghaznavid army at Dandāqān.
1055 Ṭughril Beg enters Baghdad and assumes the office of the Būyids.
1059 Iraq under the Būyid general Basāsīrī is subject to the Fāṭimids for one year.
1063–1072 Seljūq Sultan Alp Arslan; Turks break into eastern Asia Minor.
1064 Death of the Spanish politician, lawyer, prose writer and religious philosopher Ibn Ḥazm.
1071 Battle at Manzikert begins the Turkization of Asia Minor.
1075–1094 al-Muqtadī.
1076 Damascus falls to the Seljūqs.
1082 The leader of the religious reform party of the Almoravids, Yūsuf ibn Tāshfīn, has created a united realm in north Africa.
1085 Conquest of Toledo by King Alfonso VI of Castille.
1090 Yūsuf ibn Tāshfīn removes the Spanish petty princes.
c. 1090 Foundation of the secret society of the Assassins by the Nizārī Ḥasan-i-Ṣabbāḥ (d. 1124).
1092 Niẓām al-Mulk, vizir of the Seljūq sultans, murdered by the Assassins.
1094–1118 al-Mustaẓhir; the 'Revivification of the sciences of religion' by al-Ghazzālī (d. 1111), synthesis of religious law and mysticism.
1096 First Crusade.

1099 Jerusalem conquered by the crusaders; it becomes a Latin kingdom.

c. 1100–1130 Ibn Tūmart founds the party of religious reform in North Africa and the Empire of the Almohads, the 'Followers of Unity'.

After 1100 Ḥarīrī (d. 1122) gives its greatest lustre to the new literary genre of the *maqāma*.

1105–1118 New unification of the Seljūq empire under Muḥammad ibn Malikshāh.

1118–1135 al-Mustarshid; dissolution of the Seljūq empire into separate princedoms under the Atabegs, and ultimate downfall.

1118–1157 Sanjar holds the Persian possessions of the Seljūq dynasty.

1127 Transference of the emirate of Mosul to Zengī (murdered 1146).

1132 Construction of the Palatina of Monreale near Palermo by Roger II (until 1140).

1133–1163 Almohads consolidate their power in North Africa under 'Abd al-Mu'min. Start of construction of the Kutubiyya mosque in Marrākesh.

1135–1136 ar-Rāshid.

1136–1160 al-Muqtafī II; the Ṣūfī 'Abd al-Qādir al-Jīlī (d. 1166) combines religion of the law with ecstatic individualism.

1140 Foundation of the dynasty of the shāhs of Khwārezmia.

1144 Zengī wins back Edessa from the Christians.

1145 Death of the last Almoravid prince Tāshfīn ibn 'Alī; the Almohads gain a foothold on the Iberian peninsula.

1147 Second crusade.

1150 The mountain tribe of the Ghūrids destroys Ghazna.

1154 Nūr ad-Dīn, son of Zengī, conquers Damascus; Idrīsī (d. 1162) completes his famous description of the earth, in Sicily.

1160–1170 al-Mustanjid; Ibn Ṭufail (d. 1185) writes a philosophical novel concerned with the harmony between reason and revelation.

1164 The Persian Nizāriyya proclaims the 'great resurrection'; Paradise on earth and the abrogation of the law.

1170–1180 al-Mustaḍī'; the great Spanish philosopher and commentator of Aristotle Ibn Rushd (Averroës; d. 1198). Building of the Almohad mosque in Seville with its minaret, now the Giralda.

1171 The Ayyūbid Ṣalāḥ ad-Dīn puts an end to the Fāṭimid dynasty in Egypt.

1175 Recognition by the Caliph of the sultanate of Ṣalāh ad-Dīn over Egypt, Palestine and Syria.

1180–1225 an-Nāṣir; final rise of caliphal power.

1187 Saladin inflicts a crushing defeat on the Franks at Ḥaṭṭīn and occupies Jerusalem.

1189–1192 The German emperor and the kings of France and England participate in the third Crusade to the Holy Land.

1193 Death of Saladin; partition of his empire.

1194 The shāh of Khwārezmia defeats the last Persian Seljūqs.

1195 The Almohad Ya'qūb al-Manṣūr (1184–1199) wins an important victory over the Castilians at Alarcos.

1199–1220 The empire of the shāh of Khwārezmia Muḥammad II enjoys its highest floraison and then collapses before the Mongols under Temujin (supreme ruler as Genghis Khan since 1206).

1223 Civil wars and wars of succession cause the fall of the Almohad dynasty.

1225–1226 aẓ-Ẓāhir.

1226–1242 al-Mustanṣir; Ibn 'Arabī (d. 1240) directs mysticism towards pantheistic monism.

1229 Sultan al-Malik al-Kāmil (1218–1238) of Egypt makes a peace treaty with Frederick II and hands over Jerusalem to the Christians.

1229 Death of Yāqūt whose compilation of the Biographical Handbook is a landmark of scholarship.

1234 Death of Ibn al-Athīr, author of a monumental world history.

1236 Dissension among Muslims enables Ferdinand III of Castille to take Córdoba.

1238 The Naṣrids, last Islamic dynasty in Spain, hold out in Granada (until 1492).

1242–1258 al-Musta'ṣim, the last 'Abbāsid caliph.

1244 Jerusalem lost by the Christians for the last time.

1248 Seville falls to the Castillians.

1249 Louis IX of France occupies Damietta on the sixth crusade.

1250 Beginning of the rule of the Mamlūk, Turkish military slaves in Egypt (until 1517).

1256 Genghiz Khan's grandson Hülägü advances westward; destruction of the Assassin stronghold of Alamūt.

1258 The Mongols under Hülägü take Baghdad; end of the 'Abbāsid caliphate.

Bibliography

GENERAL STUDIES

J. J. Saunders, *A History of Medieval Islam* (London, Routledge and Kegan Paul, 1965). Most up-to-date and interpretative textbook study of Islamic History. More information on development of Islam in Iran and among the Turks than most. Includes important period from eleventh-century 'Abbāsid decline to the rise of the Ottoman Empire in the fourteenth century.

Bernard Lewis, *The Arabs in History* (London, Hutchinson, 1950; New York, Torchbook, Harper and Row, 1960). Arab Islam to the fall of the 'Abbāsids. Emphasis on social and economic interpretation. Little attention to eastern Islam.

Carl Brockelmann, *History of the Islamic Peoples* (New York, G. P. Putnam, 1947; Capricorn Books, 1960). Detailed account of Islamic history to modern times. Extensive information on the medieval period of Islam and on the Persians and Turks as well as the Arabs. Unlike Saunders and Lewis, covers the Ottoman Empire, World War I, and the inter-war period until 1939. Emphasis on names and dates, with little effort at synthesis and interpretation. Added section on the Middle East from 1939 to 1947 by Moshe Perlmann.

Philip K. Hitti, *History of the Arabs from the Earliest Times to the Present* (ninth edition, London, Macmillan and Co., New York, St Martin's Press, 1967; London, Papermac, 1967). Emphasis on Islam to the twelfth century, although some information is also given on later times. Stress on Arab Islam, with little attention to the Persians and the Turks. Reliance on Arabic primary sources provides considerable information not found elsewhere, particularly on Islamic culture, arts, and sciences.

OTHER REFERENCE WORKS

Jean Sauvaget, *Jean Sauvaget's Introduction to the History of the Muslim East: A Bibliographical Guide*, ed. and revised by Claude Cahen (University of California Press, Berkeley and Los Angeles, 1965). Annotated bibliography of Islam through the eighteenth century, with particular emphasis on the classical and medieval periods.

J. D. Pearson, *Index Islamicus, 1906–1955. A Catalogue of Articles on Islamic Subjects in Periodicals and other Collective Publications* (Cambridge, Heffer, 1958).
——, *Index Islamicus Supplement, 1956–1960* (Cambridge, Heffer, 1962).
———, *Index Islamicus Supplement, 1961–1965* (Cambridge, Heffer, 1967)

The Encyclopaedia of Islam. First ed., ed. by M. Th. Houtsma and others, 4 vols. and Suppl. (Leiden and London, 1913–1938). New Edition, ed. by J. H. Kramers, H. A. R. Gibb, Bernard Lewis, and others (Leiden, Brill and Co., 1960 to date). Authoritative articles on all aspects of Islamic history. Indispensable reference work.

C. E. Bosworth, *The Islamic Dynasties* (Edinburgh, Edinburgh University Press, 1967)—Islamic Surveys 5. Most up-to-date chronology of Islamic dynasties and reigns.

F. Wüstenfeld and Joachim Mayr, *Wüstenfeld–Mahler'sche Vergleichungs-Tabellen zur Muslimischen und Iranischen Zeitrechnung mit Tafeln zur Umrechnung orientchristlicher Ären*, ed. Bertold Spuler (Wiesbaden, Franz Steiner Verlag, 1961). Best available concordance of Muslim and Christian dates. Includes many specialized Muslim calendars, including the Ottoman financial calendar.

R. Roolvink, *Historical Atlas of the Muslim Peoples* (Amsterdam, Djambatan, 1957; Cambridge, Mass., Harvard University Press, 1958). Best available collection of maps showing the situation of the Muslim World at important periods in its history.

Guy Le Strange, *The Lands of the Eastern Caliphate: Mesopotamia, Persia and Central Asia, from the Moslem Conquest to the Time of Timur* (Cambridge, Eng., 1905; 3rd impression, Frank Cass, London, 1966). Excellent gazetteer and geographical study of eastern Islam in mediaeval times.
——, *Palestine under the Moslems* (Cambridge, Eng., Cambridge University Press, 1930). Best available historical gazetteer of Palestine and parts of Syria in Islamic times.

André Miquel, *La géographie humaine du Monde Musulman jusqu'au milieu du onzième siècle: Géographie et géographie humaine dans la littérature arabe des origines à 1050* (Paris, Mouton, 1967). Best available study of the land and peoples of the Islamic Middle East in medieval times.

Xavier de Planhol, *Les fondements géographiques de l'histoire de l'Islam* (Paris, Flammarion, 1968). Interpretation of Islamic history in terms of its geographic and social situation.

PRE-ISLAMIC ARABIA

Sabatino Moscati, *Ancient Semitic Civilizations* (London, Elek Books, 1957).

Adolf Grohmann, 'al-'Arab, (i) The Ancient History of the Arabs', *Encyclopaedia of Islam: New Edition*, vol. I, pp. 524–527.

George Rentz, 'Djazīrat al-'Arab', *Encyclopaedia of Islam: New Edition*, vol. I, pp. 533–556.

E. de Lacy O'Leary, *Arabia before Mohammed* (London, Kegan Paul, Trench, Trübner, and New York, E. P. Dutton, 1927).

MUHAMMAD

Maxime Rodinson, *Mahomet* (Paris, Seuil, 1961). Controversial sociological interpretation of the rise of Islam.

F. Gabrieli, *Muhammad and the Conquests of Islam* (New York-Toronto, McGraw-Hill Book Company, 1968).

W. Montgomery Watt, *Mohammad at Mecca* (London, Oxford University Press, 1953).

——, *Mohammad at Medina* (London, Oxford University Press, 1956). Analysis of the life and work of the Prophet in the context of the social and economic conditions of the time. Summarized in *Muhammad, Prophet and Statesman* (London, Oxford University Press, 1961, Oxford Paperbacks, 1964).

Tor Andrae, *Mohammed, the Man and His Faith* (New York, Barnes and Noble, 1935; Harper Torchbook, 1960). Presentation of the more traditional approach to the Prophet's life, analysed primarily in terms of his religious background and experience.

Frants Buhl, *Das Leben Mohammeds* (Leipzig, 1930, 2nd ed., Quelle und Meyer, Heidelberg, 1955). Most detailed and authoritative account of the Prophet's life and works.

'Abd al-Malik Ibn Hishâm, *The Life of Muhammad*, tr. by Alfred Guillaume (London, Geoffrey Cumberlege, 1955). Translation of one of the main primary Arabic sources for the Prophet's life, that of Ibn Ishâq, as edited by Ibn Hishâm in the early ninth century.

ISLAM

Duncan B. Macdonald, *Development of Muslim Theology, Jurisprudence, and Constitutional Theory* (New York, 1903, repr. Beirut, Khayat, 1965).

Duncan B. Macdonald, *The Religious Attitude and Life in Islam* (2nd ed., Chicago, 1912; repr. Beirut, Khayat, 1965).

W. Montgomery Watt, *Islamic Philosophy and Theology* (Edinburgh, Edinburgh University Press, 1962)—Islamic Surveys 1.

H. A. R. Gibb, *Mohammedanism: An Historical Survey* (2nd ed., London–Oxford, Oxford University Press, 1949; frequently repr., Mentor Books, New York, 1955; A Galaxy Book, New York, 1962).

A. J. Wensinck, *The Muslim Creed, Its Genesis and Historical Development* (Cambridge, England, 1932; repr. London, Frank Cass and Co., 1965).

Louis Gardet, *L'Islam* (Paris, Desclée de Brouwer, 1968).

——, and M.–M. Anawati, *Introduction à la théologie musulmane, essai de théologie comparée* (Paris, J. Vrin, 1948).

A. J. Arberry, *Revelation and Reason in Islam* (London, Allen and Unwin, 1957).

THE ORTHODOX CALIPHATE

L. Veccia Vaglieri, 'Il conflitto 'Alî-Mu'âwiya e la sucessione kharigita riesaminati alla luce di fonti ibadite', *Instituto Universitario Orientale de Napoli. Annali*, n.s. vol. IV (1952), pp. 1–94; vol. V (1953), pp. 1–98. The struggle between 'Alî and Mu'âwiya and the rise of the Umayyad dynasty.

——, 'Sulla denominazione Hawāriğ', *Rivista degli Studi Orientali*, vol. XXVI (1951), pp. 41–46.

R. Veselý, 'Die Anṣâr im ersten Bürgerkriege (36–40 d.H.), *Archiv Orientální*, XXVI (1958), pp. 36–58. The role of the Medinan supporters of the Prophet during the first civil war of Islam.

A. Butler, *The Arab Conquest of Egypt and the Last Thirty Years of the Roman Dominion* (Oxford, 1902). Obsolete, but not yet superseded.

E. L. Petersen, ''Alî and Mu'âwiyah: The Rise of the Umayyad Caliphate, 656–661', *Acta Orientalia*, vol. XXIII (1959), pp. 157–196.

THE UMAYYADS

J. Wellhausen, *The Arab Kingdom and Its Fall* (Calcutta, 1927; repr., Beirut, Khayat, 1964). Authoritative and detailed study of the Umayyad period Unsurpassed effort to go beyond traditional 'Abbāsid-sponsored criticism of the Umayyads by reference to contemporary sources, particularly the chronicle of Ṭabarī.

H. A. R. Gibb, 'An Interpretation of Islamic History', *Studies on the Civilization of Islam* (Boston, Beacon Press, 1962; Boston, Beacon Paperback, 1968), pp. 3–33.

——, 'The Evolution of Government in Early Islam', *Studies on the Civilization of Islam*, pp. 34–46.

——, 'The Fiscal Rescript of 'Umar II', *Arabica*, vol. II (1955), pp. 1–16.

——, 'Arab-Byzantine Relations under the Umayyad Caliphate' *Dumbarton Oaks Papers*, vol. XII (1958), pp. 219–233.

THE 'ABBĀSIDS

Bernard Lewis, ''Abbâsids', *Encyclopaedia of Islam: New Edition*, vol. I, pp. 15–23. Interpretative survey of 'Abbāsid history. Concise but comprehensive.

Claude Cahen, 'Points de vue sur la Révolution 'Abbâside', *Revue Historique*, no. 468 (1963), pp. 295–338. Survey of the different interpretations of the 'Abbāsid revolution.

D. Sourdel, *Le Vizirat 'Abbâside de 749 à 936 (132 à 324 de l'Hégire)* (Damascus, Institut Français de Damas, 2 vols., 1959–60). Authoritative account of the development of the institution of the Vizierate under the 'Abbāsids.

Harold Bowen, *The Life and Times of 'Alí b. 'Ísà, 'The Good Vizier'* (Cambridge, Cambridge University Press, 1928).

Guy Le Strange, *Baghdad during the 'Abbâsid Caliphate* (Oxford Oxford University Press, 1924).

Reuben Levy, *A Baghdad Chronicle* (Cambridge, Cambridge University Press, 1929).

E. Herzfeld, *Geschichte der Stadt Samarrâ* (Hamburg, Eckardt und Messtorff, 1948).

ISLAMIC SOCIETY UNDER THE 'ABBĀSIDS. ECONOMIC DEVELOPMENT. SOCIAL AND RELIGIOUS MOVEMENTS. INSTITUTIONS

G. E. von Grunebaum, 'The Sources of Islamic Civilization', *Der Islam*. In preparation for 1970.

——, 'Muslim Civilisation in the 'Abbâsid Period', *Cambridge Medieval History*, vol. IV, *The Byzantine Empire*, part I, *Byzantium and its Neighbours*, ed. J. M. Hussey (Cambridge, Cambridge University Press, 1966), pp. 662–695.

G. E. von Grunebaum, *Medieval Islam* (2nd ed., Chicago, University of Chicago Press, 1953; revised German ed., Zurich and Stuttgart, Artemis, 1963).

——, *Unity and Variety in Muslim Civilization* (Chicago, University of Chicago Press, 1955).

H. A. R. Gibb, *Studies on the Civilization of Islam*, ed. S. J. Shaw and W. R. Polk (Boston, Beacon Press, 1962; Boston, Beacon Paperbacks, 1968).

D. Sourdel and J. Sourdel-Thomine, *La Civilisation de l'Islam classique* (Paris, Arthaud, 1968).

A. Mez, *The Renaissance of Islam* (London, Luzac, 1937).

T. W. Arnold, *The Caliphate* (Oxford, 1924; repr. with additional chapter by S. Haim, London, Routledge and Kegan Paul, 1965).

E. Tyan, *Histoire de l'organisation judiciaire en pays d'Islam* (2 vols., Paris, 1938–1943; vol. I of 2nd ed., Leiden, Brill, 1960).

——, *Institutions du droit public musulman* (2 vols, Paris, Sirey, 1954–1956).

D. C. Dennett, Jr., *Conversion and the Poll Tax in Early Islam* (Cambridge, Mass., Harvard University Press, 1950).

M. Gaudefroy-Demombynes, *Muslim Institutions* (2nd ed., London, Allen and Unwin, 1954).

J. Schacht, *The Origins of Muhammadan Jurisprudence* (Oxford, Oxford University Press, 1950).

A. A. A. Fyzee, *Outlines of Muhammadan Law* (3rd ed., London, Oxford University Press, 1964).

E. I. J. Rosenthal, *Political Thought in Medieval Islam* (Cambridge, Cambridge University Press, 1958).

N. J. Coulson, *A History of Islamic Law* (Edinburgh, Edinburgh University Press, 1964)—Islamic Surveys 2.

W. Heyd, *Histoire du commerce du Levant au Moyen-Âge* (Leipzig, Dessau, 1885–6, repr., Amsterdam, Hakkert, 1959, 2 vols.).

Antoine Fattal, *Le Statut légal des non-musulmans en pays d'Islam* (Beirut, Imprimerie Catholique, 1958).

S. Goitein, *Studies in Islamic History and Institutions* (Leiden, Brill, 1966).

S. Goitein, *A Mediterranean Society. The Jewish Community of the Arab World as Portrayed in the Documents of the Cairo Geniza*, vol. I, *Economic Foundations* (Berkeley and Los Angeles, University of California Press, 1967).

Reuben Levy, *The Social Structure of Islam* (Cambridge, England, Cambridge University Press, 1957; repr. and paperback, 1965).

Archibald Lewis, *Naval Power and Trade in the Mediterranean, 500–1100* (Princeton, N.J., Princeton University Press, 1951).

A. S. Tritton, *The Caliphs and Their non-Muslim Subjects: A Critical Study of the Covenant of 'Umar* (London, Milford, 1930).

W. J. Fischel, *Jews in the Economic and Political Life of Mediaeval Islam* (London, Royal Asiatic Society, 1937; repr., 1968).

Jean Sauvaget, *Alep: essai sur le développement d'une grande ville syrienne, des origines au milieu du XIXe siècle* (Paris, Geuthner, 1941).

R. Brunschvig, ''Abd', *Encyclopaedia of Islam; New Edition*, vol. I, pp. 24–40. Exhaustive study of the institution of slavery in Islam.

Ira M. Lapidus, *Muslim Cities in the Later Middle Ages* (Cambridge, Mass., Harvard University Press, 1967).

Duncan B. Macdonald, *Aspects of Islam* (New York, The Macmillan Company, 1911).

D. Donaldson, *The Shi'ite Religion: A History of Islam in Persia and Irak* (London, Luzac, 1933).

J. N. Hollister, *The Shi'a of India* (London, Luzac, 1953).

A. J. Arberry, *An Introduction to the History of Sufism* (London and New York, 1943).

——, *Sufism* (London, Allen and Unwin, 1950).

Louis Gardet and M.-M. Anawati, *La Mystique musulmane* (Paris, J. Vrin, 1961).

Margaret Smith, *An Early Mystic of Baghdad: A Study of the Life and Teaching of Ḥārith b. 'Asad al-Muḥāsibī* (London, Sheldon, 1935).

Josef van Ess, *Die Gedankenwelt des Ḥâriṭ al-Muḥâsibî* (Bonn, Selbstverlag des Orientalischen Seminars der Universität Bonn, 1961).

W. Montgomery Watt, *Free Will and Predestination in Early Islam* (London, Luzac, 1948).

——, *Muslim Intellectual: A Study of al-Ghazali* (Edinburgh, Edinburgh University Press, 1963).

Margaret Smith, *Al-Ghazali, the Mystic* (London, Luzac, 1944).

Louis Gardet, *L'Islam, religion et communauté* (Paris, Desclée de Brouwer, 1967).

Henri Laoust, *Les schismes dans l'Islam: Introduction à une étude de la religion musulmane* (Paris, Payot, 1965).

Hermann Stieglecker, *Die Glaubenslehren des Islam* (Paderborn, Ferdinand Schöningh, 1962).

ISLAMIC CULTURE UNDER THE 'ABBĀSIDS. LITERATURE, SCIENCE, AND THE ARTS. THEOLOGY AND PHILOSOPHY

I. Goldziher, *Gesammelte Schriften*, ed. J. De Somogyi (2 vols., Hildesheim, Georg Olms, 1967–68).

——, *Muhammedanische Studien* (2 vols., Halle a.S., Niemeyer, 1889–90; repr., Hildesheim, Georg Olms, 1961).

——, *Muslim Studies*, tr. and ed. by C. R. Barber and S. M. Stern, vol. I (London, Allen and Unwin, 1967).

Alfred Guillaume, *The Traditions of Islam: An Introduction to the Study of the Hadith Literature* (Oxford, Clarendon, 1924; repr. Beirut, Khayat, 1966).

W. Montgomery Watt, *Islamic Philosophy and Theology* (Edinburgh, Edinburgh University Press, 1962)—Islamic Surveys 1.

Henri Corbin, *Histoire de la philosophie Islamique. I. Des origines jusqu'à la mort d'Averroës* (Paris, Gallimard, 1964).

Richard Walzer, *Greek into Arabic* (Oxford, Bruno Cassirer, 1962)—Oriental Studies I.

T. de Boer, *The History of Philosophy in Islam* (2nd ed., London, 1933; repr., New York, Dover Paperback, 1967).

Louis Massignon and Roger Arnaldez, 'La science arabe', *Histoire Générale des Sciences*, ed. R. Taton, vol. I, *La science antique et médiévale* (Paris, Presses Universitaires Françaises, 1957), pp. 430–471.

T. W. Arnold and A. Guillaume, ed., *The Legacy of Islam* (Oxford, Oxford University Press, 1931).

R. Nicholson, *A Literary History of the Arabs* (2nd ed., Cambridge, Cambridge University Press, 1930, repr., Cambridge, 1966).

H. A. R. Gibb, *Arabic Literature: An Introduction* (2nd ed., Oxford, Clarendon, 1963).

——, and Jacob M. Landau, *Arabische Literaturgeschichte* (Zurich and Stuttgart, Artemis, 1968). Gibb's *Arabic Literature*, brought up to date by Landau.

Franz Rosenthal, *Das Fortleben der Antike im Islam* (Zurich and Stuttgart, Artemis, 1965).

E. G. Browne, *A Literary History of Persia* (4 vols., Cambridge, Cambridge University Press, 1902–1904, repr., 1968).

J. Rypka, ed., *History of Iranian Literature* (Dordrecht, D. Reidel, 1968).

Richard Ettinghausen, *Arab Painting* (Lausanne, Skira, 1962).

Basil Gray, *Persian Painting* (Lausanne, Skira, 1961).

K. A. C. Cresswell, *A Short Account of Early Muslim Architecture* (London, Penguin Books, 1958).

EGYPT UNDER THE ṬŪLŪNIDS AND THE FĀṬIMIDS

Zaky Mohamed Hassan, *Les Tulunides: Étude de l'Égypte musulmane à la fin du XIe siècle*, 868–905 (Paris, 1933).

Bernard Lewis, *The Origins of Ismailism: A Study of the Historical Background of the Fāṭimid Caliphate* (Cambridge, Eng., Heffer, 1940).

Marshall G. Hodgson, *The Order of Assassins* ('s-Gravenhage, Mouton, 1955).

Marius Canard, *Les Institutions des Fâtimides en Égypte* (Algiers, La Maison des Livres, 1957).

Wilferd Madelung, 'Fatimiden und Bahrainqarmaten', *Der Islam*, XXIV (1959), pp. 34–88.

——, *Der Imam al-Qāsim ibn Ibrāhīm und die Glaubenslehre der Zaiditen* (Berlin, de Gruyter, 1965).

Bernard Lewis, *The Assassins: A Radical Sect in Islam* (New York, Basic Books, 1968).

Gaston Wiet, *L'Égypte arabe de la conquête arabe à la conquête ottomane 642–1517*, in *Histoire de la nation égyptienne*, ed. G. Hanoteaux, Vol. 4 (Paris, Société de l'histoire Nationale, 1937).

THE COLLAPSE OF THE CALIPHATE. THE LATIN STATES. RISE OF THE TURKS

Claude Cahen, 'Buwayhids or Būyids', *Encyclopaedia of Islam: New Edition*, vol. I, pp. 1350–1357.

A. K. S. Lambton, *Landlord and Peasant in Persia* (London, Oxford University Press, 1953).

The Cambridge History of Iran, vol. 5, *The Saljuq and Mongol Periods*, ed. J. A. Boyle (Cambridge, Cambridge University Press, 1968).

Bertold Spuler, *Iran in früh-islamischer Zeit* (Wiesbaden, Franz Steiner, 1952).

H. Busse, *Chalif und Grosskönig. Die Buyiden in Baghdad*, 945–1055 (Beirut, 1968).

C. E. Bosworth, *The Ghaznavids: Their empire in Afghanistan and Eastern Iran*, 994–1040 (Edinburgh, Edinburgh University Press, 1963).

W. Barthold, *Turkestan Down to the Mongol Invasion* (3rd ed., with additions by C. E. Bosworth, London, Luzac, 1968).

Claude Cahen, *La Syrie du nord à l'époque des croisades* (Paris, Paul Geuthner, 1940).

——, 'Crusades', *Encyclopaedia of Islam: New Edition*, vol. II, pp. 63–66.

——, *Pre-Ottoman Turkey* (London, Sidgwick and Jackson, and New York, Taplinger, 1968).

Kenneth M. Setton, ed., *A History of the Crusades*, vol. I, *The First Hundred Years*, ed. M. W. Baldwin (Philadelphia, Pa., University of Pennsylvania Press, 1958; repr., Madison, Wisconsin, University of Wisconsin Press, 1969); vol. II, *The Later Crusades*, ed. R. L. Wolff and H. W. Hazard (Philadelphia, Pa., University of Pennsylvania Press, 1962; repr., Madison, Wisconsin, University of Wisconsin Press, 1969).

Sir Steven Runciman, *A History of the Crusades* (3 vols., Cambridge University Press, Cambridge, England, 1951–1954; New York, Harper Torch-books, 1968).

F. Gabrieli, ed., *Arab Historians of the Crusades* (University of California Press, Berkeley and Los Angeles, 1969).

Ibn al-Qalânisî, *The Damascus Chronicle of the Crusades*, tr. H. A. R. Gibb (London, Luzac, 1932).

Usâmah ibn Munqid, *An Arab-Syrian Gentleman and Warrior in the Period of the Crusades*, tr. P. K. Hitti (New York, Columbia University Press, 1929).

H. Gottschalk, *al-Malik al-Kāmil* (Wiesbaden, Otto Harrassowitz 1958).

THE ARABIC WEST. THE ALMORAVIDS AND ALMOHADS

Mohamed Talbi, *L'Émirat Aghlabide*, 184–296/800–909 (Paris, Adrien-Maisonneuve, 1966).

Henri Terrasse, *Histoire du Maroc des origines à l'établissement du Protectorat français*. Vols. 1, 2 (Casablanca, Editions Atlantide, 1949/1950).

Michele Amari, *Storia dei Musulmani di Sicilia*. 2nd ptg. ed. C. A. Nallino. Vols. 1–3 (Catania, F. Guaitolini, 1933–1939).

Hady Roger Idris, *La Berbérie orientale sous les Zirides, Xe-XIIe siècles*. Vols. 1, 2 (Paris, Adrien-Maisonneuve, 1962).

Georges Marçais, *La Berbérie musulmane et l'Orient au Moyen-Âge* (Paris, Aubier, 1946).

Ramon Menéndez Pidal, *La España del Cid* (Madrid, Plutarco, 1929).

Jacinto Bosch Vilá, *Los Almóravides* (Tetuán, Marroquí, 1956).

Ambrosio Huici Miranda, *Historia política del Imperio almóhade* (2 vols.; Tetuán, Marroquí, 1956/1957).

Roger Le Tourneau, *Fès avant le protectorat. Étude économique et sociale d'une ville de l'occident musulman* (Casablanca, Société Marocaine de Librairie et d'Édition, 1949).

M. Vonderheyden, *La Berbérie orientale sous la dynastie des Benoū'l-Aṛlab*, 800–909 (Paris, Geuthner, 1927).

WITHDRAWAL AND MYSTICISM

Classicisme et déclin culturel dans l'histoire de l'Islam. Actes du Symposium international d'histoire de la civilisation musulmane (Bordeaux, 1956), directed by R. Brunschvig and G. E. von Grunebaum. (Paris, Besson 1957).

Classizismus und Kulturzerfall, ed. G. E. von Grunebaum and Willy Hartner (Frankfurt am Main, Klostermann, 1960). Lectures.

Hellmut Ritter, *Das Meer der Seele. Mensch, Welt und Gott in den Geschichten des Farîduddîn 'Aṭṭâr* (Leiden, Brill, 1955).

INDEX

The index contains the names of persons, places, and countries that are mentioned in the text as well as Arabic terms and many subject headings. The Arabic article *al* has been disregarded in the alphabetical order.